BOARD COMMITTEES HANDBOOK

Sue Lawrence

First published 2020

Published by
CGI Publishing Limited
Saffron House
6–10 Kirby Street
London EC1N 8TS

© CGI Publishing Limited, 2020

All rights reserved. No part of this publication may be reproduced, stored in a retrieval system, or transmitted, in any form, or by any means, electronic, mechanical, photocopying, recording or otherwise, without prior permission, in writing, from the publisher.

Typeset by Paul Barrett Book Production, Cambridge
Edited by Benedict O'Hagan
Cover designed by Anthony Kearney

British Library Cataloguing in Publication Data
A catalogue record for this book is available from the British Library

ISBN 978-1-86072-798-6

As with all legislation, the provisions of the Companies Acts and related legislation are open to interpretation and must be assessed in the context of the particular circumstances at hand, the articles of association of the company in question, and any relevant shareholders' agreement or other pertinent ancillary agreements. While every effort has been made to ensure the accuracy of the content of this book, neither the author nor the publisher can accept any responsibility for any loss arising to anyone relying on the information contained herein.

Contents

About the author	v	
Acknowledgements	vii	
Introduction	ix	

1 Introduction to committees 1
  Benefits 1
  Legal requirements 2
  Advisers 3
  Diversity and committee dynamics 3
  Values and culture 4
  Development 4
  Internal governance audit for the board 5
  Conclusion 6

2 What is a committee? 7
  What is a committee? 7
  Constituting a committee 7
  Decision making 8
  Reporting 9
  External reporting 10
  Conclusion 10

3 Implementing a committee 11
  Terms of reference 11
  Committee chair and secretary 12
  Committee membership 13
  How many members? 14
  Individual committee membership 15
  Committee member tenure 16
  Committee size and quorum 17
  Frequency of meetings and notice 18
  Reporting responsibilities 19
  Conclusion 19

4 Operational aspects of committees 21
  Committee meetings 21
  Committee chair 21
  Committee packs 22
  Agenda 26
  Time keeping 26
  Committee minutes 27
  Reporting 28
  Review 28
  Oversight of committees 31
  Digital meeting support 31
  Wider interaction beyond the committee 34
  Supporting committees 35
  Conclusion 36

5 Executive committee 37
  Role of the executive committee 38
  Terms of reference 39
  Duties, responsibilities and tasks 40
  Committee membership 48
  Interaction beyond the committee 48
  Reporting 48
  Supporting the committee 50
  Conclusion 51

6 Audit committee 53
  Role of the audit committee 53
  Terms of reference 54
  Duties, responsibilities and tasks 56
  Three lines of defence model 66
  Committee membership 68
  Interaction beyond the committee 68
  Reporting 69
  Supporting the committee 71
  Conclusion 72

7 Risk committee 73
  Risk in general 76
  Role of the risk committee 78
  Terms of reference 78
  Duties, responsibilities and tasks 81
  Risk subcommittees 87
  Committee membership 88

Interaction beyond the committee	89	
Reporting	91	
Supporting the committee	92	
Conclusion	93	

8 Remuneration committee — 95
Role of the remuneration committee — 96
Terms of reference — 100
Duties, responsibilities and tasks — 100
Committee membership — 105
Interaction beyond the committee — 107
Reporting — 110
Supporting the committee — 112
Conclusion — 114

9 Nomination committee — 115
Role of the nomination committee — 116
FCA guidance for nomination committees — 117
Terms of reference — 118
Duties, responsibilities and tasks — 119
Committee membership — 126
Boardroom dynamics and diversity — 128
Interaction beyond the committee — 130
Reporting — 131
Supporting the committee — 132
Conclusion — 134

10 Other committees — 135
Committee versus project — 136
Operational practicalities — 137
Ongoing monitoring — 138
Examples of other committees — 138
Compliance committee — 139
Safety, health and environment committees — 141
Environmental, social and governance committee — 142
Corporate social responsibility committee — 144
IT and technology committee — 147
Markets committees — 149
Investment committee — 151
Relocation committee — 151
Employment committee — 152
Social committee — 153
Niche examples of committees — 154

External committees to the company — 155
Subcommittees — 157
General — 158
Conclusion — 158

11 Subsidiary boards — 161
Legal standing — 161
Similarities to committees — 162
Operations of subsidiary boards — 163
Setting strategy — 163
Subsidiary board members — 164
The role of a subsidiary board member — 165
Overseas subsidiaries — 166
Internal non-operating subsidiaries — 167
Accounting records — 167
Subsidiary governance — 167
Subsidiary oversight — 169
Subsidiary risks — 170
Conclusion — 171

12 Other boards as formal forums — 173
Advisory boards — 173
Shadow boards — 174
Pension trustee boards — 176
Charity funding boards — 177
Employee ownership trust board — 178
Conclusion — 179

13 Conclusion — 181

Appendices: The Chartered Governance Institute terms of reference — 183
Appendix 1 – Terms of reference for the audit committee — 185
Appendix 2 – Terms of reference for the remuneration committee — 199
Appendix 3 – Terms of reference for the nomination committee — 207

Directory — 215
References — 215
Referenced published annual reports — 216
Resources — 216

Index — 219

About the author

Sue Lawrence is an experienced independent director having been appointed to a wide variety of board, trustee and committee positions in the UK for over 15 years, including trading companies, operating subsidiaries, start-ups, trustee boards, funding boards, charities and Employee Owned Trusts. Having been a successful divisional Managing Director in the professional and financial services sectors, she is now enjoying a portfolio career as an independent director and trustee for a diverse range of UK incorporated companies drawing on her past experience as well as her professional training as a Chartered Director with the Institute of Directors.

In addition, she is the founder of Independent Directors and Trustees Limited a company that provides independent directors to the boards of UK subsidiaries of overseas companies and SMEs seeking to develop a robust governance framework. Trustee appointments relate to employee ownership trusts where the board of trustees represents the employees of a business as beneficiary owners. The roles include coaching and mentoring fellow directors and trustees, as well as supporting governance reviews on behalf of clients.

Acknowledgements

In writing this book, the author drew on her experience of, and fascination with, governance in all its aspects. Personal thanks are also extended for the additional contribution made by Jonathan Lawrence, Partner (and no relation) and Enis Hallacoglu, Trainee Solicitor at K&L Gates LLP for their invaluable assistance in sourcing relevant legal cases, as well as Elise Perraud and the team at NEDonBoard for sharing their wide-ranging expertise and knowledge.

Introduction

Most large companies, and many smaller companies, delegate some authority from the board in order to progress discussions on a specific topic or where additional technical knowledge is required. Where this is a formal delegation of decision making this is most frequently constituted as a committee of the board, with clear and specific terms of reference. Indeed, without these committees taking responsibility for certain aspects of a company's governance, it is difficult to see how a board can be effective and a robust governance framework be evidenced.

Effective use of committees by a board of directors can broaden the capabilities of a board and ensure that a business can maintain its success, balancing the internal and external requirements of a business when seeking growth and success.

The aim of this book is to introduce the concept of committees and explain the practical implementation and operations of committees. It will be particularly useful to those who support committees in a company secretarial role, as an advisor or subject matter expert in attendance or as a provider of information to committees to support their effective function. It will also underpin the knowledge required at board level in implementing a committee, understanding the opportunity that having an effective committee can have in supporting the board as well as recognising the importance of clarity of the scope of each committee.

As a handbook, it will provide further detail on the most prevalent committees that are implemented. It primarily focuses on requirements in the UK; however, the contents will be useful for those tasked with implementing, maintaining or supporting a governance framework which includes committees as the fundamentals on committees are relevant to all companies globally.

While specifically focused on committee requirements for listed companies as defined by various bodies, the framework of a committee can be usefully applied in other businesses where their implementation would aid the effective development of a successful business. In these cases, where there is no regulatory requirement to implement specific, or in some cases any, committees, the use of ad hoc, multi-focused or time-limited committees can be invaluable and this handbook will give a framework and ideas for what and how these can be used.

Reference is made throughout this book to the UK Corporate Governance Code (the 'Code') and specifically that published in July 2018 which can be found on the website of The Financial Reporting Council (www.frc.org.uk). At the heart of this Code is an updated set of Principles that emphasise the value of good corporate governance to long-term sustainable success. By applying the Principles, following the more detailed Provisions and using the associated guidance, companies can demonstrate throughout their reporting how the governance of the company contributes to its long-term sustainable success and achieves wider objectives.

Throughout the chapters, examples will be given from publicly available sources. These are taken from the published annual reports of UK companies, primarily those that have been nominated for the 2018 and 2019 The Chartered Governance Institute awards. Annual reports are an invaluable source of information that readers should consult as reference documents having been written by, or on behalf of, committee members as experts. As the nominated reports from The Chartered Governance Institute, the examples given are best practice in the current industry.

Chapter 1 will introduce the **concept of committees** in more depth, including the benefits and legal requirements of a committee as well as the use of advisers. It will also introduce the concept of diversity and committee dynamics, plus the role of the committee in promoting the values and culture of a company, as well as the opportunity that committee membership can give in supporting individuals at the outset of their corporate career.

Chapter 2 will delve into the **constitution of a committee** and the method of delegating authority from the board and the importance of clear terms of reference in setting the responsibilities and authorities of the committee and its members. It will touch on the reporting requirements of the committee, both internally and externally.

Chapter 3 will provide more detail on **implementing a committee**, including the content of the terms of reference for a committee given the importance that this has in setting the boundaries and expectations of each committee. The terms of reference sit at the heart of each committee and guide the expectations of deliverables, responsibilities and constraints. Without it being in place there is a great risk of duplication of effort or conflict between the board and the committee. This chapter will reflect on its importance while referring to example contents, including the terms of reference included as appendices. Further detail is also provided on membership of committees and documenting the deliverables from the outset.

Chapter 4 will review the **operational aspects of committees** through their reporting, decision making, company secretarial support and day-to-day workings. It will introduce The Chartered Governance Institute support materials available when creating or reviewing meeting packs as well as the practical actions of the committee and its support network, such as agendas, time management and minutes. This chapter will also touch on the interaction beyond the committee and its support network.

Chapters 5 to 9 introduce the five primary committees with standard chapter formats including an introduction to the committee; its roles, responsibilities and tasks; the terms of reference; committee membership; interaction outside of the committee; reporting and supporting the committee. Throughout these chapters, extracts are included from a range of published annual reports of UK companies to provide examples to support the narrative.

Chapter 5 will explain the operational functions of the **executive committee** as a committee of the board, although often without formal terms of reference. The chapter examines the functions of this forum, its interaction with the board and its composition of both board members and other senior functional heads. Details are included on the roles and responsibilities of the executive committee, as well as examples of reporting within annual reports.

Chapter 6 specifically focuses on the **audit committee**, a required committee of the majority of large companies and those within financial services. This committee may also be known as the finance committee and may have a wider remit than purely audit. This chapter will specifically look at finance and audit and will cover the importance of the audit committee on appointing external auditors to the company, the independence it brings to internal audit and the skills required of audit committee members. In addition, this chapter includes an explanation of the three lines of defence model and the benefit that internal audit can bring to its effective implementation within a company. It also presents this model as a concept, whether implemented in totality or as a means of considering the oversight of risk and the role that audit plays in mitigating the financial risk of a company.

Chapter 7 provides greater clarity on the **risk committee** in having oversight of risk within a business as well as embedding and maintaining a risk culture throughout the business. In medium-sized companies, risk may also be included in the terms of reference of the audit committee so the contents of this chapter may be equally important for those interested in the workings of the audit committee. In addition to the risk committee, the concept of a risk subcommittee in larger, more complex organisations is introduced.

Chapter 8 considers the **remuneration committee**, specifically in reference to listed companies and the requirement that executive management should not be in a position to set their own remuneration packages, which incorporates salaries, deferred income via pension contributions, share options and other incentives. As a highly visible committee of listed companies, the workings of the remuneration committee should not be underestimated, especially as shareholders will have a vote on the workings of this committee at each AGM. Remuneration committees have very public failures but very private successes and need to be transparent in all the actions they take.

Chapter 9 covers the **nomination committee** and the role it plays in ensuring that the board of the company is effective and that succession plans are in place for senior roles. Primarily composed of non-executive directors, in smaller companies this committee may be combined with the remuneration committee. The specific guidance provided by the FCA to nomination committees is included, as is a section on boardroom dynamics and diversity.

Chapter 10 will pick up on **other committees** that are set up either through the needs of an individual company or sector, touching on their difference to a project and the need for ongoing review of their purpose. Examples are provided of different types of committees that can be incorporated, including market-facing committees where the success of a business may be closely aligned to market changes and developments, such as in the technology sector or investment committees for investment companies. It will also cover those that are time-limited or purpose focused, set up for a specific purpose with committee members drawn from internal and external experts within the specific remit of the committee. These have the delegated authority from the board to progress matters and deliver specific goals. Examples include property committees where a business may be consolidating offices or HR committees where a significant organisation change is being implemented. The chapter also introduces external committees incorporated by industry bodies and associations with members drawn from their member firms with a purpose to often share knowledge and contribute to sector development, reviews and legislative change. Finally, the chapter introduces the broad concept of **subcommittees** which are particularly prevalent in multi-national organisations where the matrix of reporting within committee structures may sit alongside subsidiary roles and responsibilities. It will bring a reminder that knowledge held within committees in isolation may be detrimental to a business and introduces the importance of effective reporting upwards, across and downwards from committees.

Chapter 11 looks at **subsidiary boards as a committee** of the main group board despite its separate legal entity status, reflecting on what is delegated to a subsidiary board versus what is decided at main group level with implementation at local subsidiary board level. It will reflect on the conflict between acting under the umbrella of a main board or executive while also maintaining local requirements of a legal entity with board responsibilities. Subsidiary board membership is also covered, while The Chartered Governance Institute subsidiary governance framework is introduced as a beneficial framework to underpin the oversight of subsidiary organisational structures.

Chapter 12 introduces **other formal forums of a company** that are constituted as a board, either with a direct link into the main board or as an independent body. This includes pension trustee boards who increasingly have an important part to play in the success of a business, especially given the frequency of pension regulation changes and the prevalence of pension deficits negatively impacting on the success of a business. Employee ownership trusts will also be introduced given the growth of employee-owned business. Other examples include funding committees for charities. It will also introduce the concept of a shadow board as a forum to introduce a wider group of employees to the expectation of board membership, strategy setting and business oversight. Similarly, it will introduce advisory boards as a means to support main boards through a formal channel to extend knowledge, skills and contacts without widening board membership.

Chapter 13 brings a conclusion and summarises the main features of a robust business utilising committees to deliver effective corporate governance.

Throughout this book, the roles of various committees are examined and explained. Where a company does not have a specific committee, the assumption is that the roles defined are maintained with the board of the company. Hence the content is beneficial for companies where a committee structure would not be beneficial due to size or cost, but the board still has the roles and responsibilities.

1 – Introduction to committees

Introduction

All large companies have a responsibility, and in some cases a legal requirement, to delegate some authority from the board to a committee implemented with specific terms of reference. Indeed, without these committees taking responsibility for certain aspects of a company's governance, it is difficult to see how a board can be effective and a robust governance framework be evidenced.

Equally, smaller companies and those acting in specific sectors see the benefit of implementing a committee structure, with either permanent or time-limited committees to support the board and ensure effectiveness of the business.

Committees give a board the opportunity to delegate lengthy or technical discussions, decisions and oversight to a subset of the board with the addition of committee members with specific relevant expertise. They can also support the board's effectiveness by delegating agreed matters to this alternative forum, thus enabling the board to utilise their time on other subjects with a higher priority need for their time and expertise. From this perspective, all boards would benefit from at least considering the creation of at least one committee to benefit themselves and their organisation.

In fact, committee structures and their implementation can be invaluable, as long as their remit is clear and their deliverables are monitored.

Benefits

In large companies, fully functioning individual committees add significant value and under certain legislation they are a mandated requirement or defined best practice. In smaller companies, committees are often combined to cover multi-functions such as an audit and risk committee or remuneration and nomination committee. Except in certain circumstances, there are no hard and fast rules on what committees should be implemented. Logically it is those areas of sufficient requirement that cannot be covered by the board as a group due to time constraints, expertise, breadth of the topic, importance for the particular business. Boards of directors choose to set up a committee to support them in being more effective.

The implementation of committees also has some beneficial side effects that a business may benefit from including identifying and testing board candidates for the future, developing staff in governance matters, drawing expert advice from external third parties, promoting the substance of a robust governance framework within a business and demonstrating that the board recognises and values the contribution of those outside the boardroom. The benefit of utilising a committee should not only be seen as the ability of the board to delegate, the add-on benefits in generating engagement from, and contribution by, the wider business should also be accepted, encouraged and embraced.

Legal requirements

Under the Code, specific committees for audit, risk, remuneration and nomination are recommended with an expectation that they will be established in all large listed companies as well as those acting within the financial services sector. In November 2009, the Walker Review of Corporate Governance in the UK Banking Industry gave detailed recommendations on the requirements of audit, risk, remuneration and nomination committees reflecting the importance these committees have in the financial sector.

Under the FCA Handbook (recommendation 2.4A) the management body of the relevant company must:

(a) define and oversee the implementation of governance arrangements that ensure the effective and prudent management of the [company] in a manner which promotes the integrity of the market, which at least must include the:
 (i) segregation of duties in the organisation; and
 (ii) prevention of conflicts of interest;
(b) monitor and periodically assess the effectiveness of the [company's] governance arrangements; and
(c) take appropriate steps to address any deficiencies found as a result of the monitoring under paragraph (b).

Where the company is significant, a nomination committee must be implemented unless it is prevented by law from selecting and appointing its own members. This nomination committee must engage a broad set of qualities and competences when recruiting persons to the management body, and for that purpose, must have a policy promoting diversity on the management body. (Further details of these requirements are included in Chapter 9, Nomination Committee.)

The Charity Commission, in its guidance for larger charities, references the implementation of risk, audit and nomination committees to support the effective governance of the charity by the board. Charities may also implement a funding committee with specific focus on generating funding within their charitable sector, although it should be noted that larger charities may also constitute this as a separate legal entity with a funding board specifically focused on identifying and generating additional opportunities for revenue generation to support the aims of the charity.

Although not legally required, smaller companies may benefit from delegating discussions and decision making to a committee or alternative forum either on a permanent basis, for a specific time period or to deliver on a specific topic. This can be particularly beneficial when senior input would be useful, but the company does not want to increase the membership of its board, either for cost or practical reasons. By delegating to a committee, experts can be co-opted as committee members to share their expertise without the legal responsibilities of becoming a director. This often takes the form of a management committee, similar in nature to an executive committee, which takes responsibility for operational aspects of the company (see Chapter 5).

Advisers

As with boards, committee meetings may welcome attendance by experts and advisors to specific meetings to contribute to specific discussions. For example, if a topic is to be discussed at one meeting but is not part of the standing agenda items, having an expert present, to be available for the discussion and questions is invaluable and further enhances the expertise already within the committee.

This also gives advisers a way of understanding their clients' business better, using their time spent working with and presenting to the committee as a way of generating a productive and knowledge-based client relationship. Committee presentations or attendance can sit alongside the adviser's work with the company but, it should be noted that the company should not use this as an alternative way to gain knowledge that should otherwise be contracted or received as formal advice that can be relied on at a later date.

As an example, a legal adviser may attend a committee meeting to introduce the concept of new legislation, such as may have been the case when GDPR legislation was introduced. This would take the form of generic guidance, however, if specific advice on its implementation by the business is required, the expectation would be that this would be in the form of formal legal advice, paid for by the company.

Partners at audit firms would expect to be invited to relevant audit committee meetings to enable them to answer questions or explain matters in more detail. However, they should not expect to attend all meetings in full or be a committee member given their relationship to the company as a service provider.

Diversity and committee dynamics

As with the board, committee composition is an opportunity to engender diversity within its membership, bringing different experience, knowledge and outlook from members to each discussion. Differences in professional experience, knowledge and understanding is key to ensuring that discussion topics cover as wide a view as possible before decisions are made. Equally having diverse backgrounds will energise discussion, bring differing viewpoints and identify a broader outlook for the committee.

Members of a committee may reflect the existing or target diversity of a company or its board. It may also create an opportunity to bring fresh viewpoints and ideas.

Diverse membership may also create an opportunity to mirror a company's customer, community or market. In particular, a markets committee focused on identifying and developing new products would benefit from having representation of the target market in its membership or, as a minimum, as committee advisers. There are many examples of organisations that include representatives of their customers or markets on their board or committees, from social housing organisations having residents within their membership to membership bodies having members on their boards or committees to consumer goods companies utilising customer feedback forums to develop existing and new products.

Increased diversity within a committee brings new dynamics to meeting discussions. Embracing and enhancing this new dynamic is crucial to being able to benefit from diverse membership. New or inexperienced committee members should be mentored, respected for their views, be proactively provided with opportunities to contribute and, above all else, should be respectfully listened to. Without this, the benefit of incorporating diversity into committee membership is completely negated and it has the risk of merely delivering a good metric or soundbite without adding the real value.

Values and culture

Committees have delegated responsibilities from the board and have an equal requirement in the leadership of a business or organisation. The values and culture of an organisation are set by the board and the leadership team through their actions and example. Committees should reflect the same values and culture ensuring that their behaviour, both in committee meetings and outside of formal forums, reflects the same values. Being a committee member is a position of responsibility both in the actions that are undertaken within the committee and also in the interactions with all members of the wider organisation as well as other stakeholders.

Development

In addition to the support a committee gives to board members, it can also be a useful forum to support the learning and development of individuals within a business. Becoming a member of a specifically tasked committee gives an individual exposure to the formal workings of a group of experts with a defined purpose. It is a forum where an individual can find their voice through engagement and discussion on a topic in which they are an expert, by sharing knowledge, understanding the purpose of the committee, receiving committee packs with a broader content than their specific knowledge and engaging in discussion in a productive and positive manner with fellow committee members. Where an individual has previously provided information for board or committee meetings, this is the opportunity to understand the value of a good meeting pack and the benefit of having clear content.

In an ideal scenario, HR teams should incorporate committee attendance and membership as part of a development programme for staff members identified as having the potential to lead the business in the future. Committees are invaluable on-the-job training forums where confidence can be gained in a collegiate and supportive forum attended by colleagues. In this respect, HR teams should discuss this aspect with relevant board members, or members of the nomination committee if there is one and they have responsibility for committee membership.

Internal governance audit for the board

Effective committees can also act as an internal check of board delivery, either directly or indirectly. With actions delegated from the board to a committee, the residual work undertaken by the board can become more effective. Committee board reports should be clear and concise identifying areas for board decision or contribution. All other content should be limited to a brief update which evidences that the committee is effectively delivering against its terms of reference without encouraging board debate of the same topics as this would replicate considerations, negate committee benefit and evidence poor delegation.

If the board continues to own, discuss and review actions delegated to a committee, the perception is that the wider remit of the board is being neglected or avoided. It may also imply that the board is unable to delegate, they have been unclear on the requirements and deliverables within the terms of reference of the committee or have appointed ineffective committee members. In most of these cases, the resultant negativity, disillusionment or frustration that will be created in the wider company due to lack of delivery or wasted time and effort, will be directed at the board, not the committee or its members. Hence the committee will be ineffective and respect for the board will be diminished with reduced morale across the company due to governance inadequacies.

As an example, if the production, review and monitoring of a risk register are formally delegated to a risk committee, any excessive time spent reviewing the risk register in minute detail by the board is negating the work of the committee, undermining their expertise and results in the board duplicating effort. It also takes time away from board meetings that should be spent on other board discussions.

As a minimum, implementation of committees should reduce micromanagement by the board as a whole and by individual directors. Although, if a director is also a member of the committee, this trait may merely be moved down the organisational chain, in which case review of the committee membership would be sensible.

One way to evidence board and committee effectiveness is to undertake an audit of the two forums through review of meeting packs, agendas and minutes. If the time spent by the board remains the same, or increases, after a committee is formed, its benefit is not being evidenced. In this case, either the committee has not been effectively incorporated with clear delegation or the board is unwilling or unable to delegate the topic. Either way, it needs to be addressed or the committee may as well be terminated, although this is not an option if its existence is a legal requirement.

Conclusion

Creating a committee enables a topic that is extensive, or requires specific knowledge, to be discussed in more detail outside, and on behalf of, the board. They are not implemented as a substitute for the board, to work in isolation or conflict with the board. It should be remembered that the committee is set up by, and for, the board. Effective use of committees is empowering to a board, ineffective use of committees can have the opposite effect.

If care is taken to define the purpose of a committee prior to its implementation, with continued support, it can be a powerful support for the board and solution for the company in terms of resource and time utilisation.

2 – What is a committee?

Introduction

With reference to a committee implemented by a board of directors, a committee can be defined as a group of individuals appointed by a company to act on behalf of, but not instead of, the board of directors, under the framework of defined terms of reference in respect of a particular subject matter with pre-agreed duties and responsibilities. The committee has no direct powers other than those duties delegated in writing by the board.

All committees have a responsibility to act in the best interests of the company via their role in supporting the board of directors. Crucially, it is a delegated forum working on behalf of the board. It is not a forum in and of itself and does not act independently.

What is a committee?

As a delegated forum of the board of directors of a company, a committee is formally set up to cover a specific topic that requires more time and/or expertise than the board can commit to giving during the normal course of board meetings. By delegating specific roles, duties and responsibilities, the board does not divest itself of its own obligations and authorities. Crucially, the committee only acts on behalf of the board; it does not act instead of the board or on its own behalf.

Constituting a committee

Specifically, a committee is set up under defined and documented terms of reference which are discussed, agreed and approved by the board. These terms of reference then constitute the purpose of the committee. Their content must clearly define the remit of the committee as well as any points or decisions that have been delegated to the committee by the board. It should be noted that while the committee may make decisions concerning the role they are performing, they do not have the authority to make decisions on behalf of the board.

Further detail of the content of the terms of reference can be found in subsequent chapters both in general and concerning specific committees and reflects the importance of having this documented with clarity of content and purpose.

Best practice would be for the terms of reference of each committee to be reviewed regularly to ensure they continue to be fit for purpose. During their life, external factors will influence and affect the purpose of a committee as well as the best composition of membership. The committee chair, as a member of the board of directors, should raise the review of the committee on a defined regular basis, for example every three years. Also, if, as chair, they see a reason to review the terms of reference during this period, they should discuss this with their fellow board members and, if relevant, the members of the committee.

On occasion, committee members themselves may raise the topic of review of the terms of reference or committee membership. This should be raised with the chair who should then discuss with the board of directors. This ensures that the role of the committee as a delegated forum remains intact. If a committee member has an issue with the chair of the committee themselves, they should raise their concerns with an alternative board member in a confidential manner.

Decision making

It should be emphasised that a committee should not make decisions independently of the board unless specifically authorised to do so in writing, either under the terms of reference or via a formal instruction from the board. Care should be taken if authorisation is given verbally or by a single board member without the agreement of the wider board or, at the very least, a quorum of board members. Decisions made by a company are made by or on behalf of the board and, for future protection of both the board and the committee and their members, having a documented audit trail will reduce any potential future conflict if decisions are subsequently seen to be incorrect or ill-advised.

Any forum other than the board making a decision without documented delegation is exposing both themselves and the board to claims that a decision has been made invalidly or contrary to a decision that may subsequently be found to be mistaken or that with the passing of time or with receipt of subsequent information may be seen to be incorrect.

> **EXAMPLE: Litigation arising from unauthorised corporate decisions**
>
> Forums, such as committees, should have their authority agreed in writing and approved by the relevant authorising body, usually the board of directors of a company. Equally any quorum for making such a decision, whether at board or committee level, should be documented and adhered to. Implied authority, where repeated action is uncontested, should also be avoided as it can cause confusion between the authorities of the various forums and may lead to future litigation where the decision is contested by one party or another and creates a drain on resources, cash and time.

> Where these written requirements are not followed, subsequent claims can be made that the decision was invalid, even if the decision was made for the right reasons or based on incorrect information.
>
> *Smith v Henniker-Major & Co [2001] 10 WLUK 465*
> The claimant, a director of the company 'the Company' sued the defendant, a firm of solicitors the 'Firm' for professional negligence, relying on a purported assignment of the company's cause of action against the Firm to the Company.
> The assignment was found to be invalid because the relevant resolution to assign the cause of action had been passed without the requisite quorum of directors, and therefore no valid board meeting had taken place.

Where decision-making powers have been delegated these should be clearly evidenced in writing.

An example would be where the audit committee has been specifically tasked with reviewing the role of auditor on a regular basis with a delegated authority to re-appoint auditors annually and replace auditors on a three-year rolling cycle. The actual appointment of auditors would be ratified and documented by the board via their board minutes but the appointment of the auditors would be agreed by the committee. Given the increasing focus on auditors and their use, especially where companies have gone into default, it is imperative that the choice of auditor to appoint is transparent and documented clearly.

For clarity, any decision made by a committee should either be:

(a) a decision made within the powers of the committee and as evidenced by the specific delegation of decision making to the committee; or
(b) a decision made that is ratified by the board prior to its implementation.

Reporting

As a minimum, all committees should provide a written report to the board for each board meeting. Its purpose is to report, document and evidence the actions of the committee and include details of decisions made, decisions to be ratified or approved by the board and advice to the board for the board to make a decision. Additionally, board reports should include sufficient detail that the board maintains their confidence in the application of the terms of reference by the committee and their continued effectiveness in their role.

Board reports should not be so detailed that the board meeting reviews and re-discusses the topics covered by the committee. If this is happening the committee's expertise and abilities are being undermined while the available time of the board to discuss their other responsibilities is reduced. Further detail on composition and content of board reports by committees is included in Chapter 4: Operational Aspects of Committees.

Best practice is for each report of the committee to the formal board meeting to clearly disclose any decisions that have been made in the previous period for the board to ratify them. This ensures that committee decisions are noted and approved by board members on whose behalf decisions have been made. Equally, it ensures that the board is aware of committee decisions that have been made on their behalf.

External reporting

Committees within listed companies will have an additional responsibility to provide a written report to be included in the published annual report of the company. Specifically, this includes audit, remuneration, risk and nominations committees. Such reports should include detail of the role and remit of the committee as well as how they have discharged their responsibilities during the relevant financial year. Reporting is specifically to investors as readers of the report and is a consolidation of the work undertaken in the specific year.

Under the Companies (Miscellaneous Reporting) Regulations 2018, Regulation 16, remuneration committee reporting is required to provide information to be included in the annual report in respect of reporting on remuneration and pay ratio matters. Further detail is included in each specific chapter.

Conclusion

The addition of a committee can add significant value to a company and its board in broadening the expertise and time available to delve more deeply into specific topics. Even where a committee is constituted with no decision-making powers, having a committee to review, consider, discuss and contribute additional knowledge can support the effectiveness of board considerations and their decisions.

While some committees for certain types of companies are best practice or required by legislation, committee implementation in general by all boards should be considered, even if this is only constituted for specific periods or purposes. Having the ability and open mind-set to be able to delegate and devolve to another forum can, in itself, enable the board to be more focused on its own deliverables. It also builds a board culture of identifying and accepting the additional advice and knowledge of others to support the collective expertise already prevalent on a board.

3 – Implementing a committee

Introduction

New committees should be implemented by the board at a formal board meeting, where the requirement for, and implementation of, the committee is documented in a board minute. This should refer to the terms of reference for the committee which should be agreed and approved by the board. Without this formality, the committee lacks formal guidance on its purpose as well as the documented evidence of its implementation.

Documentary evidence of the implementation of the committee is also a useful tool for explaining the purpose of the committee to potential committee members as well as others who may have dealings with the committee and its members, either formally or informally.

Example wording for inclusion in the minutes would be: 'The board, after due care and consideration, agrees to implement a [ ] committee for the purpose of [ ] in accordance with the term of reference of such committee as hereby approved by the board.'

Where a committee is being implemented urgently, the board may discuss, agree and document via the minutes of the board meeting, the purpose of the committee. However, formal written terms of reference and immediate appointments to the committee may be delegated to a board member. Where this responsibility is delegated to an individual who is not a board member, the board should be satisfied that the nominated individual understands the purpose of the committee, with specific reference to deliverables, delegated authorities and reporting requirements.

Terms of reference

The terms of reference of all committees should clearly document the purpose of the committee as well as any responsibilities, duties or roles delegated from the board to such committee. The terms of reference will form the basis for the operations of the committee. Hence, ensuring clarity of content, and that all board members have agreed to such content, is imperative to enabling the committee to be effective.

As a minimum, the terms of reference should include the following general matters:

- membership;
- chair and secretary;
- quorum for decision making;
- frequency of meetings;
- notice of meetings;
- duties; and
- reporting responsibilities.

The practical terms of reference for a committee should mirror those of the board from which they have been implemented, sharing best practice, support functions and timetables. For example, minutes should be of a similar nature and format following company preference as to the depth of content and confidentiality. The quorum for decision making should also be based on the same framework as the board, often based on percentages. For example, 25% of members of an eight-person board requires at least two members to be present for it to be quorate.

To support this consistency, it is preferable for the company secretary to attend and minute committee meetings, although this is best practice rather than a definitive requirement. The benefit is that the company secretary can ensure consistency of meeting approach, minutes, administration and terms of reference across multiple committees and forums. They can also then provide feedback to the board, specifically its chair, as to the workings of the committees as individual forums and their interactions between themselves as the combined governance structure of the company.

The key point that the terms of reference should include is the duties of the committee, documenting the remit and responsibilities delegated from the board. It is this that will form the framework of the committee, its discussions and its work. Specifically, it should document any points where the committee has the ability to make decisions independently with notice to, but not prior approval from, the board. Similarly, any areas where prior board approval would be required, or where decision making remains with the board, should be clearly documented. Given the final responsibility rests with the board, any areas where it is unclear which forum should have decision-making responsibility should default to board level.

Examples and further details of the specific duties of each committee are incorporated into specific committee chapters later in this book.

Committee chair and secretary

Best practice is for the chair of the committee to be a member of the main board of directors so that they can straddle the two forums. They have a key responsibility to ensure that the committee works within its terms of reference and that it reports effectively to the board. When at board meetings, they will be the main spokesperson for the committee and are able to address any queries arising from the board report that the committee will have presented.

As a committee chair, it is expected that the individual will have experience of both the subject matter and chairing a board, formal meeting, committee or another similar forum. Knowledge of the subject matter may not be extensive given the members of the committee are those that bring the specific expertise required to drive the discussion and decision making. As an example, it is unlikely that the chair of a finance and audit committee would not have had some exposure to working with finance professionals, appointing auditors or leading internal finance functions to gain and maintain peer respect. It is also likely that they will have formal qualifications in accountancy or another finance-based qualification, although this is not a prerequisite to being effective in their role.

The chair of the committee has responsibility for the overall governance of the committee working with administrative support, whether provided by the company secretary or otherwise, to ensure that the committee is effective. They provide the framework for the working of the committee and the effectiveness of each committee meeting. As such, they drive both the agenda and the contents of the committee meeting pack. They also have the ability to delegate from the committee to other sub-groups or contributors, as long as this ability is not specifically restricted under the terms of reference.

As with the chair of any meeting, they must facilitate the contribution by all committee members. This is particularly important when introducing new or inexperienced committee members who may need support, guidance, coaching or mentoring to be able to contribute at their best in initial meetings. These members, plus experienced or long-standing committee members, by their interaction with each other, and contribution as a collective, form the basis of a robust and effective committee. A successful chair is only as effective as the committee members they lead.

They should also monitor the composition of the committee and make recommendations for new members and/or, as the purpose of the committee progresses, the removal of those who no longer have the relevant knowledge or skills to contribute or the availability to commit. As with board composition, committee membership should straddle the twin aims of maintaining momentum and effectiveness through having experienced members while also addressing new requirements and refreshing the composition. Board effectiveness reviews can equally be undertaken for committee composition aligned to the purpose of the committee, although formal evaluation by external reviewers may not be required.

Committee membership

Members of the committee are appointed for their expertise within the specific remit of the committee. It should be noted that in the same way that diversity of experience, knowledge and outlook for the board is key to having an effective board, the same applies to committee membership. For example, while an audit committee will, by its nature, have a majority of members with an accounting background, diversity of discussion can be facilitated through having members with alternative backgrounds and experience of financial matters. Additional members could have experience of appointing auditors in an executive capacity or operational experience of receiving financial reporting.

Composition of the wider committee is dependent on the terms of reference of the committee, the specific drivers to implementing a committee and the nature of the business. It is the contribution of the committee as a whole that brings added value rather than the strength of any one individual. Hence it is important that the committee as a collective body is appointed with individuals bringing complementary skills and knowledge. Appointing for a new committee enables the composition of the members to be considered as a group, identifying those areas where different skills may be beneficial. As an example, a committee set up to monitor markets, consider opportunities and identify new product development in the technology market would benefit not just from technology expertise but also development skills, multiple technology and digital experience, consumer use of technology and experience of working in competitor organisations. The skills to monitor markets and competitors could be beneficial and may not be from the technology sector while customer knowledge and marketing could also add additional value to discussions. If the committee is only composed of technology experts the opportunity to discuss more widely and discuss and develop outside of the norm within the sector could be missed.

How many members?

The number of members of each committee should be defined in the terms of reference; however, it is most frequently defined by stating the minimum number of members that should be in place at any one time. Consideration should also be given to the size of the company, whereby a large committee may not be appropriate for a smaller organisation or for one with a narrow focus. Consideration should also be given to the culture of the company and whether this should be reflected in, or challenged through, the composition of the committee.

If relevant, it should be noted in the terms of reference if members of one committee should also sit on another committee. For example, the terms of reference may state that the audit committee membership should also include a representative of the risk committee and vice versa.

Consideration should be given to the purpose of the committee and the skills and expertise that would benefit the deliverables identified. Through this, individual members' attributes can be identified and the number of members that would be required to be able to provide such expertise.

The effectiveness of the committee should also be reflected in its size, given that a large committee membership will drive lengthy discussion and long meetings, potentially resulting in sub-committee meetings. Given this, smaller committees may be more effective in time management and effectiveness, especially if combined with utilising external contributors or sub-committee forums for topic-specific or technical knowledge.

Having specific skills represented by committee members does not preclude the committee also requesting experts to contribute and/or attend committee meetings to share their expertise. An individual who attends a meeting as a non-member would be documented in the minutes as in attendance 'by invitation'. They may attend all, or just the relevant part, of the committee meeting. This is particularly beneficial where a topic is being discussed that may not be a standing agenda topic in the future. An example could be the attendance of a legal representative to explain new legislation being implemented and how it may affect the scope of a particular committee. As a specific example, a legal attendee, or submission paper, to a sales and marketing committee may be used to explain new legislation impacting on the distribution of knowledge via social media and the legal requirements that digital marketing may have to align to.

A beneficial consideration when deciding whether to appoint new committee members, rather than occasional contributors, is to consider if the topic will be a standing agenda for each meeting. In this case, a committee member with specific responsibility would be beneficial. The consideration of what knowledge would be required to understand and present the topic should be given. If existing members have neither sufficient knowledge nor available time, may not be required, noting that the nominated committee member may draw on expertise outside of the committee to enhance their personal knowledge. If existing members have neither sufficient knowledge nor available time, the appointment of a new committee member should be considered, discussed and agreed.

The quorum and voting of committees should be defined in the relevant terms of reference, noting that a minimum quorum for each meeting should be included, whether in person, via telephone or other electronic means. Having an uneven number of committee members ensures that voting or decision making can be by a majority, although absences may require the chair to have the casting vote. The ability for the chair to have the casting vote, if appropriate, should be documented in the terms of reference.

Individual committee membership

When being appointed to a committee, each member should have a clear and documented understanding of:

- the period of their appointment and if it can be renewed;
- their roles, responsibilities and deliverables and that of the committee to which they are appointed;
- any areas of specific focus for them as an individual;

- the process and frequency of evaluation of the committee they are a member of and themselves as a contributor; and
- the processes of the committee including meeting schedules, meeting packs, agendas and other practical considerations.

Specific requirements of committee membership skills, attributes and experience would be reviewed by the chair, the CEO, and the board or, if there is one, the nomination committee.

The board should also be mindful of overlap between committees and their membership ensuring that duplication, conflict or mistaken [absence] does not occur. Board members, especially independent board members, are most frequently members of the committee and usually the committee chair. The board should ensure that committee membership does not replicate the board, as this will stifle independent, fresh discussion and may blur the lines between the two forums.

Equally, both individuals on their own account, chairs and board as a collective, should be mindful of time commitment by individuals to ensure that they have the bandwidth to contribute.

As delegated forums of the board, membership of each committee should align to the skills and experience of board members ensuring the company and the board get the best value out of independent directors in supporting the success of the company.

While appointment to the board and committees may be on the recommendation of the nomination committee, the board should recognise the benefits of diversity and effective governance through boardroom dynamics. Each individual member should recognise where they can escalate any concerns they may have, including beyond the chair of the forum of which they are a member if discussing concerns with the chair would be inappropriate.

Committee member tenure

Terms of membership of committee members should mirror that of the board. If there is a time limited term, such as nine years, the same should apply to the committee, given that the reasons for time limiting board membership would equally apply to committee membership.

It should be noted that, where a committee membership is aligned to a representative of the board, the board membership will define their term as a committee member. However, there is no legal requirement for committee membership to be terminated at the same time as termination of board membership unless the committee membership is linked to their position on the board. As an example, the terms of reference of the committee membership may state that the finance director should be a member of the audit committee. A change in finance director at board level would have a linked change to the individual sitting on the audit committee. In this case it is the role of the finance director that is the committee member not the individual.

Equally, if a board member's appointment is terminated due to their conduct or their resignation from the company, the termination of the membership of the committee would be effective at the same time.

It should be noted that minuting the termination of a board member at board level does not automatically terminate their appointment as a committee member. The termination of their appointment as a committee member should be documented by the relevant committee, even if the board minutes additionally note the termination of their committee appointment alongside their termination as a board director.

Committee size and quorum

There are no prerequisites for the size of a committee although, as with a board of directors, it must be of sufficient size to be meaningful and beneficial without being so large that meetings are too long or discussions do not enable all members to contribute. Similarly, it is important that all members have the ability to contribute as equals.

The size of a committee is determined by its terms of reference and the areas of expertise that are required. As a combined group, committee members should be able to address all matters evidenced in the terms of reference. Hence if the terms of reference are narrow with a limited remit on topic, deliverables or decision making, it would be sufficient to have a small committee. Larger committees would be justified where the remit of the committee is broad in topic, requiring broad experience and knowledge to be evidenced and contributed. Hence a combined committee of finance, audit and risk, as a minimum, would require members who have experience and can, between them, confidently discuss all three areas of responsibility. It would also be beneficial to have more than one expert on each topic to ensure that a wide approach to knowledge is available as a foundation for discussions.

What should not be ignored is that all committee members should expect to contribute to all topics under discussion so, as a minimum, should be confident in their ability to contribute on the contents of the terms of reference as a whole, not just a small sub-section.

Where a committee member is the acknowledged expert on any given topic, they should also be mindful that colleagues will have at least some relevant knowledge that will support a broadened discussion. The strength of a committee in its discussions, decisions and ultimate success is the combination of knowledge. An unchallenged expert on a committee will not support the delivery of an effective committee or support the dialogues and decision making that the board has delegated.

Diversity of knowledge and experience in committee members is equally as important as it is in board composition and should be the aim when creating a new committee or replacing retiring members.

Practically it is advantageous to have an uneven number of committee members to avoid stalemate in any decision making. Good practice may also determine that the chair should have a casting vote in cases of equal voting, however, as a committee, it is equally possible, where a decision has strong views for two outcomes, for both sides to be taken to the board for a final decision at board level. However, this should remain for significant committee decisions and only those occasions where stalemate cannot be avoided. If every committee decision is taken to the board for resolution, the value of the committee is diminished, and members may best serve as board advisers rather than having the formal role of committee members.

Frequency of meetings and notice

Frequency of committee meetings is noted in the terms of reference. As best practice, they should mirror the board meeting schedule, given they report into each board meeting. Hence quarterly board meetings should create at least quarterly committee meetings. However, if the committee covers active areas of concern or focus, more frequent committee meetings would be appropriate. In particular, topic-specific or time-limited committees meeting for a defined purpose may require active meeting schedules.

An example could be a committee to drive forward a new product launch on behalf of the board. Given the need for rapid implementation, this committee may meet weekly or fortnightly to monitor and have oversight of the implementation. Equally an organisation with a strong focus on risk and a broad risk-based culture may require an active risk committee meeting monthly to have oversight or operational risks as well as the functionality of the risk-based culture across the business.

Finance-related committee meetings would expect their annual meeting schedule to include meetings aligned to budget setting, the financial year-end and audit reporting. For example, the audit committee of Just Eat Plc reported in their 2018 annual report that they met five times, with two of these meetings focused particularly on the audit tender process. The remaining three meetings were scheduled around full-year results, half-year results and year-end accounting, with additional standing agenda topics such as audit, tax and risk.

Scheduling committee meetings prior to board meetings with sufficient time to contribute to board packs makes practical sense. Standing committees aligned to board meeting schedules would benefit from meeting two to three weeks prior to each board meeting to ensure that committee submissions to the board are available and current.

Notice periods for committee meetings should mirror that set at board level to ensure consistency, noting that this may be significantly in advance of the meeting and is often set either at the end of each meeting or against an annual calendar.

Distribution of meeting packs before each meeting should enable sufficient time for contents to be current, balanced with the need for members and participants to have sufficient time to read the contents before the meeting. This is usually at the very least 48 hours in advance and preferably longer, especially where the meeting pack is extensive.

Reporting responsibilities

Committee reporting responsibilities are primarily to the board given that they are acting on their behalf. As noted above, submissions to each board meeting in a format that is consistent with general board reporting packs should be provided ahead of each board meeting.

It should be noted that day-to-day deliverables of the committee should be documented in committee minutes rather than incorporated in board reports. If full information is provided for discussion at the board level, the benefit of delegation to the committee is lost to the board as discussions and decisions would be duplicated.

It should be further noted that board reports should clearly document and include any decisions taken by the committee on behalf of the board for ratification by the board. Equally, any decisions requested by the committee to be made by the board should be clearly evidenced, including any relevant supporting narrative to support the board in making such decisions.

When reporting to the board it should be remembered that the implementation of the committee was to act as an effective delegate of the board thus reducing the board's requirement to have detailed discussion of the delegated topics. If the board duplicates discussions held at committee level, the purpose of the board is negated. Ensuring this occurs is the responsibility of both board and committee members.

Conclusion

Practical implementation of a committee should be seen alongside the requirements of the board, ensuring that the terms of reference have clarity of the purpose and the deliverables. The board as a whole should be supportive of the process and see the benefit of both implementing the committee and implementing it as quickly as possible so that the benefits can be seen promptly.

Ideally, practical application of the requirements is delegated to a senior supportive team, such as the company secretarial or legal function. They can then ensure that the new committee is constituted in a standard form to the board and other committees. The nominations committee, if there is one, should be tasked with identifying the skills required within the committee and subsequently seeking potential candidates.

The chair of the board, plus the designated board member who will be a member (or chair) of the relevant committee if this is not the chair of the board, should be the primary drivers to conclude the process. Where there is no nomination committee in place, these individuals should also lead the process for identifying and appointing members.

The board should confirm the implementation of the committee in its minutes once it is concluded. There should also be clarity on the required reporting and how any escalations will be accepted, discussed, approved and monitored.

Finally, there should be a regular documented review of all committees undertaken by the board based on their contribution against the terms of reference and their deliverables. Early intervention where a committee may be veering away from required deliverables will have more impact and be more easily applied than late or slow recognition that the committee is no longer supporting the board.

Implementation is primarily an administrative process, but it needs the full support and backing of the board if the committee is to be able to deliver from the outset.

4 – Operational aspects of committees

Introduction

Once constituted with agreed terms of reference and members, the practical actions of the committee can commence. These are best aligned to the operations of the board to ensure that consistency is seen across the governance framework of the company.

This chapter provides clarity on the key operational aspects of committees, giving a framework for committee meetings themselves, as well as committee packs, reporting and review. It also gives consideration to measuring the effectiveness of board packs in their support of the committee in its role to support the board and contribute to the success of the company as a whole.

Committee meetings

As with board meetings, it is imperative that the meetings of every committee are documented through formal minutes as a record of discussions, decisions and actions agreed.

Each committee meeting should have a set agenda based on the roles and responsibilities identified in the terms of reference. The agenda may have annual actions that should be included as well as those included at each meeting.

Committee chair

The committee chair should have a one-to-one relationship with the chair of the board of directors ensuring that any significant or time prioritised issues can be raised immediately in a non-formal way if necessary. The board of the company and the committee will have different priorities and focus areas so it is important that the chair of the committee is able to recognise, understand or be notified of board priorities so that these can be accommodated and delivered by the committee. The committee should recognise that the board has a holistic overview of the whole company and all committees so it may direct specific committees to prioritise review of a particular topic that, while not a priority for the committee, may be part of a wider priority of the company.

Through this connection, the chair of the committee should also seek feedback on the effectiveness of the committee and any areas where additional responsibility, duties or roles should or could be delegated to the committee to benefit the board.

The chair should also take personal responsibility for setting the agenda of each committee meeting, both standing agendas and ad hoc meetings. They should work collegiately with the company secretary/administrative support to ensure that the agreed agenda covers all the topics required as well as including any points or actions to be taken forward from previous meetings. The chair should also ensure that committee packs are collated and shared with members in a timely manner.

When at the committee, the chair should ensure that all attendees have an opportunity to contribute to the discussion, ensuring that individual expertise is drawn on and that fresh ideas can be shared and discussed. As chair it is their responsibility to ensure that the committee does not fall into any of the four types of dysfunctional behaviour prevalent in ineffective boards or committees, namely:

1   Group think, of the collective members.
2   Conflict due to different perspectives, background, role or behaviour.
3   Overly operational in focus rather than effective oversight and challenge.
4   Passivity of individual board members or a general tick-box mentality.

The role of the chair is multifaceted, and the various responsibilities they have in ensuring that the committee is effective should not be underestimated. They need to have abilities that straddle administration, knowledge, intellect and emotional intelligence. They are both a coach to the members and a leader of the committee. There is a reason why the chair of a committee is remunerated at a higher level than committee members.

Committee packs

Much has been written about board packs and how to generate meaningful packs to support the purpose of the board rather than simply focusing on reporting raw data. Committee packs have the same potential for containing multiple reports and data dumps without addressing the needs of the attendees at the meeting. The results of a survey on board packs conducted by The Chartered Governance Institute and Board Intelligence in December 2017 reported that over 70% of respondents saw board packs as too long and, understandably as a result, too time-consuming to prepare.

Additionally, over 50% saw them as too operational, internally focused and backward looking, surely something that the executive committee should have oversight of, rather than the board receiving full detail as well. Ensuring board and committee packs are generated for the correct forum, without overlap or duplication, can support more effective meetings. Challenging contributors on why and how their meeting report supports the forum in their discussions, roles and responsibilities, may assist those producing reports to become more aware of the impact good reporting can have. Equally, clarity of data submission and including this as an appendix for reference if required rather than in the main body of the report, enables focus to be on the report content rather than the data itself.

Reflecting this, more concerningly, in the survey was that 51% of respondents felt that it was hard to extract the key messages from the board pack while 30% thought they were not readily understandable. If this same metric is shared by all those who receive committee packs, it is unclear how a governance framework can be working in the best interests of the company or how the constituent members can add the value that their experience and expertise could bring.

How can this be addressed?

Follow up work from that same survey resulted in three tools being produced to help organisations with the preparation and presentation of their board reporting:

- the cost calculator, to enable organisations to work out how much time and money they currently spend on reports for the board and its committees;
- a self-assessment tool to enable organisations to assess the length and balance of their board packs and identify ways in which they might be made more user-friendly and better focused; and
- guidance to assist company secretaries and governance professionals in addressing some of the challenges identified by this research.

Cost calculator

The cost calculator is available on The Chartered Governance Institute website and allows users to uncover the hidden costs of board and committee reporting, reflecting the resources used in terms of time and money in producing meeting reports. Specifically, it covers the time spent writing, reviewing, compiling and distributing board and committee papers as well as the time spent by committee members reading these papers. The results provide a simple image of the time and cost of preparing meeting packs, whether these are effective packs or not.

Self-assessment tool

The self-assessment tool produced by The Chartered Governance Institute enables companies to assess their board reports in the following three areas:

- Style – the quantity and accessibility of their reports.
- Scope and content – the quality and effectiveness of their reports.
- Process – the efficiency, security and timeliness of their board reporting cycle.

Guidance

The guidance consists of four sections which give a framework for the development of a board pack:

1 Identifying the information the forum needs.
2 Commissioning meeting papers.
3 Writing meeting papers.
4 Collating and distributing the meeting pack.

While aimed at supporting those collating and producing the meeting pack itself, the first point, identifying what information is needed, is the foundation for the production of a meeting pack that beneficially supports the discussions held at each meeting.

Taking the terms of reference of the committee as a starting point, the committee chair, working with their company secretary, can identify those topics that should be prioritised as opposed to those that are for information purposes only. Drafting the agenda and the form of the meeting pack to reflect this then creates a foundation for effectiveness.

Over time priorities will inevitably change and need to be adapted, while significant escalations, emerging issues or immediate concerns will often overtake the formalities of the meeting for good reasons. Reviewing the standing agenda and adapting it for each meeting may be time well spent ahead of meeting packs being collated, rather than when the agenda is discussed. This advanced planning will help to identify the key items for discussion and will enable the production of a supportive meeting pack.

When new committee members are appointed, part of their induction should include a walk through the previous meeting packs, the agendas and meeting minutes. Given the expertise of these appointees, this is also an opportunity to review the content based on their experiences, good and bad, when appointed to other committees or formal forums.

Operational content

When comparing board packs and committee packs, it should be noted that, depending on its terms of reference, the committee may, in fact, be the forum where operational matters are discussed given their oversight role, or in the case of the executive committee, their day-to-day responsibilities as a forum and individuals. If this is the case, the benefit of a committee as oversight for operational matters may reduce this content in board packs but may, as a consequence, increase it in committee packs. Hence, the balance of what to include in the committee pack is just as important as that for board packs.

Care should be taken that the simplest option of providing the same report and data to both the committee and the board is not taken. These are two different forums with different objectives and, as a result, different needs in terms of information provision. Time spent by the contributor tailoring their submission to the needs of the relevant forum will not only use the forum members' time more effectively it will also aid the discussion and reduce the level of queries resulting from that discussion. After all, if operational matters are presented in detail to both forums, there is a natural result that this detail will be reviewed and commented on by both. The contributor then receives two sets of comments, and potential actions back, with the risk that these contradict each other. Hence short-term focus on requirements may result in long-term gains in terms of focused responses and required actions.

Questions to consider

In a follow up to the survey, The Chartered Governance Institute collated helpful tips that were provided by survey respondents and subsequent submissions. This proposed 12 simple questions that companies could consider when reviewing their board packs for content, collation and distribution. This has been adapted here to reflect the considerations of committees when reviewing their committee packs:

1 Purpose: What parts of the terms of reference of the committee are being covered in each committee meeting? Is the committee clear about how it wishes to divide its time between these roles and responsibilities within the committee meeting?
2 Authority: Is the committee clear about which decisions it has authority to take? Is it clear when decisions must be escalated to the board, either for ratification or decision? Is it clear which decisions are not relevant to the committee?
3 Content: Is the committee clear on the criteria for determining when other matters are significant enough to be brought to their attention? Is the submission relevant to the purpose and discussions of the committee and, if not, why is it included? Do the forward meeting plans, individual agendas and meeting packs reflect the committee's priorities? Do the agenda and individual papers make clear what action or input is needed from the committee? Do papers set out all the relevant considerations and implications of which the committee should be aware?
4 Collation: Are responsibilities for commissioning, writing, reviewing and collating the board pack clear? Are contributors properly briefed on why the committee wants the paper, what information it needs and how it should be presented?
5 Format: Do you have or need standard formats for different types of committee papers? Is training and support available to contributors?
6 Distribution: Is the meeting pack easy to navigate and readily accessible for committee members? Is the meeting pack distributed with sufficient time before the meeting for members to review the content without the content becoming too historical?
7 Storage: Are the methods by which the committee pack is stored and distributed secure? Are committee members and contributors clear on their responsibilities regarding the storage of meeting packs, particularly any confidential data?

8   Feedback: Does the board give feedback on the clarity and usefulness of the papers it receives?

The aim remains for the forum, in this case, the relevant committee, to be effective in its purpose and efficient in its use of time. Succinct, meaningful committee packs aligned to the terms of reference of the committee will enable committee members to contribute their expertise and support the board through their contribution.

Agenda

Best practice, once the formalities of the meeting such as attendees and absences noted and any conflicts of interest have been completed, is for the actions agreed at previous meetings to form the core of the meeting agenda. This action list should be in a format that identifies all actions agreed at previous meetings, their timetable for completion and the party responsible for completion. By keeping this as the core of the committee, progress can be tracked against critical actions.

The agenda should also cover any issues that have been raised within reports to the committee or as a result of a committee member's review of the submission.

Standing agendas should include an initial review of agreed actions from previous meetings to ensure they are on target to deliver against expectations and identify if any additional resources or time is required to facilitate their completion. Thereafter agenda items should firstly follow any new urgent actions or issues to address, followed by review, update and discussion based on submitted reports.

There are differing views on the benefits of including 'any other business' as the final agenda item. Some believe this is a detrimental inclusion as it may extend the length of meetings to accommodate unimportant or superficial matters and that significant points should have been included in the main body of the agenda for discussion, Conversely, it can provide attendees with an opportunity to raise a topic that wasn't covered within the substance of the meeting and that remains a concern for themselves.

Whether any other business is included as a final agenda item or not, best practice is for the chair to allow sufficient time at the end of each meeting to specifically ask all attendees if there are any final points they would like to raise before the close of the meeting. By doing this, the chair ensures that all members are formally included in the meeting and have had an opportunity to contribute, even if they have not contributed during the main part of the meeting.

Time keeping

Frustration in meetings is most often evident when a meeting runs over its allotted time. The best practice is to allocate sufficient time for discussion of each topic, noting this alongside each topic on the agenda.

Company secretaries and those facilitating or supporting meetings are integral to avoiding lengthy meetings that overrun their allotted time.

A confident and experienced chair will enable focused discussion, moving lengthy discussions outside the formal meeting if they require more in-depth consideration. This may include the creation of a sub-committee to meet on a specific topic and report back either before or at the next meeting.

Care should be exercised when moving discussion outside of the formal committee meeting to document the purpose, scope and attendees at any such subset of the committee. Clarity of purpose and reporting will protect all members from the possibility of decisions being made, or actions taken outside of the formal forum that have not been agreed.

The benefit of a subset discussion on a particular topic by a smaller group is that it can be more focused and effective. However, often these subsets are populated by experts on the subject, so do not benefit from the challenge of the combined committee bringing their diverse viewpoints. Hence, best practice is for any subset discussions to be brought back to the full committee for final challenge, review and ratification to ensure that the expert group-think benefits from wider input.

Committee minutes

Minutes of each committee should follow the standard format adopted by the company at board level. This should include whether the minutes are detailed in content or, conversely, should only identify and document discussion topics in a headline, decisions made or escalated, and significant points.

Members should ensure that the minutes reflect the discussion at the meeting they attended. They should specifically note and ensure the inclusion of any points they, as an individual, made that they feel should be documented in the minutes. This is particularly important where a collective decision has been made that an individual has raised concerns over. These concerns should be minuted, if relevant and substantial, and the individual's dissent to the approval included.

Discussions held outside the formality of the meeting should not be included in the minutes unless they were additionally discussed at the meeting itself.

Minutes may include ratification of decisions made by other forums on their behalf and in line with their authority. Where actions have been escalated to the board, including requests for approval, these should be documented in the minutes. Their resolution or further actions should be monitored at subsequent meetings and in their relevant minutes.

Distribution of draft minutes should be as agreed by the committee as a whole, whether immediately subsequent to the meeting or just prior to the next meeting.

As with any formal forum, the minutes of the previous meeting should be presented and approved at the subsequent meeting.

Reporting

The committee should be clear on its reporting responsibilities including what needs to be reported and to whom.

> **EXAMPLE: Reporting and monitoring**
>
> Committees should ensure that they report their concerns to the board as an escalation point and should be conscious of when this escalation should be immediate and urgent or when it can flow through the scheduled meeting channels. Where actions are agreed by the board, the committee may also be asked to monitor compliance. This example reflects how and when a committee may become involved, in this case, the safety and ethics committee is responsible for HSE and reports its actions during the year in the annual report. The full report contains a number of areas of improvement and agreed actions of which the below is a brief extract.
>
> *Rolls-Royce Holdings plc, Annual Report 2018 (extract)*
> The Committee, however, remains concerned that the number of major and high potential incidents in 2018, while fewer than in 2017, is still unacceptably high. The most serious injury in the year was a fall from height in which an employee in Derby suffered a fracture of both wrists. The UK Health and Safety Executive conducted an investigation across our Derby and Hucknall sites, also engaging with me directly. Corrective actions were required, which the Committee is overseeing to ensure full implementation.

Review

Where a committee has been incorporated by the board with full terms of reference, the practicalities of board meetings, actions and reporting should have already been agreed and documented. However, over time, this may change as different needs and responsibilities are identified and added to the remit of the committee. Given this, it is best practice for the committee to diarise review and update of the terms of reference on a regular basis to ensure that the needs and requirements of the board continue to be met. This review should informally be part of the chair's ongoing considerations. A formal review should be undertaken when any member leaves the committee for whatever reason, or after three years if no review has been instigated due to membership change.

Regular review of membership should also be undertaken by the nominations committee or if there isn't one, the board chair. This should focus on the continuing ability of committee members to contribute to the topics being covered by the committee. Over time, as the focus of the committee changes and the needs of the board change, the requirements of, deliverables from, and knowledge by, committee members will also need to adapt for the committee to continue to be effective. It is important that the membership continues to be able to support the changing needs and is relevant to the purpose of the committee. The review may include committee member evaluation, skills and knowledge comparison to updated terms of reference, monitoring of the length of service, the dynamics of the committee in its meetings and the benefit that new members may bring in terms of re-energising discussions or bringing diversity to avoid stagnation or group-think.

The review should also align with the strategy of the company and the contribution of the committee to its development, deployment and ongoing effectiveness. Where a committee is closely aligned to the strategy, such as a markets committee, the expectation would be for frequent review and re-alignment as the strategy develops and changes. For example, if a company strategy is to enter a new product, service or geographical markets, the markets committee should consider adding new members with relevant experience if the board believes this is a key strategic focus. This new addition may, or may not, be a new board member as well.

Committee review checklist

There is no set format for a committee review process, although this checklist may provide a useful starting point for implementation:

1 Terms of Reference:
   a. Review current terms of reference for obvious areas that are no longer required or are missing
   b. Review terms of reference against residual responsibilities of the board
   c. Identify any overlap with other committees and resolve ownership
   d. Consider any additional requirements from the board to add to the terms of reference
2 Committee Output:
   a. Review at least one year's output (minutes) to ensure annual topics are captured in the review
   b. Review committee minutes against roles and responsibilities detailed in the terms of reference
   c. Is there any topic that has not been covered by the committee? Is there any reason for this omission? Should it be removed from the terms of reference? Or should the committee be reminded of this responsibility?
   d. Are there any committee topics that are also covered in detail by the board or another committee? [Review against minutes of the board and other relevant committees]
   e. Is the level of escalation to the board correct, too much, too little?
   f. Is the committee working within its terms of authority?
   g. Is the committee following the relevant company processes and procedures?

3. Administration:
   a. Is the committee adequately supported?
   b. Do the meeting packs support and facilitate relevant discussion? If not, consider reviewing board pack processes, contributions and format
   c. How many times has the committee met? Have all members been able to attend? If not, is there a better way to convene meetings?
   d. Have meeting packs and minutes been distributed within agreed timelines? If not, can anything be done to support the distribution process?
   e. How many non-members attend each committee meeting? Are they required? Do they bring additional value? If not, consider reviewing and restricting attendance protocols
4. Membership
   a. Undertake a member skills matrix versus the terms of reference
   b. Are any skills missing from the current members? If so, consider adding additional member(s) to contribute these skills
   c. Are there any topics in the terms of reference that consistently require external input? If so, is this significant enough to add an additional member(s) with this knowledge and expertise?
   d. Does the committee as a group, or any individual members, have any training needs?
   e. Is the committee too large or too small?
   f. Are there succession plans in place for committee members?
5. Costs:
   a. Apply The Chartered Governance Institute cost calculator to the committee
   b. Include resource costs and those of third-party contributors to the calculation
   c. Include any duplication of effort with the board, other committees or other forums
6. Action Plan
   a. Act on the results based on:
      i. Terms of reference amendments
      ii. Membership
      iii. Administration and processes
      iv. Costs

Identify an individual, either internal or external, to undertake the review and provide feedback for consideration. Agree who will receive the feedback and agree on action points.

Discuss the checklist topics with individual board and committee members based on consistent questions to ensure feedback can be analysed.

Oversight of committees

As committees are constituted on behalf of the board, the board then has oversight responsibility to ensure that each committee continues to meet its terms and purpose. They should also ensure that overlap between committees is kept to a minimum, that their resourcing is sufficient and that they continue to benefit the functioning of the board and the company as a whole.

Delegation of the composition of committees can be delegated to the nominations committee; however, the overarching collective view of all committees is a board requirement.

Having clear definitions of each committee and their purpose can help to support an annual consideration of any changes, additions or reductions in responsibilities of committees. Based on the level of work each committee undertakes, this is also an opportunity to consider whether committees should be split into smaller more focused forums or, conversely, combined into a single forum. For example, consideration of whether a finance and risk committee should be split could be based on the level of emerging risks versus the complexity of audit and finance oversight.

Digital meeting support

Increasingly boards are being supported through the application of digital board solution enabling information to be shared with all members and support staff in a secure and timely manner. Where possible, these should also be utilised for committee meetings to ensure consistency in approach and format as well as a timely and effective interaction between forums.

Notable benefits of digital meeting support include:

- Security: data held in a secure environment utilising leading technology including encryption and accessibility protocols.
- Accessibility: content available to all committee members, support staff and contributors, with access restricted based on company guidelines.
- Adaptability: to new requirements of the committee whether internally driven, such as updated terms or reference, or externally, such as legislative requirements.
- Efficiency: with the ability to share notes, approve minutes and distribute effortlessly. Equally all records of the committee are automatically stored in a secure environment creating an effective audit trail for decisions, meetings, authorisations, actions and content.
- Consistency: ensuring that all content is shared to all users, while templates can be incorporated to drive consistent format.
- Immediacy: updates and amendments shared with users immediately via a single portal.
- Flexibility: most tools can now be accessed through all digital hardware.

EXAMPLE: Board and committee responsibilities
Great Portland Estates, Annual Report 2019, Division of Responsibilities

Board

- six scheduled meetings a year
- sets strategy
- provides oversight of purpose, culture and risk
- approves major transactions
- provides oversight of governance

> See Board activities on pages 96, 98 and 99
> See biographies of the directors on pages 70 and 71
> See division of responsibilities of the directors on page 101

Board Committees

Audit Committee
- four scheduled meetings a year
- oversees financial reporting
- monitors risk management and internal controls
- evaluates the external and internal auditor

> See Audit Committee report on page 107 to 114
> See risks management reports on pages 74 to 88

Remuneration Committee
- six scheduled meetings a year
- establishes remuneration policy
- sets executive remuneration schemes
- reviews Executive Committee member objectives and achievements
- approves senior management remuneration and LTIP awards
- approves executive bonus plan and LTIP targets
- approves the Directors' remuneration report

> See Directors' remuneration report on pages 116 to 142

Nomination Committee
- four scheduled meetings a year
- recommends Board appointment
- approves senior management appointments
- oversees succession planning
- responsible for Board effectiveness evaluation

> See Nomination Committee report on pages 102 to 106

OPERATIONAL ASPECTS OF COMMITTEES 33

Management Committees

Executive Committee
- meets weekly
- implements the Group's strategy
- oversees transactions
- monitors risks and opportunities
- responsible for succession planning, resourcing and people development
> See Strategic Report on pages 1 to 88

Sustainability Committee
- meets four times a year
- provides oversight on climate change risk and resilience
- reviews progress and development of sustainability strategy
- monitors environmental compliance
> See Sustainability on our website
www.gpe.co.uk/sustainability

Health and Safety Committee
- meets four times a year
- reviews the Group's Health and Safety compliance and performance
- provides oversight on Health and Safety strategy
- identifies and reviews opportunities for improvement
> See Sustainability on our website
www.gpe.co.uk/sustainability/working-safely

Community and Charity Committee
- meets four times a year
- oversees the implementation of the Group's community strategy
- ensures that charitable donations made are in accordance with the Group's charitable donations policy
> See Strategic Report on pages 1 to 88

Figure 4.1: Division of Responsibilities

While not the solution for all companies, particularly those with simpler structures or smaller budgets, the use of digital technology to support meetings is becoming wide spread and standard in larger more complex organisations.

> **EXAMPLE: Supporting the board and committees**
>
> *Taylor Wimpey Plc, Annual Report 2018, Nominations Committee report (extract)*
> The Group Legal Director and Company Secretary acts as Secretary to the Board and its Committees and he attends all meetings. It is Board policy that wherever possible a formal agenda and reports are issued electronically to Directors in respect of all Board and Committee meetings at least one week prior to the meeting, in order to allow sufficient time for detailed review and consideration beforehand. Formal minutes are prepared in respect of all Board and Committee meetings and are then circulated and submitted for approval at the next meeting. All Board papers are circulated electronically and Board meetings have been effectively 'paperless' for several years, which has worked well and aided the overall efficiency of the wider Board process.

As these develop, cost considerations of their use by smaller companies may be offset by the efficiencies they can bring, particularly in terms of time spent, consistency and reliability of storage.

When moving to a digital solution, care should be taken on planning the time and cost that may be initially duplicated versus the long-term benefit.

Wider interaction beyond the committee

Historically, independent board members and their role within committees has been seen as a way to include wider experience and knowledge of other organisations into the governance framework of an organisation. Their broader roles and previous experience will have provided alternative insights as well as a different pool of external contacts from which to draw knowledge.

While the role of the committee is to support the board with this independent voice, increased interaction between committee members and the wider organisation is being seen, including by independent directors.

Committee members may seek to interact with the wider company to underpin their knowledge of the company, gather knowledge from a wider pool of employees, extend their contact beyond written reports and the executive team or, in the case of executive committee members, extend their knowledge beyond the function to which they are aligned. In some companies, the wider experience of committee members is used to benefit the company and its workforce by mentoring or coaching rising talent within an organisation.

It may also be beneficial for individual committees to work together on specific topics, or to share knowledge between the two forums. This is prevalent where there are full committees in place with close topics on which to focus but with some overlap to another committee. Some committees actively engage with each other as full forums while others rely on individual members to cross-reference the workings of the two committees, most commonly the chair. Most frequently this is seen where there is a separate risk and audit committee given the overlap in terms of financial risk oversight.

> **EXAMPLE: Committees working collegiately**
>
> *BP, Annual Report 2018 (extract)*
>
> *Joint meetings of the audit and safety, ethics and environment assurance committees*
>
> The audit committee and SEEAC hold joint meetings on a quarterly basis to simplify reporting of key issues that are within the remit of both committees and to make more effective use of the committees' time. Each committee retains full discretion to require a full presentation and discussion on any joint meeting topic at their respective meeting if deemed appropriate. The committees jointly met four times in 2018, with the chairmanship of the meetings alternating between the chairman of the audit committee and chairman of the SEEAC. Topics discussed at the joint meetings were the quarterly ethics and compliance reports (including significant investigations and allegations) and the 2019 forward programmes for the group audit and ethics and compliance functions.

Supporting committees

Ensure meeting packs are provided with sufficient time for committee members to read the content before the meeting.

Work with the chair to ensure:

- the right length;
- the agenda prioritises the actions the committee needs to deliver;
- that reports for information only do not become full agenda items; and
- that previous actions agreed by the committee are documented and reviewed for completion.

Ensure reports submitted to each committee support the discussion to be held and reflect the agenda priorities. That the content is informative, not data only. That consideration has been undertaken by the report compiler as to the content, the purpose and their specific knowledge. Don't submit data-only reports for committee members to have to firstly review the data to identify the findings that the data is evidencing. Within committee reports, any data should support the report. As a process, the compiler of the report analyses the data, disseminates their findings from this analysis and presents these findings in the report. The role of the committee is to reflect on the report itself and the findings being presented. Committee members may refer to the data when considering the report or to validate or challenge the findings but should not undermine the compiler's knowledge and expertise by reviewing the data in isolation or dismissing the compiler's report and findings. To ensure this is the case, it is often best practice to include data as an appendix to the report for reference only if needed, instead of incorporating it in the main body of the report.

Review agendas and report contributions for effectiveness in supporting the committee's roles and goals.

If in a position to influence, ensure that the terms of reference are reviewed and re-approved by the board on a regular basis and that all board members respect the contribution of the committee.

When working with the board, ensure that the work of each committee is not duplicated or undermined by the meetings of the board. If they are, both the board and the relevant committee becomes ineffective.

Conclusion

Considered in totality, the operational aspects of constituting and maintaining an effective committee may seem daunting, both to board members and to those that support the governance of a company. In some cases, this is so daunting that the board continues to cling on to significant issues, thus denying themselves the additional expertise, band-width and resources that a committee can deliver. Building a robust framework and mapping the operations of each committee to that of the board itself can serve to give board members comfort that a committee is invaluable in supporting them in their effectiveness and can mitigate any limitations that the board may have, in particular, that of time.

Maintaining oversight at board level with constant light-touch review can also ensure the continued effectiveness of each committee. Where this is aligned to more formal reviews, each committee can add a significant contribution to the success of a company and their contribution can be easily tracked, audited and valued.

Successful committees not only have clear responsibilities and deliverables, they also have an operational framework and support team that enables their contribution to be beneficial and measurable. The combination of this plus engaged committee members and a supportive board are fundamental to the success of each committee. Hence discussing, aligning and agreeing the operational aspects of each committee is time well spent that will deliver future benefit.

5 – Executive committee

Introduction

The executive committee (commonly known as the 'ExCo') is a subset of the board with responsibility for the day-to-day running of the business. It has no non-executive members, instead reporting to the board on all operational matters of the company. Members take specific responsibility for aspects of the business, i.e. sales and marketing, service delivery, finance, HR.

More than any other forum of a company, the executive committee sets the tone and creates the culture of a company. Its members are the visible face of the company for the majority of its employees and personally represent the company values, whether formally defined and communicated or not. Members, between them, have responsibility for all operational aspects of a company as well as being the primary forum for discussion and agreeing the future strategy for review by the board as a whole.

Often within a large company the functions of the executive committee are assumed to be understood by all employees, however, best practice would be to be transparent and openly share the responsibilities of this forum with all employees and stakeholders, as well as identifying any areas where the board retains sole responsibility.

As a subset of the main board with operational responsibility and no non-executive director representation, this committee maintains the hands-off independent nature of the non-executives appointed to the board. Executive committee members take leadership responsibility for specific areas of the company and may, or may not, also be full board members.

The executive committee is chaired by the chief executive officer ('CEO') of the company who brings together the members to ensure that the company has a forum taking responsibility for operational effectiveness, the implementation of the near-term business plan and the long-term strategy. The CEO reports to the independent chair of the board working closely with them for the benefit of the company.

Unlike other committees, it is not usually a formally implemented committee of the board with defined delegated responsibilities. Instead it is assumed that the purpose of the executive committee as a collective forum is known and understood, with individual members having clear roles, responsibilities and deliverables.

Its members comprise the C-suite of the company, namely the 'chief of' the various functions of the company. Aside from the chief executive officer, other core members are the chief financial officer (CFO), chief operating officer (COO) with the addition of sales & marketing and HR. Depending on the nature of the business, additional roles may be represented such as technology, product development, client relationship or sales and marketing. Functions of a business that are represented through a committee of the board, such as a risk committee, do not automatically have a seat on the executive committee. For example, the head of the risk function may report to the chief finance officer who then reports on operational risk at executive committee level, rather than the head of risk having a permanent position on the executive committee.

Role of the executive committee

It is unusual for an executive committee to have formal terms of reference given their responsibilities are clear. Sitting alongside their responsibility of oversight of the effective delivery of services within the business, there is also the expectation that they are responsible for the implementation of the strategy as discussed and agreed at board level, often also setting the strategy to be discussed, agreed and ratified by the board.

Conflict often occurs where the executive committee strays into developing, extending and changing the overall strategy of the business in isolation of the wider board, as the board often provides the challenge needed when agreeing on a strategy. This challenge is invaluable given it is not hindered by operational considerations or personal relationships and can bring an independent view based on external knowledge and experience. Where elements of a strategy need external validation or market testing, the board may be able to provide first stage feedback that enables more focused market testing resulting in faster and more economic development and implementation.

EXAMPLE: Role of the executive committee

Legal and General Group Plc, Annual Report 2018 (extract)

The role of the Executive Committee
The Group Executive Committee (Exco), chaired by the Group Chief Executive, brings together the heads of Legal & General's business units with the executive committee members … 'Exco' is responsible for the day-to-day implementation of strategy agreed by the Board. 'Exco' meets regularly to ensure continued cooperation between the business units and the effective adoption of our culture, a key focus for the group. 'Exco' also monitors and manages risk, ensures efficient operational management and adherence to compliance and addresses key issues such as health and safety, diversity and environmental and corporate social responsibility.

The focus is on operational delivery by the company, whether in respect of external customers and suppliers or the internal functions supporting the business. Oversight of financials, cost of delivery and profitability are core responsibilities.

In addition, the executive committee should be the forum to agree and track delivery of the short-term business plan and associated budgets. More long-term discussion on the strategy of the company should also start in this forum and be brought to meetings of the board for discussion and approval.

Boards often arrange strategy days to specifically challenge the strategy and agree on future focus. These strategy days would be attended by the full board plus those members of the executive committee who are not board members, as well as any other relevant attendees, both internal and external to the company.

Terms of reference

Rarely, if ever, does the executive committee have a formal, documented terms of reference in place, with the forum being more informal in its purpose and flexible in its meeting schedule aligning itself to the needs of both the business and the CEO. Having said this, it is a core part of the governance framework of the company given its responsibility for driving effective operations. Simple terms of reference for the executive committee can be beneficial for employees in the wider organisation so they can understand and appreciate the roles and responsibilities of members of this forum. It is also an opportunity to document for those reporting to members of the executive committee or compiling reports, what the deliverables of this committee are. A standard form for a terms of reference for an executive committee could be based on those provided in the Appendices, with duties, reporting responsibilities and authority clearly defined. Documenting the delegated authorities given to the executive committee is highly beneficial given their operational responsibilities. This may take the form of identifying those authorities that are reserved for the board rather than attempting to provide a complete list of operational scenarios. Matters reserved for the board may include acquisitions, sales of significant parts of the business, business investment above a certain financial cost, new geographical expansion or significant organisational restructure.

In general, the executive committee meets frequently, often formally on a monthly basis and ad hoc on specific topics. Attendees are primarily the heads of the various functions within a business, although they may not be formal board members.

It is important that both the board and the executive committee members are clear where authority for decision making lies, where board approval is required and where the executive committee can take full ownership. This is often, though not always, based on financial value or quantum of resource allocation with exceptions for acquisitions, divestments or new product launches. Given the seniority of executive committee members, the expectation is that they will have a high level of authority to act autonomously.

> **EXAMPLE: Transparency of executive roles and responsibilities**
>
> *Taylor Wimpey Plc*
> As disclosed in their annual report, the roles and responsibilities of all senior positions are available to all employees on their internal system:
>
>> ... The Group has clearly defined policies, processes and procedures governing all areas of the business, which will continue to be reviewed and refined in order to meet the requirements of the business and changing market circumstances. Defined authority limits continue to be closely monitored in response to prevailing market conditions. Any investment, acquisition or significant purchase or disposal of land requires detailed appraisal and is subject to approval by the Board or the Chief Executive, depending on the value and nature of the investment or contract.
>>
>> There is a clearly identifiable organisational structure and a framework of delegated authority approved by the Board within which individual responsibilities of senior executives of Group companies are identified and can be monitored. The Operating Framework, within which delegated authorities, responsibilities and related processes are explained in detail, is available for review and guidance online by any employee through the Company's intranet. These activities are reinforced through process compliance and other audits conducted by Internal Audit...

Despite the lack of formal terms of reference, it is imperative that minutes of meetings are maintained and that any actions agreed are tracked to completion. These minutes can then also form the basis of reporting to full meetings of the board and are a useful tool for tracking delivery against both the short-term business plan and the long-term strategy of the company. Given the close interaction between the board and the executive committee, the company secretariat function would document both forums ensuring that consistency is maintained between the two.

Duties, responsibilities and tasks

The roles and responsibilities of the members of the executive committee vary depending on the company, its services and sector. However, in general, the core responsibilities can be grouped into specific areas. These are then reviewed and discussed at each executive committee meeting with regular reporting back to the board by the CEO both informally and formally to each board meeting.

Attendees and members of the executive committee will have responsibility for specific areas delegating through their part of the company and ensuring that resourcing is adequate to be able to deliver.

Depending on the stage of the company, different areas will have greater or lesser focus at any one time. For example, where a company is seeing a downward trend in revenue generation, business development, and sales and marketing will be a core area of discussion, noting its impact on and potential contribution by, the other operational areas, such as HR and Finance.

EXAMPLE: Reporting on the executive committee

Hammerson Plc, Annual Report 2018 (extract)

Managing the business

The Group Executive Committee (GEC), which is chaired by David Atkins, supports the Board by providing executive management of Hammerson plc within the strategy and Business Plan approved by the Board. The GEC has responsibility for operational matters, including the implementation of the Group's Business Plan and strategy. The chief responsibilities of the GEC are set out on page 70. During the year a decision was made to increase the breadth of membership of the GEC and several new appointments were made.

The GEC meets formally once a month. The members also meet most weeks for informal discussion on day-to-day issues.

At its meetings during the year the GEC received a number of regular reports including on finance, trading and marketing, the property portfolio, human resources, corporate communications and the Group's Risk Management Framework. It also received regular update reports from each of the Committees which reports to the GEC, which are set out in the governance structure overleaf. The GEC also received regular updates on the Value Retail and VIA Outlets businesses, which are externally managed.

The GEC monitored the progress of the strategic and operational objectives set by the Board, through the delivery of the Business Plan. It reviewed the Group's Risk Management Framework and internal controls in conjunction with the Risk and Controls Committee. It also ensured that development and succession plans were in place so that the business had people of the right calibre and skills to deliver the Business Plan for the current year and in the future.

In addition to the regular reports described above, the GEC also spent time on the following activities:

- Oversaw strategic planning to prepare for the proposed acquisition and integration of intu in the period before the Board withdrew its offer to acquire intu
- Oversaw plans to ensure compliance with the General Data Protection Regulation which came into force in May 2018
- Reviewed Hammerson's Modern Slavery and Human Trafficking Statement for recommendation to the Board for approval and publication on the Group's website
- Received and discussed feedback from the Great Place to Work Employee Survey

> - Received the annual Health and Safety Report including an update on the Company's review of its assets and audit of building cladding following the Grenfell Tower fire in June 2017
> - Oversaw a project to review the Company's strategy, and reviewed the proposed revised Business Plan 2019 and accompanying papers for the Board's October Strategy Day
> - Reviewed the proposed changes in the UK Corporate Governance Code published in July 2018 and how they would impact the business.
>
> Meetings regularly take place between members of the GEC and senior management as a whole. For example, in May, the Chief Executive and Chief Financial Officer hosted a leadership forum in London. This was an opportunity for senior colleagues to meet, discuss the current market environment and future direction of the business and share ideas. Feedback from the event was reviewed at a subsequent GEC meeting. The feedback also helped to inform the Board's consideration of Hammerson's reshaped strategy.

In effect, the executive committee is the forum for ensuring the effective functioning of the company. Depending on its size, the executive committee may have sub-teams responsible for specific divisions or functions. Larger organisations may have also applied a matrix organisational structure whereby support functions, such as finance or HR, spread across product, service or geographical divisions. In these complex structures, the executive committee needs to ensure that the model continues to be fit-for-purpose and that its effectiveness continues to support the success of the company as a whole. Too often a large matrix organisation can result in functions or divisions that work in silos in isolation of each other to the detriment of the company. The executive committee must ensure that this is mitigated through their combined focus and shared responsibility.

The CEO of a company will have over-arching responsibility for the company and may take the lead on a specific area based on their expertise. Equally, they may move across areas as the company develops, focusing their time and effort on the function that requires the most attention, resources or need at any one time. Generally, the CEO's main responsibility is in respect of the strategy, ensuring that it is in place, that all elements are progressing, that actions related to the strategy are progressing and that the day-to-day operations of the company continue to align to the strategy. Their main reporting line is to the chair of the board ensuring that the day-to-day operations of the business are visible to the chair and the wider board of directors.

While rarely documented, the roles and responsibilities of the executive committee can be categorised into seven core areas of focus, documented here as a reference.

Objectives and strategy

The board sets and approves the strategy based on the input received from the executive committee and their teams. In effect, the executive committee will recommend objectives and strategy for the company as a whole to develop its business, having regard to the interests of its shareholders, customers, employees and other stakeholders. Strategies are primarily focused on the longer-term success and direction of the company, aligned to the vision and mission of a company. Long-term is generally considered to be a strategy for three years or over, most frequently for five years and beyond, although this may differ between companies and sectors, with fast-moving sectors needing a much more dynamic, energised and short-term strategic focus.

Short-term the executive committee should focus on the application of near-term objectives under the strategy ensuring they are agreed and cascaded to the relevant division or function of the company. This is then the foundation of the business plan of the company, identifying and agreeing on objectives, deliverables and related policy guidelines to drive the near-term success of the business aligned to the longer-term strategy.

In effect, the executive committee is responsible for the ideas underpinning the strategy agreed at the board, the identification of related actions that underpin it and the implementation of the agreed strategy through execution of those actions.

Performance and operations

Operationally the executive committee must have a strong grasp on the financials of the company, presenting proposed short-term budgets and long-term plans to the main board. Following their adoption, they should closely monitor the adoption and achievement of both the budget and the plan, challenging delivery and recognising areas that may need additional resource or support.

Key performance indicators for the company should be set at the board with the executive committee monitoring performance against these targets, objectives and indicators. The cascade of these deliverables to the relevant forums, divisions, functions and teams is the responsibility of the executive committee, as is the oversight, particularly where teams may be delivering against the same targets.

Ongoing monitoring of budgets, reviewing business plans of parts of the company, aligning team delivery to targets and the strategy is a core responsibility as is optimising the allocation and adequacy of resources to fulfil the agreed targets.

Too frequently large organisations end up with silos within the company where interaction is competing against each other rather than collegiate in delivery against common company purposes. The executive committee should be mindful of this and seek to minimise any conflict within and across the company to ensure that the common goals remain the primary focus of all parties. In some organisations the executive committee includes the heads of divisions or subsidiaries as members, or as invited attendees to every meeting, to minimise the potential for thinking and acting in silos. Where implemented, this also has the advantage of sharing company-wide knowledge to all attendees enabling cross-fertilisation of knowledge, ideas and contacts.

Human resources

Human resources, the cost of the workforce and related activities is often the highest cost to any business. As such, its oversight in terms of return on cost is a key area of focus for the executive committee. While individual focus may be on the senior management team and their deliverables, as the senior forum, this also needs to link with the wider workforce and the deliverables, returns and benefits implemented across the company.

In respect of the senior management team, the executive committee should ensure that appropriate levels of authority are delegated to senior management and that they have relevant and adequate management development opportunities. Part of this includes succession planning for senior roles as well as for their own position within the executive committee.

The executive committee should take responsibility for creating and implementing an appropriate remuneration structure within the company that supports the strategy of the company while engaging appropriate behaviours and deliverables. This should align with the responsibilities of the remuneration committee in respect of board members and senior executives as well as the head of HR in respect of the wider workforce.

Development of the workforce to meet the requirements of the future business aligned to the strategy should be reflected in the training and development plans that are created and cascaded throughout the company with messaging of this alignment to ensure understanding across the company.

Business structure and risk management

The executive committee sits at the top of the organisational structure of the company and, as such, has responsibility for ensuring that the organisation structure is fit for purpose at all levels. While constant change of an organisational structure creates unwanted uncertainty across the workforce with resultant decreases in productivity; the executive committee should keep the structure under review. Recommendations for changes to organisational structure should be made to the board with clear focus on outcomes and cost/benefit analysis.

The nature of the company and its organisational structure also reflects the culture of the company; therefore alignment to the strategy should be part of the consideration. Key areas of delegated and devolved responsibilities and decision making give a clear indication of the nature of the business, its culture and the workforce that is needed to deliver success. There is no one correct organisational structure or culture for a company which is often driven by the personalities at the top, the nature of the growth that is achieved, the size and the sector in which the company operates. By being mindful of the importance of culture in driving success, the executive committee should be aware of their own impact on this, both as individuals and as a combined forum.

The executive committee should also take responsibility for ensuring that the control, co-ordination and monitoring within the company of risk and internal controls are effective. This may be delegated to the risk and audit committees, as well as the head of the risk and internal audit functions, with oversight by the executive committee. The aim is for this to be proportionate to the company, effective in its application and meaningful in its outcome. Alongside this, the executive committee should safeguard the integrity of all internal reporting including management information and financial reporting systems, while simultaneously receiving and using the provided data to underpin their discussions and decision making.

All companies must comply with relevant legislation and regulations both in general and specific to their industry and company type. The executive committee takes ownership for this, albeit that application and understanding of both existing and future requirements may be delegated to other functions, such as the company secretariat, legal or finance teams. It should be noted here that legislation affecting customers and clients will have an additional indirect impact on a company and should be part of the review delegated within the company.

Business development

In its widest sense, business development underpins the growth of a business without which any company will plateau or contract.

As part of its strategic focus, the executive committee should identify and ensure successful execution of new business opportunities outside the current core activities, including business acquisitions, joint ventures, partnerships, new product development and geographic diversification. This is the significant and forward-looking business development that ensures the business continues to drive to further growth.

The executive committee should examine all trade investments, divestments and major capital expenditure proposals, often grouped under mergers & acquisitions. Aligned to the strategy, acquisition of competitors or acquisition to move into a new sector is an opportunity to grow a business by size, product, service or geographical reach in a relatively short space of time and can deliver much faster results than pure organic growth. The executive committee should consider all such opportunities aligned to the strategy and make recommendations to the board of those which, in a group context, are material either by purpose or cost.

Approval of all strategic or material alliances and partnership agreements, including all joint venture agreements should sit with the executive committee. The definition of material will be company-specific and should be agreed and communicated to ensure that significant decisions are not made without executive committee knowledge and approval. Equally, in a large company, the executive committee should not be the decision-maker for every new contract or opportunity, so *de minimus* levels should be identified below which the authority is delegated elsewhere in the company.

Service delivery

Depending on the nature of the company and its services, a key relationship is between the company and its customers. The executive committee will drive the framework for engagement with customers, both relationship management and service delivery.

Utilising customer metrics and understanding the intersection of the company to its customers, the executive committee should identify a customer charter that clearly positions the how, when and by whom customer interaction is driven. This could also include outsourcing the initial customer contact through external call centres with the resultant oversight required in relation to the outsourcing contract.

Business-to-customer (B2C) companies with a direct relationship to the consumer market will have different customer drivers to business to business (B2B) service delivery and professional service firms. Even the terminology is different with B2C identifying customers and B2B companies largely referring to clients.

The executive committee should also take responsibility for significant client escalations that may have an impact on the company as a whole and, whether direct or through the risk committee, should have oversight of resolution of issues.

In some companies, executive committee members also take personal responsibility as the leading client relationship manager for significant clients. These may be defined by contract size, future potential, market position, external visibility or other definitions. It would also include significant relationships with suppliers and joint venture partners.

Similarly, the executive committee is likely to take responsibility for significant supplier relationships or have close oversight of the related contracts and their application. This will extend to business process outsource ('BPO') providers as well as significant supply chain partners.

Policies

There are certain policies that all companies must have under law or by legislative best practice. These vary depending on the size, sector and focus of the business. While core policies often have recommended best practice guidelines for their content and format, the executive committee should ensure that drafted policies are fit for purpose for the specific company, are consistent, have been approved and communicated across the company and are being effectively applied and monitored.

Specific policies also underpin the legal requirements of the board; for example, the board has a legal duty to include health and safety as an agenda item with the related policy and its application supporting this. Depending on the industry, health and safety metrics may be submitted at each board meeting with mitigations, actions and monitoring results also included. While all directors have personal liability for its implementation, the executive committee would be responsible for its application across the company. Executive committee members can draw additional input from their employees, advisers and external information sources. In this instance the Health and Safety Executive is a UK government body that provides advice, support and knowledge in this space.

Developing and implementing group policies can be split into those required for regulatory purposes, noting that some sectors and industries are more highly regulated than others so have more policies to implement. However, there are certain policies that all companies should implement, particularly in relation to employment practices.

Each company should also consider policies that are relevant to their company and how they want to do business. These should not be confused with procedures for how to implement the policy or deliver a service which would be owned, controlled and monitored by the relevant function themselves.

Where there is a risk committee, the executive committee may delegate the oversight and monitoring of policies to this forum; however, the over-arching decision-making for an effective policy framework would sit with the executive committee on behalf of the board. The executive committee in their considerations should also ensure that policies are fit for purpose without detracting from the purpose of the company itself. It is key that they are robust and applied effectively across the company.

Examples of specific policies include, but are not limited to:

- codes of ethics and business practice (including bribery prevention and whistleblowing policies);
- risk management policies;
- Treasury policies;
- health and safety policies;
- environment and sustainability policies;
- communications policy (including procedures for the release of price-sensitive information);
- corporate social responsibility policy (including environmental, employee communications and employee disability); and
- charitable donations policy.

Where new policies are being drafted, external bodies, associations and advisers can provide a useful source of input, for example a whistleblowing policy may benefit from including direct reference to guidance and further information that is available from Protect (previously Public Concern at Work), including frequently asked questions and free confidential advice to individuals thinking about raising their concerns.

Committee membership

As has been mentioned, the culture of a business is set from the top at the executive committee level. Hence the interaction and dynamics between executive committee members will set the tone for cascade throughout the business. Collegiate and supportive executive committee members with defined static deliverables will provide a different cultural tone to a company than challenging and energised change-driven discussion at the executive committee level. Both have their place in the right company scenario and executive committee composition is as much about creating the correct culture as the skills and experience that members bring to their role. However, given the research led benefits of having diversity in leadership, executive committee membership should reflect skills required and positive interaction, in preference to group-think and uniformity.

Appointment to the executive committee will be led by the CEO, with the support of the board chair and the nominations committee. Where the role of CEO is being appointed the chair of the board will lead, with the support of relevant board members, alongside the nomination committee. Remuneration of this senior leadership team, whether board members or not, will be reviewed and driven by the remuneration committee.

Interaction beyond the committee

Clearly the executive committee and its members have a pivotal role in the success of the company. Their interactions are internal and external in equal measure and they lead the business in all its endeavours.

A key relationship is with the board and the non-executive directors thereon, ensuring that they communicate effectively, liaising when necessary and reporting frequently.

Reporting

External
The annual report of larger companies will include reporting from the executive reflecting the composition of this committee, their roles and deliverables. In some cases, this is provided as part of wider reporting included in strategic reporting or operational reports

Reporting should also include any key issues, drivers or objectives of the business that the executive committee is facing, delivering on or considering. While risk in itself would be reported by the risk committee, its application in respect of the operations of a company is the responsibility of the executive committee.

The executive committee will also interact with significant external contacts including clients, advisers, suppliers, investors and, more frequently, the local community in which the company is situated. Members are the day-to-day face of the company and, as such, undertake an ambassadorial role alongside other members of the board. Often the target for external parties to identify as decision-makers and business generators, their time is often stretched, and delegation may be difficult to achieve in very large, active or visible companies. Being able to manage external time commitments against internal responsibilities and delivery is a juggle that members of the executive committee will need to make when fulfilling their role to full effectiveness.

Internal

The executive committee, more than any other forum of a company, has a key responsibility to report to, and engage with, employees to share company knowledge and gain engagement from staff.

EXAMPLE: Employee engagement by the executive committee

Vodafone Group plc, Annual Report 2019 (extract)

Our leaders have a critical role in setting the tone of our organisation and championing the behaviours we expect to see. The Executive Committee led campaigns and engagement throughout the year to highlight our values and beliefs. Various indicators are used to provide insight into our culture, including employee engagement, health, safety and wellbeing measures and diversity indicators. We regularly assess the state of our culture, through activities such as compliance reviews and we address behaviour that falls short of our expectations.

Internally the executive committee will be sharing progress reports, updates and general strategic communications with employees on a regular basis, with best practice to utilise all formats for such communication. These may include personal correspondence from the CEO, such as emails, monthly reporting via management teams to be delegated to all staff, quarterly 'town halls' as a forum for the leadership team to present and also be available for questions, staff newsletters and any other forms of communication. When delivering on an internal communications plan, consideration should also be given to the engagement and contact with the company by employees themselves. Remote or mobile workers will not have the same connectivity to a company as those with head office-based roles. Those with customer-focused engagement will have different views to those in internal functional roles. Having a clear message about the strategy of the business, the short-term business plan and current standing of the company are all important areas to address and share.

The depth and breadth of these communications would be company-specific and, to ensure they are meeting the requirements of employees as stakeholders, feedback should be gained on the communication strategy.

In the majority of companies, employee costs are the highest costs of the company and, as such, ensuring that communication to employees delivers well and engages employees with their company and leadership should not be underestimated.

Supporting the committee

Governance and secretarial support of the executive committee should mirror that of the board ensuring that minutes of meetings and decisions made therein are accurately recorded. It is equally important to manage and support colleagues who contribute to this forum, whether through attendance or reporting.

This is a downwards-focused forum in terms of company focus, with the additional responsibility of reporting into the board and enabling the strategy. The executive committee is also the forum that will make significant and often difficult decisions that may impact heavily on the wider company, so discretion is key. Often the CEO will have a close team of administrators to support this specific forum to ensure that confidence is maintained.

This forum may also set up project teams to deliver specific projects which may, or may not, be constituted as an ad hoc committee of the board. Where it is implemented as a committee of the board, it is important that the wider board is party to the implementation, signs off on the terms of reference, agrees to any areas where the committee can take discretion and receives reports on the actions taken. Without this formal documented sign off at board level, there is a risk that executive committee members and members of the committee may be exposed if any subsequent decisions are taken that the wider board disagrees with or that result in issues arising.

As the chief leadership team of a company, the executive committee will set the tone for the business. Being able to support this forum and align it to the wider board is often a delicate supportive role that needs tact and diplomacy. Particularly where a company is undertaking significant change, perhaps through acquisition, rapid growth or significant losses, the tensions in the executive committee can be extreme and, if the discussions are confidential, the reporting out of this forum, as well as the undocumented comments, can heavily impact on the wider company and its workforce. Too often the silos of a business are a reflection of division within the executive committee and, where supporting or contributing to this forum, it is important to not become part of any internal conflict or to inflame any tensions.

Being a supporter or contributor to this forum can be personally very rewarding given the extent of its remit and its alignment to the board and the company strategy. It also enables personal exposure to senior executives who are looking at talent identification and successor planning, so any individual with career aspirations would do well to have positive connections to this forum and its members.

Conclusion

The executive committee is the heart of any company, leading by example, ensuring delivery and operations are effective. Its members sit at the heart of the governance framework of a company, setting the tone in terms of culture and values. They are the leaders from a day-to-day perspective in terms of strategy and its application.

The personalities in the executive committee and their interaction will guide the wider business on colleague interaction. While the board as a whole is the primary forum for leading the business and ensuring its effectiveness, the executive members on the board are embedded daily in the functioning of the company.

Having an effective executive that works well with non-executives on the board as well as colleagues throughout the business will put a company in a position of strength, especially when paired with transparency and clarity of roles, responsibilities and deliverables at all levels in the organisation.

6 – Audit committee

Introduction

The audit committee, sometimes known as the finance and audit committee, delivers oversight of internal and external audit as well as the financial reporting and controls operating within a company. As such, it is largely backwards-facing, reviewing existing processes and procedures for efficacy and historical reviews of financials, actions and issues. The main area of divergence from this backward face is in respect of reviews of audit plans and their alignment to strategy and the future of the company.

The audit committee is often merged with the risk committee in which case, the oversight of risk as a whole is monitored. Where these committees are separate, the audit committee would maintain oversight of financial risk within the company, with co-ordination with the risk committee to ensure that no risks fall between these two forums or are duplicated.

Within the Code (Provision 24) there is specific reference to establishing an audit committee to support the board in establishing formal and transparent arrangements for considering how they should apply the corporate reporting and risk management and internal control principles and for maintaining an appropriate relationship with the company's auditors. Hence, the audit committee is a required committee of large listed companies while most large unlisted companies also benefit from having a separate forum for this purpose. Guidance from the FRC provides a useful framework for the roles and responsibilities of the audit committee noting that arrangements should be proportionate to the task, and will vary according to the size, complexity and risk profile of the company

Conversely, there is no legal requirement for any company to have an internal audit function. In this scenario, oversight of the internal finance function by the audit committee has greater importance with committee review of internal controls and their effectiveness being a key priority.

Role of the audit committee

The audit committee is an oversight committee with two main areas for the focus of financial reporting and controls and internal and external audit.

Within financial reporting and controls, the audit committee provides specific oversight of:

- the financial reporting systems in place within the company and their effectiveness;
- the controls and associated financial risk management systems;
- compliance with applicable laws and regulations; and
- where requested, the annual report and other external financial reporting on behalf of the board.

Oversight of internal and external audit incorporates:

- the audit process itself, reflecting the process where an internal audit function exists or where this function is not in place;
- the interaction between internal and external audit processes; and
- the appointment process for external auditors.

Terms of reference

While the prevalence of an audit committee is relatively universal in large companies across countries, differences in its roles and responsibilities can be seen under different legislation and should be considered if looking at the audit committee across jurisdictions or when expanding governance controls across multiple countries.

In general, the framework for the audit committee terms of reference is standard concerning the meeting schedule aligning to audit and financial reporting timetables (see Appendix 1).

EXAMPLE: Audit committee

The audit committee of Just Eat Plc, which is combined with its risk committee and has a financial year-end of 31 December. Their annual report for 2018 notes that:

'We met five times as a Committee during the year, with two of these meetings focused particularly on the Audit tender. The Chief Financial Officer and senior representatives of the finance management team also attend meetings, as do representatives of both the external and internal auditors. The Committee also meets privately with the external auditor at least once per year.'

As further detail on the above, their annual report noted the following schedule and actions spread throughout 2018:

- Analysis of 2017 full-year results presented by management.
- Review of 2017 full-year results presented by the external auditor.
- Review of going concern, internal controls and fair balanced and understandable statement in the Annual Report.

- February:
  - Review of the Group's Annual Report for 2017.
  - Discussion with the external auditor in the absence of management.
  - Recommendation to the Board for approval of the Annual Report including the Report of the Audit Committee.
  - Review of the Group's whistleblowing procedures.
  - Review of internal audit planning and resourcing.
  - Introduction of future audit partner.
- July:
  - Analysis of 2018 half-year results presented by management.
  - Review of half-year results presented by the external auditor.
  - Review of 2018 draft half-year results announcement.
  - Review of 2018 audit plan with the external auditor.
  - Agreement of plans for audit tender.
  - Group risk update and adjustments to the internal audit plan.
- September & October
  - Audit tender update.
  - Review of the results of the FRC's Audit Quality Review.
  - Recommendation to the Board in relation to the proposed external auditor.
- December
  - Progress in year-end accounting presented by management.
  - Updates to the 2018 audit plan presented by the external auditor.
  - Review and approval of 2019 internal audit plan.
  - Review of tax matters including tax strategy for publication.
  - Review of the Committee's terms of reference.

Alongside these specific points during the year the Committee also had the following standing agenda items:

- Report of the Chief Financial Officer.
- Report of the external auditor.
- Report of Director of Internal Audit and Risk.
- Minutes and actions from previous meetings.

Given the importance of the financial oversight that the audit committee undertakes, and its reporting to the board, the audit committee should also report to shareholders, most prevalently via the annual report, the details of any issues that remain outstanding between the committee and the board.

The terms of reference should reflect the size and requirements of the company including whether an internal audit function is in place. Where it is not, the audit committee role should include an annual review as to whether one should be implemented and, if the audit committee errs towards its creation, should advise the board accordingly. The decision of whether to implement an audit function or not then rests with the board or the executive committee on their behalf. If the board decides not to implement an audit function against the recommendations of the audit committee, this should be documented in both the board and audit committee minutes, with content reflecting why the decision was made and any additional considerations given.

Duties, responsibilities and tasks

Detail within the terms of reference will reflect the dual role of oversight of financial reporting and controls and internal and external audit. Financial reporting and controls encompass all elements of financial reporting, related systems and controls and the application of regulatory and legislative requirements and responsibilities.

Financial reporting

There is a wide variety, form and timetable of financial reporting within all companies and the integrity of the data to underpin wider decision making is key. The audit committee role in ensuring that this integrity is intact should be at the heart of the purpose of an audit committee.

To undertake this, the committee should monitor all financial statements distributed by and within the company. This should include its annual and half-yearly reports, interim management statements, preliminary announcements and any other formal statements relating to its financial performance. These should be critically reviewed with any significant financial reporting issues reported to the board along with any judgements which those statements contain. This should also have regard to any matters communicated to it by the auditor.

EXAMPLE: Financial reporting

Prudential PLC, Annual Report 2018, Audit Committee report (extract, further details provided within the annual report)

One of the Committee's key responsibilities is to monitor the integrity of the financial statements and any other periodic financial reporting. During the last year, items reviewed by the Committee included the 2017 Annual Report and Accounts, the 2017 Solvency and Financial Condition Report and associated Pillar 3 returns submitted to the Group's regulator, the 2017 Environmental, Social and Governance Report, the 2017 Tax Strategy Report, the 2018 Half Year Report and Accounts, and the key accounting judgements for the 2018 Annual Report.

In reviewing these and other items, the Committee received reports from management and, as appropriate, reports from internal and external assurance providers, which in some cases were provided at the explicit request of the Committee.

> When considering financial reporting, the Committee assesses compliance with relevant accounting standards, regulations and governance codes. During 2018, the Group adopted IFRS 15 'Revenue from contracts with customers' and, as described in note A2, this had no material effect on the Group's financial results. The Committee also reviewed the potential impact of accounting standards that are effective in the future, including IFRS 16 'Leases' and IFRS 17 'Insurance Contracts'. The approach to adopting these standards is further discussed in note A2. The Committee requested regular updates from management on the progress against plans for implementing IFRS 17 given its particular significance.

This review should extend to internal management accounts reported across divisions of a large company to ensure consistency, alignment and lack of duplication. For example, where costs are allocated across multiple statements or financial support is cascaded from group borrowing to multiple profit and loss areas, the audit committee should be confident that the allocation is neither misleading nor inconsistent in application and does not duplicate allocation. In effect, the sum of the whole should equal the sum of the cascaded allocations.

The audit committee should also ensure that reporting correctly reflects the application of significant accounting policies and any changes to them. They should review the methods used to account for significant or unusual transactions with consideration of the reason why specific approaches are applied where alternatives are possible.

The committee should make an independent judgement, based on the expertise and experience of its members, of whether the company has adopted appropriate accounting policies and made appropriate estimates and judgements. This should take into account the external auditor's views on the financial statements without using the auditor as the sole source.

The audit committee should also review the financial elements of all reporting by the company, including within strategic reports, governance statements and reports to shareholder or regulators.

Where the committee has concerns or is not satisfied with any aspect of the proposed financial reporting by the company, it should report its views to the board as a matter of priority.

Within the annual report, the board should confirm that the contents of the annual report provide a true and fair representation of the business. The audit committee should be prepared to review the annual report on behalf of the board in support of the board making this statement within the accounts.

Financial controls and systems

The audit committee should review the company's internal financial control systems that identify, assess, manage and monitor financial risks. Within this, they should review the resourcing available to ensure that controls and systems are maintained and working. This should also extend to risk management systems concerning financial risks, in co-ordination with the risk committee where there is one or for all risks where there isn't.

The audit committee should review and approve the statements to be included in the annual report concerning internal control, risk management and the viability statement.

Where a company has multiple divisions or locations, the controls and systems of the business are, by necessity, complex, multi-layered and often applied as a matrix. The audit committee should be mindful of the interaction between reporting and ensure that the systems and controls are applicable both at the top within group-level reporting and in isolation by each specific division or function.

EXAMPLE: Internal financial controls

AA Plc, Annual Report 2019, Audit Committee report

Internal financial controls

The Committee works closely with the Risk Committee and has completed its review of the Group's systems of internal financial controls and their effectiveness for the 2019 financial year and has done so in accordance with the requirements of the Code. It should be noted that the Group's risk management systems are designed to manage rather than eliminate the risk of failure to achieve business objectives and they can only provide reasonable and not absolute assurance against material misstatement or loss.

In the Committee's opinion, there were no significant failings noted from this review and overall there has been an improvement in the overall control environment. However, a number of recommendations have been made, particularly in respect of the IT controls environment and these are being addressed.

While not an IT committee, the audit committee should be mindful of the sources of data, the transposition of data between systems and the differences between them. This may be as simple as the language used to define terms or the periodicity of recognising revenue. As an example, a client relationship management (CRM) system may recognise new sales revenue from contract signing date while finance systems may variously account on service delivery, invoice or receipt of payment from the customer.

Legal compliance

The committee should review the adequacy and security of the company's arrangements for its employees and any contractors to raise concerns about possible wrongdoing in financial reporting or other matters. They should also ensure that such reporting can be undertaken in confidence and to a neutral third party. The committee should also ensure that the processes and procedures once a concern has been raised allow for a proportionate and independent investigation and that appropriate follow up action can be taken. Where a concern has been raised, it would be expected that this would be reported to the committee by the relevant reporting function after which the committee should monitor the resolution and any resultant actions agreed to be taken.

EXAMPLE: Whistleblowing oversight

Prudential Plc; Annual Report 2018, Audit Committee Report (extract):

Whistleblowing
The Group continues to operate a Group-wide whistleblowing programme ('Speak Out'), hosted by an independent third party (Navex). The Speak Out programme receives ad hoc reports from a wide variety of channels, including a web portal, hotline, email and letters. Reports are captured, confidentially recorded by Navex, and flagged for investigation by the appropriate team. Under the Senior Managers Certification Regime (SMCR), the role of the Whistleblowing Champion continues to be carried out by the Chair of the Prudential Assurance Company (PAC) Audit Committee, an independent non-executive director of PAC.

The Committee is responsible for oversight of the effectiveness of the Group's whistleblowing arrangements. The Committee receives regular reports on the most serious cases and other significant matters raised through the programme and the action taken to address them. The Committee is also briefed on emerging Speak Out trends and themes. The Committee may, and has, requested further review of particular areas of interest.

The Committee reviewed the Group's Speak Out programme arrangements during the year, satisfying itself that they continue to comply with regulatory and governance requirements. The Committee also noted the consistency of approach adopted across subsidiary committees. This was facilitated through greater visibility of significant regional issues (addressed by subsidiary audit committees) and their outcomes. The Speak Out process has been further enhanced this year by focusing on (post-reporting) management action and, where relevant, sharing of lessons learnt.

The Chair and Committee spent time privately with the Group Resilience Director, to ensure that investigations were adequately resourced and appropriately managed, that there had been no retaliation against anyone making a report and that investigations were not improperly influenced. The Committee was also updated on arrangements for promoting Group-wide awareness of the Speak Out policy (including computer-based training tailored for each business unit) and a refresh of Speak Out communications across the Group.

The audit committee should also review:

- the company's procedures for detecting fraud and the reporting of the application of such procedures. An example of this may be in the form of monthly KPIs from IT noting any system checks that have been run to identify potential or actual breaches of systems. Alternatively, it may be a check of password security and regular passwords changes by all employees of all systems including financial or banking;
- the company's systems and controls for the prevention of bribery and should receive reports on non-compliance;
- where relevant to the company, the regular reports from the money laundering reporting officer and the adequacy and effectiveness of the company's anti-money laundering systems and controls; and
- regular reports from the compliance officer and keep under review the adequacy and effectiveness of the company's compliance function.

In some companies the responsibility for the above reviews may be undertaken by or shared with, other committees in existence such as the risk committee or a regulatory committee. Where this is the case, the chair of each of the committees should co-ordinate their oversight responsibilities to ensure there is no overlap or areas overlooked.

The audit committee should also co-ordinate with the general counsel of the company, or the company's legal advisers, with regard to any new legislation that is planned or implemented to ensure that any new requirements have been captured by the company and whether their oversight responsibilities have been changed or extended as a result. Individual committee members should also bring to the attention of their fellow committee members any new or changed legislation they are aware of through their wider connections. The committee should then ensure that they have notified the board of these and have ensured that appropriate action is being taken or responsibility delegated adequately.

Audit

Oversight of the internal and external audit incorporates:

- the audit process itself, reflecting the process where an internal audit exists or where the function is not in place;
- internal and external audit processes and their interaction; and
- the appointment process for external auditors.

The audit process

Where there is an internal audit function, the audit committee should be part of the review of the role of head of audit and their appointment and ongoing effectiveness in their role, working with the board, HR function and, if they exist, the nomination and remuneration committees. As an ongoing responsibility for ensuring effectiveness, the audit committee should ensure that the head of audit has access to the chair of the board as well as heads of functions and is able to deliver in their functions independently of influence or involvement of senior executives. Where a senior representative of the internal audit function flags concerns they may have in respect of their ability to undertake their role, the audit committee should seriously consider their concerns and identify appropriate solutions for discussion and agreement with the board. Where concerns are raised relating to the influence of specific senior executives, this should be undertaken confidentially, usually with the chair of the board as initial contact.

Alongside this, they should ensure that the role and mandate of the audit function itself are effective and it has the ongoing resources required to fulfil all identified deliverables. If, during their ongoing oversight of the audit function, the audit committee believes that resources are not sufficient, they should ensure that their concern is shared with the board and should press for the board to consider adding additional resource whether inhouse or through external providers and consultants.

As support to, and oversight of, the audit function, the audit committee should review and challenge the internal audit plan. This should focus on the review of previous issues as well as new areas aligned to strategic focus and ensure that lesser risk areas have sufficient focus. Also, where there is one, the audit committee should review the audit charter on an annual basis ensuring that it continues to meet the changing needs of the company.

After each planned internal audit, and any emergency audits conducted, the audit committee should review the resultant report, approve any associated actions and oversee the conclusion of any such actions within the timeframes identified and agreed.

Alongside ensuring that the audit function has sufficient resources, the audit committee should ensure that the audit function has unrestricted scope, the necessary resources and access to information to enable it to fulfil its mandate. It should also ensure that there is open communication between different functions and that the internal audit function evaluates the effectiveness of these functions as part of its internal audit plan.

Members of the audit committee should be mindful of the appropriate professional standards expected of an audit function operating within a company of such size and sector and should ensure that the audit function meets such guidelines and acts within best practice guidelines.

EXAMPLE: Internal audit review

SSE Plc, Annual Report 2019, Audit Committee Report (extract)

Internal Audit Effectiveness

The Committee keeps under review the effectiveness of the activities undertaken by Internal Audit by monitoring the following:

- Internal audit feedback. Reports on the development and delivery of the internal audit plan; the delivery of actions from reviews; audit resource and expertise; and "management awareness" and priorities.
- Management feedback. Output of post Audit Surveys and the views of the Chief Executive, Finance Director and other Senior Management.
- Internal Auditor feedback. Feedback provided by the External Auditor.
- External quality assessment. An external Independent review was completed during the year, with the output of this review described below.

Having considered the external quality assessment of Internal Audit, the Committee confirms it is satisfied with the overall performance of the Internal Audit Function.

When reviewing the audit function, which from best practice would be ongoing in respect of information received and annually on a proactive basis, the audit committee should consider whether the contribution of an external assessor would be of value. If they believe it would, they should raise this with the board for their approval and be part of the appointment, implementation and review process.

EXAMPLE: External assessor of audit function

SSE Plc, Annual Report 2019, Audit Committee Report (extract)

External quality assessment of Internal Audit

During the financial year, BDO carried out an external quality assessment of SSE's Internal Audit function. The objective of this assessment was to evaluate the degree of Internal Audit's conformance with the requirements of the Chartered Institute of Internal Auditors (CIIA) standards, which includes the International Professional Practices Framework (IPPF) and the Code of Conduct. Performance against leading practices and comparable organisations were also considered. Conformance with CIIA standards requires that external assessments must be conducted at least once every five years by a qualified, independent assessor or assessment team from outside the organisation, SSE has chosen for these to be conducted every three years.

The assessment considered Internal Audit's positioning within the organisation and the quality of its planning and operational procedures. The assessment incorporated survey and sample interviews of Internal Audit's stakeholders across the Group, along with a review of working papers and outputs from a number of recent internal audits.

BDO's assessment concluded that the Internal Audit function was exhibiting a satisfactory level of maturity for the business and is generally performing to a good standard. SSE scored the generally conforms (highest) rating for 47 of the standards and a partially conforms rating for the other five. The assessment highlighted some improvement opportunities to further enhance the Group's overall Assurance Framework. An action plan has been developed to address these enhancements which will be monitored and evaluated by the Committee.

Where there is no internal audit function, the audit committee should review the financial risk, controls and reporting of the finance function and other related internal functions, as the third line of defence (see below explanation). On an annual basis, they should report to the board whether the absence of an internal audit function remains appropriate and, if not, the options that could be considered for implementing one. These options can range from implementing a fully resourced internal audit function, introducing audit contractors to work on defined elements of audit work within the company or full outsource to third-party providers of the audit function. The decision of which option is most appropriate is a decision of the board based on input by the audit committee. Consideration would be based on company requirements as well as resource availability, current concerns, cost and nature of the business.

External audit

Given the important role of external audit in monitoring financials of companies and the high profile failures that have been reported, there is an increasing amount of research and guidance on the role of the audit committee in respect of monitoring external auditors and their actions. There is also significant information provided on the role of auditors themselves, their processes when undertaking an audit and reporting thereon (see Directory, references and resources). In the UK there continues to be government, as well as industry, led reviews and consultations on the audit sector to ensure its continued transparency and professionalism. Information provided by the Financial Reporting Council is invaluable as a starting point for accountants, auditors, directors and those that interact with them in their role.

In respect of company audits, the audit committee should be heavily involved in the appointment and ongoing monitoring of the audit provider and can bring external expertise and knowledge of the external audit market-place to their considerations. Specifically, they should be part of the appointment process, reviewing audit requests, audit firm proposals as well as the audit processes themselves and the related costs. As part of this, the audit committee should apply best practice, recommendations and regulatory requirements to their consideration. As an example, a 2014 EU audit regulation provides that public interest entities should not maintain the same auditor for more than 10 years (see Directory, resources, REGULATION (EU) No 537), although the UK has implemented a derogation that this can be extended to 20 years with retendering after 10 years.

There are differing views on the benefits or otherwise of long-term tenure of the same audit firm and no doubt audit committee members will have differing views based on their own experience and expertise. From one perspective, there is the fact that a longer tenure enables an audit firm to understand a business better, identify potential fraud and thus discourage employees from instigating fraud. Conversely, longer-term appointments may give auditors too close a connection to their contacts within a company and they may become complacent in their checks. It should also be noted that audit firms themselves rotate their own employees working on company audits and an understanding of how this applies to the company should be gained by the audit committee. This may include how frequently the audit partner is changed as well as how frequently the audit managers and teams working on the data gathering are rotated.

There are audit exemptions in place for small companies or subsidiary companies that are guaranteed by their parent. However, it is expected that, if a company is of sufficient size to warrant an audit committee, such small company exemptions will not apply.

It should be noted that for listed companies, the appointment, re-appointment and removal of external auditors require approval by shareholders, usually at the Annual General Meeting.

Where an external auditor tenders their resignation, the audit committee should review the reasons why, investigating the issues and ensuring that any resultant actions are identified, allocated and completed. Given that the external auditor should be an invitee of the audit committee at each meeting, it would be unusual for the committee to not have prior knowledge of the potential resignation of an external auditor and already be involved in understanding and addressing their concerns. Appointment of an alternative auditor in these scenarios would inevitably include the new auditors tendering for the appointment to be apprised of the reasons for resignation.

External auditors must be independent of the company that they are auditing and act objectively. As such, the audit committee should ensure that this is the case and that the external auditors have access to all required data and resources to fulfil their role. As part of this, the audit committee should liaise with the audit firm and the lead partner as well as review their work on an annual basis based on published requirements for audits and ethical standards for professional services.

> **EXAMPLE: Audit committee reporting on reviewing audit independence:**
>
> *United Utilities Group Plc, Annual Report 2019, Audit Committee Report (extract)*
> There are two aspects to auditor independence that the committee monitors to ensure that the external auditor remains independent of the company.
>
> Firstly, in assessing the independence of the auditor from the company the committee takes into account the information and assurances provided by the external auditor confirming that all its partners and staff involved with the audit

are independent of any links to United Utilities. KPMG confirmed that all its partners and staff complied with their ethics and independence policies and procedures which are fully consistent with the FRC's Ethical Standard including that none of its employees working on our audit hold any shares in United Utilities Group PLC. KPMG is also required to provide written disclosure at the planning stage of the audit about any significant relationships and matters that may reasonably be thought to have an impact on its objectivity and independence and that of the lead partner and the audit team. The lead audit partner must change every five years and other senior audit staff rotate at regular intervals.

Secondly, the committee develops and recommends to the board the company's policy on non-audit services and associated fees that are paid to KPMG. The EU Audit Directive (2014/56/EU) and Audit Regulation (537/2014) (the Regulation) came into force in the UK on 17 June 2016. Associated guidance was included in the FRC's Ethical Standard, which prohibits the statutory auditor from providing certain non-audit services to public interest entities (i.e. United Utilities Group PLC) as such services could impede their independence. The FRC's Ethical Standard clarified that non-audit services would be subject to a fee cap of no more than 70% of the average annual statutory audit fee for the three consecutive financial periods preceding the financial period in which the cap will apply.

The audit committee should review the fees of the audit firm, compared to both the overall fee income of the company and the market as a whole. These should also be reviewed in respect of the audit firm itself with regard to the fee income of the firm, the particular office and the relevant partner. These should be assessed in the context of relevant legal, professional and regulatory requirements, guidance and ethical standards.

The audit committee should consider the timetable of the external auditor against the actual and proposed activities of the audit and finance functions within the company to ensure that they can all deliver within their roles. They should also review and challenge the proposed, incurred and invoiced fees relative to both the wider market and the work undertaken.

Where the board may request, or the audit firm may offer, to provide non-audit services, the audit committee should review these for independence, transparency and objectivity. There should be a specific focus on objectivity and independence of the services being provided and any conflict that may arise. Also, fees in isolation of, and in combination with, the audit fees should be reviewed. Consideration should also be given to whether the audit firm is the most suitable provider of such services. In some companies, the audit committee approves all non-audit work provided by the audit firm, either with or without minimum levels identified. Marks and Spencer Group plc notes in their 2019 annual report that 'all non-audit work performed by Deloitte was put to the Audit Committee for prior consideration and approval, regardless of size'.

Where a company has broad company interests, whether geographically or by product or service, the audit committee should be assured that the audit firm can accommodate the breadth of the company within their audit. Where this includes the use of other parties, whether different offices of the same audit practice or external third-party providers, the audit committee should review the services to be provided in their totality and ensure that they have a clear understanding of any such outsourced services and how they will be combined within the audit process and reports. Equally, consideration should be given to the audit of subsidiaries within the same process, whether these subsidies avail themselves of a subsidiary exemption or not.

As with any considerations of a committee, but specifically in relation to external audit appointment and oversight, committee members should be transparent in any conflicts of interest they may have with providers or potential providers of audit or other financial services.

The audit committee should liaise with the head of internal audit and the auditor on receipt of the audit report to identify any areas of concern or risks flagged as a consequence of the audit process or other issues that may arise. As part of this, any feedback or queries to the auditor from the company, or the board and its members, should be accommodated and addressed. The chair of the audit committee should also meet with the auditors independently to ensure that communication can be free of influence or company restrictions.

Three lines of defence model

Oversight of risk within a business, including financial risk, frequently refers to the three lines of defence. While commonly applied in large organisations across industries, an understanding of its definition and its application is beneficial, whether applied in totality or via understanding the concepts. Smaller companies may benefit from elements of its structure, whether using this as a basis for how the board considers financial risks or through adopting elements of it within their structure.

The Chartered Institute of Internal Auditors provides a clear explanation of this model reflecting the key role that internal audit plays in risk management and assurance. Specifically, they set out the delegation from the board to senior management and their role in leadership and direction provided to employees in respect of risk management. The Chartered Institute of Internal Auditors and the Institute of Directors endorse the 'Three Lines of Defence' model as a way of explaining the relationship between these functions and as a guide to how responsibilities should be divided as:

1. The first line of defence – functions that own and manage risk.
2. The second line of defence – functions that oversee or specialise in risk management, compliance.
3. The third line of defence – functions that provide independent assurance, above all internal audit.

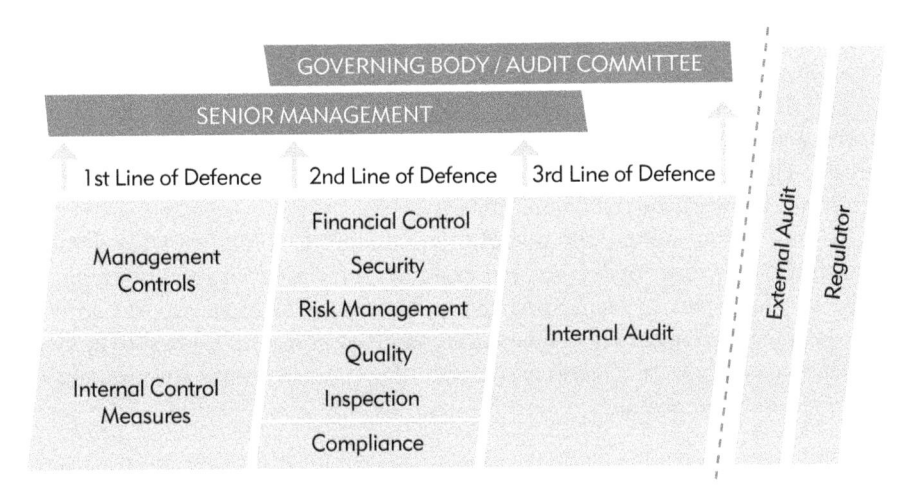

Figure 6.1: Three lines of defence model

First line of defence: Under the first line of defence, operational management has ownership, responsibility and accountability for directly assessing, controlling and mitigating risks.

Second line of defence: The second line of defence consists of activities covered by several components of internal governance (compliance, risk management, quality, IT and other control departments). This line of defence monitors and facilitates the implementation of effective risk management practices by operational management and assists the risk owners in reporting adequate risk-related information up and down the organisation.

Third line of defence: Internal audit forms the organisation's third line of defence. An independent internal audit function will, through a risk-based approach to its work, provide assurance to the organisation's board of directors and senior management. This assurance will cover how effectively the organisation assesses and manages its risks and will include assurance on the effectiveness of the first and second lines of defence. It encompasses all elements of an institution's risk management framework (from risk identification, risk assessment and response, to the communication of risk-related information) and all categories of organisational objectives: strategic, ethical, operational, reporting and compliance.

The role of the three lines of defence

Internal audit is uniquely positioned within the organisation to provide global assurance to the audit committee and senior management on the effectiveness of internal governance and risk processes. It is also well-placed to fulfil an advisory role on the co-ordination of assurance, effective ways of improving existing processes, and assisting management in implementing recommended improvements. In such a framework, internal audit is a cornerstone of an organisation's corporate governance.

The use of the three lines of defence to understand the system of internal control and risk management should not be regarded as an automatic guarantee of success. All three lines need to work effectively with each other and with the audit committee to create the right conditions.

In some organisations, the role of internal audit is combined with elements from the first two lines of defence. For example, some internal audit functions are asked to play a part in facilitating risk management or managing the internal whistleblowing arrangements. Where that happens, committees need to be aware of potential conflicts of interest and ensure they take measures to safeguard the objectivity of internal audit.

Committee membership

The audit committee as a collective should have sufficient financial acumen to deliver in their role effectively. However, this does not mean that all committee members should have a finance or audit background or an accounting qualification. A balanced committee may include members with wider experience of using financial reporting rather than producing or having oversight of such data. In fact, guidance from the Code, under Provision 24, states that at least one member should have recent and relevant financial experience, and the committee should consist of at least three members or two for smaller companies. Its guidance specifically notes that the committee, as a whole, should have competence relevant to the sector in which the company operates.

Under Code guidelines, the chair of the main board should not be a member of the audit committee (Provision 24), although other jurisdictions have different guidelines. For example, the revised AIC Code (Guernsey & Jersey) published in February 2019 permits the chair to be a member as long as they were independent on appointment, although they cannot chair the audit committee.

Interaction beyond the committee

As can be expected, the audit committee has considerable interaction with internal audit, both liaising and working with the function as well as having oversight of their actions, processes and procedures. It is imperative that there is an effective working relationship between the two, as well as a professional and proactive one between the chair of the committee and the head of internal audit. Where there is no internal audit, the audit committee will, by default, have greater interaction with the finance function, ensuring that processes and procedures within the finance function are accurate and fit for purpose. Where there is an audit function, the audit committee will still interact heavily with the finance function as part of its oversight responsibilities.

Given the reliance on the use of systems in maintaining and using data, the audit committee will interact heavily with the IT function to understand the breadth, and limitations, of systems used for financial reporting. This should be in relation to the systems themselves as well as the sharing of data between systems and any manipulation that may be undertaken. A robust audit committee will have at least one member that has relevant experience or knowledge of financial systems used within the sector in which the company operates or its use and application in financial reporting.

While there is an expectation that audit committee members will keep abreast of relevant legal and regulatory changes being planned as well as implemented, input from the legal function if there is one, or external legal advisers if not, should be provided as a standing agenda item for formal audit committee meetings. Where such changes are to be implemented, the audit committee should be in a position to provide technical financial input into board discussions and the impact that such changes will have on the company. These changes may be in relation to processes and procedures, as well as to customer relations.

External contacts are largely in relation to external auditors given the roles and responsibilities of the audit committee. Committee members should also bring personal knowledge to each meeting to ensure that the benefit of their independence and professional knowledge is being applied for the benefit of the company.

As with all committees, the audit committee supports the effectiveness of the board through direct interaction as well as through interaction with other committees of the board. Their primary relationships are in respect of any financial reporting and associated risks, actions and reporting.

Reporting

There is clear guidance within the Code (Provisions 26 and 27) of what the board should include in the annual report in respect of financial reporting, auditors and financial risks. In addition, annual reports, particularly of large or listed companies, now have requirements to include much more than pure financial data and their breadth of required topics is ever increasing. The audit committee specifically reviews the financial statements being provided as well as any narrative in relation to the financial statements and the workings of the committee. However, they should also reflect on the wider reporting in the annual report and the underlying data that is being presented.

As with other committees of the board, the annual report should include an explanation of how the audit committee undertakes its roles and responsibilities. Any areas that the audit committee has reported to the board that have not been adequately responded to should be reported with detail on how the auditors have been appointed and reviewed. It should include explanations of how any non-audit services and fees are managed by the audit firm and provide evidence of their independence. Alongside the reporting of the risk committee, and identified financial risks, mitigating actions and significant issues should be reported.

> **EXAMPLE: Escalation to the board**
>
> *BT Group Plc, Annual Report 2018, Audit & Risk Committee Report (abstract)*
> During the year, I highlighted to the Board that the committee was disappointed to note that the positive trend in reducing the volume of overdue audit recommendations had not been maintained and that the long-term overdue recommendations had also increased. We were assured that management were closely monitoring this trend and that it has been appropriately overseen by the Executive Committee. As a result of this oversight, we have seen a drop in both overdue audit recommendations and long-term overdue audit recommendations in recent quarters, and year on year, compared with 2016/17.

Best practice would be for the audit committee to review any and all financial statements that are distributed outside the company given their independence as well as their knowledge of systems and controls in place within the company. This may include shareholder reports, interim statements and updates in respect of significant events impacting the business, both positive and negative. There is also a case for the review of the processes used to compile and submit data to any regulatory bodies to ensure that the process is robust and the data is clean. This may be through *ad hoc* testing or challenging internal audit or their processes for such testing.

Internally when reviewing processes for reporting, the audit committee should be mindful of interactions between functions and divisions of a business. They should also include their knowledge of the strategy of the business when considering the actual data and its presentation, as well as the future areas of focus that the strategy may be moving towards.

The annual report should also include reference to the future deliverables and focus of the audit committee beyond its standard responsibilities as defined in the terms of reference. For example, if the audit committee has an oversight role in terms of new product development, systems upgrades, regulatory or legislative amendments or changes to internal financial reporting.

> **EXAMPLE: Forward-looking actions of the audit committee as reported in the annual report**
>
> *Marks and Spencer Plc, Annual Report 2019, Audit Report (extract):*
>
> **2019/20 ACTION PLAN**
> - Monitor the recommendations of the Internal Audit effectiveness review undertaken in 2018/19.
> - Increase focus on risk reporting and emphasising accountability for risk at business unit level.
> - Monitor the progress and pace of delivery of the Company's wider technology and cyber security transformation.

Supporting the committee

All contributors to committee packs should make sure the audit committee is getting information, not just data. Of all the committees of the board this is the most prevalent for reporting to the committee being data-heavy and information light. With meaningful reporting the audit committee will be able to review and recommend beneficial actions that will support the company. Without clear reporting the function of the audit committee may deteriorate into review of the data itself rather than the key issues that the data could be flagging. Too often reporting is purely factual, based on data extraction with no secondary manipulation or grouping of the data to reflect areas of interest. While the audit committee, with the correct skills within their membership, can tease this out of the provided data, this demeans the contribution they could provide through their wider experience. Hence, when reports are submitted to the audit committee, whether as an internal or external contributor, the initial data download should be reviewed against the requirements of the audit committee and the key issues that the data is evidencing.

It is imperative that the audit committee understands the various systems used for collating, using and reporting data and specifically, the differences between them. Proactively arranging for the IT function to provide a good overview of each to committee members and new joiners is beneficial. They should also be available to answer specific questions during and between committee meetings.

While audit committee members should ensure that they keep abreast of regulatory, legislative and legal reporting changes that may affect the company, if there is an internal general counsel or legal department they should update the audit committee on any proposed or implemented changes to ensure that these are formally noted and discussed by this forum. Any advice on required actions as a result of these discussions should then be escalated to the board.

Conclusion

As can be seen, the audit committee has much wider roles and responsibilities than can be understood from its title. It seeks assurance and has oversight of the internal audit function and external auditors as well as the internal controls, processes and procedures. Working with the management team, it can underpin the foundations for an effective framework.

As an independent team of professionals, having an effective audit committee can ensure that a company can rely on its internal controls and processes, is compliant with external requirements and has a robust financial model and financial reports themselves. Specifically, an effective audit committee will bring a level of independent challenge to the business and will report to the board on all their findings, with follow up on any actions identified and agreed.

7 – Risk committee

Introduction

Risk in all businesses must be understood, mitigated against, managed and, above all else, understood and addressed. The framework for this varies across companies, even those within the same sectors and seemingly of similar size and nature. Frequently risk remains solely with the board with no supporting risk oversight function acting on their behalf. Equally, it is often merged with the audit committee, aligning financial risk oversight with that of the wider risks of the business.

> 'I am pleased to present the report of the Group Risk Committee (GRC) which has replaced the Risk Advisory Committee, established by the previous management. As it is clearly unacceptable that Group risk was demoted to an advisory committee, the new GRC is a subcommittee of the Board and positive and significant developments have taken place in risk management during the year.'
>
> Angela Knight, Group Risk Committee Chairman, Provident Financial plc, Annual Report 2018

Writing in the Provident Financial plc annual report, Angela Knight as chair of the group risk committee was clear in her view of where operational oversight of risk should sit in relation to the board within the organisation to which she was appointed. Having this independent support can only be beneficial in a large organisation, while the focus of these forums can also act as a guide to smaller organisations without the organisational breadth to support a stand-alone risk committee.

There are primarily two forms of risk committee, the executive risk committee and a financial services risk committee.

The former, while beneficial, is most often combined with the audit and finance committee given the inter-relation of the topics that these forums have in non-financial services firms. They are rarely implemented as a stand-alone committee, although there are some notable exceptions in large organisations where the risk profile is high and diverse.

The latter is a required committee of the board in financial services businesses given the complexity of the business, the regulatory environment and the impact that financial failures have on the wider landscape.

This chapter will reflect on the role of the risk committee in general and as a stand-alone committee, not differentiating between these two forms of risk committee.

All businesses should be clear on their risk appetite and should communicate this to all employees as well as sharing it with shareholders and other stakeholders. Where there is no risk function or a risk committee is not established, the board should also confirm how risk is overseen within the company.

EXAMPLE: Risk appetite statement

Experian Limited, Annual Report 2019

Risk appetite

We assess the level of risk and our associated risk appetite to ensure we focus appropriately on those risks we face. We target risks for assessment based on gross risk and measure them based on net risk using a scoring methodology. We then prioritise them for mitigation. The Board and Audit Committee review the principal risks, of which there are currently ten, on an ongoing basis, as does the ERMC. The Board has defined risk appetites for certain principal risks that we face during the normal course of business. We use a variety of information sources to show if we are working within our tolerance for these risks and whether or not any of them require additional executive attention.

Our risk culture

The Board is committed to maintaining a culture that emphasises the importance of managing risk and encourages transparent and timely risk reporting. We work to align employees' behaviours, attitudes and incentives with our risk appetite and other governance and risk management policies. Our risk governance process reinforces and facilitates appropriate ownership, accountability, escalation and management of our principal risks. This process includes well-defined roles and responsibilities across our Three Lines of Defence model; assigning accountability for risk-taking when making key business decisions; documenting clear boundaries and behavioural expectations in policies and standards; and creating an environment that reinforces adherence and accountability.

Current areas of focus

Our risk landscape is continuously changing as both business and regulatory environments evolve. The pace of change and need for greater visibility across Experian is growing and we are developing our risk practices accordingly. We are making significant progress in advancing our Three Lines of Defence model.

> In addition to known risks, we continue to identify and analyse emerging ones through internal discussions in different forums, including the ERMC, and the results of these discussions are incorporated into our risk assessment process as appropriate.
>
> We use enterprise risk management software to give managers advanced capability for monitoring their risks. We are developing this software to expand its support capabilities across various risk management activities.

Where implemented, the risk committee is a designated committee of the board with no stand-alone authority to act other than in support of the board. Specifically, under the Code (Principle O), the board 'is responsible for determining the nature and extent of the significant risks it is willing to take in achieving its strategic objectives. The board should maintain sound risk management and internal control systems'.

Where it has been implemented, the risk committee is often aligned to those sectors where the taking of risks drives, and is closely aligned to, reward either of individuals or the company as a whole. In these instances, having a robust risk framework, oversight and culture is highly important as is its effective application.

The risk committee does not act in place of having a strong approach to risk and, as can be seen, their role is primarily one of advice, oversight or review. The culture and attitude to risk is set from the top at board level and, from there, permeates throughout the business. As has been seen in a number of businesses, where the risk appetite is large and it is applied with ineffective controls, a company is likely to fall foul of the risks that it is taking, often crashing to a public and ignominious end. Examples can clearly be seen in banking where the appetite for risk to drive company and individual reward was high but, in some notable cases, the framework of checks and balances was ineffective in challenging or controlling risk takers to the detriment of the company and, by turn the shareholders and stakeholders.

While regulation of financial firms has been enhanced and extended, there is still a balance to be seen between taking risks to generate profits against mitigating risk to such an extent that the business cannot be profitable or survive. However, by and large, the risk/reward framework has failed where individuals either deliberately, or unconsciously, work outside the risk framework of the company. There has been wide publicity of cases where individuals, and sometimes teams, have taken actions that have put the company's, or their personal profit, first, with little consideration for risk, impact, affect or outcome. Hence, having a clear and robust risk framework that openly communicates the risk appetite of the company and its alignment to market and regulatory requirements is imperative. Equally important are the checks to ensure that, not only is this cascaded through the company, but that all individuals, at all levels, understand and constantly apply its concepts. While obvious in large investment banks, this is equally important in all organisations, large and small, and particularly those with a broad customer base, environmental impact or community responsibility.

Even outside financial services, the risk a company is prepared to take must be transparent and include the application of clear policies, checks, balances and guidelines. In a theoretical example, a company processing client data through online portals has a high potential for cyber fraud or IT breaches. The culture of the business must be to minimise this, take seriously any breaches and apply consistently and aggressively all mitigations that would reduce the potential risk. Reputational and financial impacts of not applying risk protocols in this scenario would be serious and could lead to the closure of the business.

Risk in general

All companies have a responsibility to identify the risks prevalent within and affecting their business. In smaller companies, or those without a dedicated risk function and risk committee, this will remain with the board. Wherever the monitoring, oversight and review of risks sit, it is best practice to identify and document risks and review these on a regular basis. The risk appetite of the company should also reflect the level of risk that the company is prepared to accept in undertaking its business and should ensure that this is known by its workforce. The content of this chapter on the role of the risk committee can equally be applied to the board where a risk committee is not in place.

Top risks should be identified, monitored and reported to shareholders. They should also be reviewed for change as the business changes focus, makes strategic decisions or acquires or divests businesses. Risks should also be aligned to strategic focus, and the purpose of the business.

Ideally the risk appetite should be able to be shared succinctly with further detail in support. For example, Smith & Nephew plc within their annual report note that they assess their '…Principal Risks in terms of their potential impact on our ability to deliver our Strategic Imperatives'. Thereafter the principal risks are identified along with examples, actions taken and whether the risk has increased or decreased compared to the previous financial year.

EXAMPLE: Principal risk identification – business continuity and business change

Smith & Nephew Plc, Annual Report 2018, Principal Risks (extract)

Business Continuity and Business Change
Operating with a global remit, increased outsourcing, more sophisticated materials and the speed of technological change in an already complex manufacturing process leads to greater potential for disruptive events. Ensuring our ability to continually execute and operate key sites and facilities in order to develop, manufacture and sell

our products within this environment is a key strategic imperative of the organisation. In addition, the pace and scope of our business 'change' initiatives increases the execution risk that benefits may not be fully realised, costs of these changes may increase, or that our business as usual activities may not perform in line with our plans.

Examples of risks
- Failure or significant performance issues experienced at critical/single source facilities.
- Disruption to manufacturing at single or sole source facility (lack of manufacturing redundancy).
- Supplier failure impacts ability to meet customer demand (single source suppliers).
- Natural disaster impacts ability to meet customer demand.
- Significant 'change' prevents our projects and programmes such as APEX achieving the intended benefits and disrupts existing business activities.

Actions taken by management
- Comprehensive product quality processes and controls are in place from design to customer supply.
- Emergency and incident management and business recovery plans are in place at major facilities and for key products and key suppliers.
- Undertaking risk-based review programmes for critical suppliers.
- Project management governance and toolkits and project steering committee oversight to support successful execution of programme and projects.
- Executive Committee and Audit Committee oversight of risks to change programmes.
- Brexit Steering Group regularly monitors the evolving impact of Brexit and oversees our response.

Risk Tolerance
In operating our business, executing our change programmes and in managing our suppliers and facilities we have a low to moderate tolerance for this risk.

Change from 2017
No change.

Link to strategy
Our Strategic Imperative to 'Become the best owner' requires us to ensure we remain sustainable into the future and through periods of business change.

Oversight
Board

Role of the risk committee

The risk committee has a threefold role: to advise the board on risk matters, oversee risk matters in general and review the adequacy and application of risk within the company.

On behalf of the board they will be tasked with oversight and will support the board in determining the nature and extent of the principal risks the company is willing to take in order to achieve its long-term strategic objectives. At the outset of a new, refreshed or revised risk framework, they may also be tasked with the establishment of a new risk model to reflect the framework. Thereafter their role will encompass ongoing monitoring of procedures to manage risk and the internal control framework, although oversight of financial internal control most likely falls under the remit of the audit committee.

When significant decisions are being made by the board, the risk committee should review, discuss and support the board in its decision making. As an example, a due diligence framework should be implemented when looking at acquisitions to ensure that all elements of risk are considered during the acquisition process. Similarly, if a new product or service is to be launched, the risk committee should advise on the risk elements of the project across all elements of risk including financial, reputational and operational. Without replicating the work of the risk function within the business, they can be the neutral, independent adviser to the board, validating decisions made by the board through their expertise.

Terms of reference

The format of the terms of reference of a risk committee as a delegated forum of the board are generally standard in content with regard to meeting frequency, quorum, attendance and minute taking (see Appendices). As such, support of the risk committee is most often provided by the company secretarial function.

In addition to clearly defining the roles, responsibilities and authority of the risk committee, the terms of reference should also identify responsibilities that sit with other committees to ensure alignment. Specifically, the terms of reference for the risk committee should be aligned to that of the audit committee and the remuneration committee.

At its core, the risk committee has oversight of all enterprise risks, including operational risk, third-party risk, cyber risk, conduct risk, regulatory and compliance risk and emerging risks. In most financial organisations, the finance internal control framework will fall under the remit of the audit committee not the risk committee. For each of the risks identified in the risk register, which is approved by the board risk committee, and ultimately the board, the audit committee will ensure that there is an effective control in place.

When setting the duties of the committee, care should also be taken to differentiate the role of the committee as separate to that of the risk function within the company. The two are distinctly different in their deliverables and it should be clear as to the remits of each, where they interact and where the committee has authority to step in, or report findings to the board.

The head of risk should see the committee as an independent forum of risk-minded professionals that support and promote effective risk awareness throughout the business. They should also be a member of the risk committee, although not the chair.

Specific authority should be given to the committee to request any employee to attend a risk committee meeting in respect of any particular agenda topic. This is particularly applicable where the committee is reviewing specific risk-related items, such as breaches of risk limits or risk-based incidents. In these cases, the relevant attendee may be asked to attend both the committee when the incident is first disclosed and discussed, and also subsequent meetings to report updates on agreed actions to be taken to mitigate or avoid future occurrences of the same risk.

Appendix 1 provides a standard format terms of reference for an Audit Committee. If documenting a terms of reference for a risk committee from the outset, this version would be a good starting point. Care should be taken on incorporating risk related duties (section 8) reporting responsibilities (section 9) and authorities (section 11).

Sample Duties for a terms of reference for a risk committee which all boards should consider are:

1. advise the board on the company's overall risk appetite, tolerance and strategy, taking account of the current and prospective macroeconomic and financial environment and drawing on financial stability assessments such as those published by relevant industry and regulatory authorities including the Bank of England, the Prudential Regulation Authority, the Financial Conduct Authority and other authoritative sources that may be relevant for the company's risk policies.
2. oversee and advise the board on the current risk exposures of the company and future risk strategy.
3. in relation to risk assessment and subject to overlap with the audit committee:
   (a) keep under review the company's overall risk assessment processes that inform the board's decision making, ensuring both qualitative and quantitative metrics are used;
   (b) review regularly and approve the parameters used in these measures and the methodology adopted; and
   (c) set a standard for the accurate and timely monitoring of large exposures and certain risk types of critical importance.
4. review the company's capability to identify and manage new risk types [in conjunction with the audit committee].

5 before a decision to proceed is taken by the board, advise the board on proposed strategic transactions including acquisitions or disposals, ensuring that a due diligence appraisal of the proposition is undertaken, focussing in particular on risk aspects and implications for the risk appetite and tolerance of the company, and taking independent external advice where appropriate and available.
6 review reports on any material breaches of risk limits and the adequacy of proposed action.
7 keep under review the effectiveness of the company's internal financial controls and internal controls and risk management systems and review and approve the statements to be included in the annual report concerning internal controls and risk management.
8 provide qualitative and quantitative advice to the remuneration committee on risk weightings to be applied to performance objectives incorporated in executive remuneration.
9 review the adequacy and security of the company's arrangements for its employees and contractors to raise concerns, in confidence, about possible wrongdoing in financial reporting or other matters. The committee shall ensure that these arrangements allow proportionate and independent investigation of such matters and appropriate follow up action.
10 review the company's procedures for detecting fraud.
11 review the company's procedures for the prevention of bribery.
12 consider and approve the remit of the risk management function and ensure it has adequate resources and appropriate access to information to enable it to perform its function effectively and in accordance with the relevant professional standards. The committee shall also ensure the function has adequate independence and is free from management and other restrictions.
13 recommend to the board the appointment and/or removal of the chief risk officer.
14 review promptly all reports on the company from the chief risk officer.
15 review and monitor management's responsiveness to the findings and recommendations of the chief risk officer.
16 ensure the chief risk officer shall be given the right of unfettered direct access to the chairman of the board and to the committee.
17 work and liaise as necessary with all other board committees.

The list should be modified to accurately reflect the specific risks associated with the company's individual business. It should also be noted which entities the risk committee has oversight of. Standard oversight would include carrying out these duties for the parent company, major subsidiary undertakings and the group as a whole, as appropriate.

Within the duties set out there are certain duties that could be undertaken by either the audit committee or the risk committee and there is some overlap in duties. The precise allocation of responsibilities should be allocated within the respective terms of reference and should be agreed by the board. It is recommended that the board should err on the side of overlapping duties on critical issues, for example in oversight of the capability of the executive team to manage and control risks within the agreed parameters.

Risk committee reporting to the board and in the annual report are fairly standard, however, it should be made clear in the terms of reference whether there are any specific areas where the committee should provide greater clarity of depth. Reporting should also provide detail of general as well as specific risk to the company rather than reporting only on generics. Provision of clear reporting from the risk committee should provide an indication for the board and shareholders of the approach to risk identification, mitigation and acceptance as well as give comfort that internal risk monitoring is effective.

Ad hoc risk committee meetings

Given the purpose of the risk committee, it is also advisable to include the ability to convene ad hoc risk committee meetings in the terms of reference. This allows for topic-specific meetings to be held with a narrow agenda. An example may be a meeting convened to specifically review an acquisition by the company from a risk perspective or an emerging risk related to a client contract or the risk impact of external factors such as a market crash or societal unrest affecting the delivery of service.

The same governance principals apply to ad hoc meetings as to diarised committee meetings. Meeting papers should be circulated, if possible, within the set time frame and the quorum requirements must be maintained. In these cases, there may be a single agenda item and this should be adhered to. Minutes should clearly reflect the discussion and any decision, advice or concerns on the topic noted. Any actions or escalation to the board should be communicated quickly to reflect the urgency that necessitated the meeting to be convened.

Often ad hoc meetings are held at short notice so the full committee membership is not in attendance. As such, it is best practice to include the minutes from any ad hoc committee meeting in the meeting pack of the next diarised formal risk committee meeting where, if appropriate, they can be ratified by the full committee.

Duties, responsibilities and tasks

The role of the risk committee can be broken down into advice, oversight and review. These three areas cover a number of specifics that should be included in the terms of reference and applied by committee members.

Advice

The risk committee should act as a trusted and experienced provider in respect of the overall risk appetite of the company, its tolerance for risk and any and all risks sitting within, or impacting on, the strategy of the company.

The board has a responsibility to carry out a robust assessment of the company's emerging and principal risks and will delegate the operational elements of this to the risk function. The risk committee should be prepared to advise the board on the suitability of both the risks being identified as well as the implementation and actions of the risk function in relation to this.

EXAMPLE: Risk committee review of strategy and business risk appetite

Prudential Plc, Annual Report 2018, Audit and Risk Committee report (extract)

Business Plan:
As part of its role in overseeing and advising the Board on future risk exposures and strategic risks, the Committee reviewed Group Risk's assessment of the Group's Business Plan which covered a range of both financial and non-financial considerations including those associated with the demerger of M&G Prudential from the Group.

As part of the Group Risk's review of the annual Group Business Plan, Group Approved Limits were reviewed, updated and approved by the Committee.

Risk Appetite:
The Committee is responsible for recommending the Group's overall risk appetite and tolerance to the Board.

The Committee approved the Group Risk Appetite Statement, which sets aggregate risk limits in respect of capital requirements, earnings volatility and liquidity as well as maintaining the existing tolerance levels associated with each of these limits.

It is prudent for the risk committee to review emerging risks as a standing agenda item and be prepared to report to the board any areas where they believe risks may be increasing or heightened. The review should take into account the current, and prospective, macroeconomic and financial environment. In undertaking this regular review of emerging risks, the risk committee should utilise external information and data sources as well as those provided from internal sources. These external sources may include, but are not limited to, financial stability assessments such as those published by relevant industry and regulatory authorities including the relevant central bank, the relevant regulatory and legislative bodies such as the IMF, the Prudential Regulation Authority and the Financial Conduct Authority and other authoritative sources that may be relevant for the company's risk policies. Care should be taken to utilise robust data sources with their data used with a consideration of any bias that they may include in their analysis.

Before a decision to proceed is taken by the board, the risk committee should advise on proposed strategic transactions including acquisitions or disposals, ensuring that a due diligence appraisal of the proposition is undertaken, focusing in particular on risk aspects and implications for the risk appetite and risk tolerance of the company. This may include taking independent external advice where appropriate and available.

Internally the risk committee should provide qualitative and quantitative advice to the remuneration committee on risk weightings to be applied to performance objectives incorporated in executive remuneration.

As a general point, the risk committee should also advise the board on the appointment and/or removal of the Chief Risk Officer. Where a new appointment is to be made, they should work with, or provide input into, any process of appointment led by the nominations committee and the HR department.

The risk committee should be prepared to provide advice to the board in respect of their responsibility in relation to Health, Safety and the Environment (HSE). In all businesses this is a responsibility that cannot be delegated by the board and all board meetings must reflect the company's position of HSE as well as documenting any HSE incidents. The risk committee is in a position to support the board in ensuring that HSE is incorporated into company policies and that its practical application throughout the company is adequately resourced. Given the nature of HSE and the associated risks, this topic would form part of any risk committee discussion as a standing agenda item, including reporting any incidents, mitigations and resolution.

Oversight

The risk committee should oversee the current risk exposures of the company as well as the future risk strategy. Hence oversight responsibilities of the risk committee can be subdivided into those looking at the strategy of the business, the appetite for risk in the business that underpins the overall risk model, the operational mechanics of risk within the business and the output of the operational framework.

Oversight of the strategy from a risk perspective would include review, input and challenge of the strategy, reflecting on strategic long-term goals of the business; there are two elements to this. Strategic discussions often focus on the potential of strategic goals and the delivery of this through near-term business plans or strategic projects. Within this there is an element of looking at the existing risks within the business and mapping these against the enhanced or reduced risks that the strategy may create. As an example, expanding a product line may create economies of scale that reduce the capital risk but increase the exposure to and risks with third-party raw materials suppliers. Alternatively, expansion of the client base may reduce client concentration risks but increase due diligence, relationship management and oversight resourcing leading to operational cost and time risks.

Secondarily, are there new risks that the strategy may create which would have to be reviewed and mitigated from a new starting point? For example, if the strategy includes expanding into international markets, there are new risks such as local legal requirements, culture and operational delivery that would need to be reviewed, assessed and mitigated against.

The risk appetite of the business is driven by the board and the risk that the board is prepared for the business to take. The board will have looked at this and any associated mitigations that could be put in place to lessen the impact of risks. Often the risk appetite is documented by recognising the risks that a business is not prepared to take, for example not providing services to certain sectors such as gambling, the defence industry or those adding to the global impact of climate change. Equally there may be risk thresholds that are defined as part of the risk profile of a business, which may include concentration risks such as not investing more than 20% in any one sector or monitoring concentration risks against large clients. The risk committee should advise the board when these are being set. It should also periodically review them against changing board appetite and be prepared to challenge board decisions relating to both change and stagnation. Risks of a company are constantly changing so it is expected that the risk appetite will also change as risks emerge, lessen, become more understood and have mitigations applied.

Where a company outsources any part of its business processes or services, the risk committee should have oversight of the effectiveness of this delegation to a third party in respect of risk. This would include the additional risks that outsourcing creates as well as the potential to mitigate risks through this approach. Contract risk should also not be ignored when outsourcing, given the contract drives the relationship and service delivery, in the same way that the terms of reference defines the role of the committee.

Where a company warrants the implementation of a risk committee, or it has a requirement to do so under legislation or best practice, there will also be an operational risk management function headed by the Chief Risk Officer. The risk committee should be tasked with oversight of the effectiveness of this function as well as oversight of its resource requirements. The risk committee should work with the chief risk officer to understand the drivers behind the risk function and the day-to-day deliverables that are required by the team.

The committee should ensure that the risk function has adequate independence and is free from management or other restrictions. Cases have been reported where executive management has sought to limit the remit of the risk function or divert a review, to protect their own position. One such example was an executive seeking to obtain the identity of an internal informant reporting through a whistleblowing helpline. The risk committee should be aware of any such breaches and, if the culprit is at the executive level, should be prepared to address the situation directly either in support of, or instead of, the head of the risk function.

The risk committee should have oversight of the risk culture and application across the whole business. This would include oversight of risk training for all staff members to ensure that it is effective and applicable. It should also include oversight of risk reporting and processes for mitigating risks throughout the business. In part, this also incorporates the review of processes.

The risk committee should have oversight of the output from the risk function ensuring that risk reporting is adequate, clearly records the key risks of the business, documents the mitigations implemented and flags any areas for improvement. Where the risk function is large, or spread through multiple locations or divisions, the risk committee should ensure that the risk function and its reporting is consistent across all locations and topics. It should also oversee the sharing of risk knowledge throughout the business to ensure that this is shared for the benefit and protection of the business. Risk knowledge owned exclusively by the risk function can be significantly detrimental to a company. If lessons learnt in one function or division are not shared throughout the company, the same risk issues may be duplicated elsewhere impacting resources, credibility, professionalism and financials. Hence, monitoring and oversight by the risk committee should cover consistency communication and effectiveness of all material controls, including financial, operational and compliance controls.

Review

The risk committee has a number of areas where its role is to review the effectiveness of the risk function and the wider company. Within this there may be overlap with the audit committee in respect of financial risks and, where possible, it should be documented clearly where the specific review responsibilities are allocated. If the risk oversight predominantly lies with the audit committee, it would be sensible to have the risk committee have an oversight role in respect of the audit committee's review. There have been a number of cases where the actions of the finance department have been found to be in default. The audit committee may be too narrow in its focus, or too close to the finance function, to be able to adequately review from a position of neutrality. In these cases, a risk review of the finance function undertaken either by the risk committee, or by the risk function on behalf of the committee, would be beneficial.

A key role of the risk committee is to review the company's overall risk framework and the risk assessment processes that sit beneath this. This is the basis that informs the board in its decision making; therefore it is imperative that the framework and the processes are robust. Within this review the risk committee should specifically ensure that:

- both qualitative and quantitative measures are used;
- the parameters that are identified continue to be relevant and beneficial;
- standards for the accurate and timely monitoring of large exposures or concentration risks are in place; and

- risks are adequately defined with any risks of critical importance being effectively monitored and managed.

The risk committee should also ensure that any new or emerging risk types can be adequately identified, mitigated where possible and monitored. Given their nature, this is a developing part of any risk function's remit, therefore, the oversight and review by the risk committee is highly beneficial where independent risk experts may bring alternative views or existing knowledge of a new risk.

At formal committee meetings the risk committee should review any material breaches of risk limits and reflect on the adequacy of proposed actions. It should also review any proposed risk actions in relation to other, non-material risks, given that their non-completion may cause a subsequent material breach due to a continuation of the issue or an increase in impact. At subsequent risk committee meetings the progress of risk-related actions should be tracked to a conclusion. As part of this the risk committee may make recommendations to the risk function for changes or updates in procedures or policies which the risk function should consider implementing. As part of this, they should review management responsiveness to findings and actions, including the indication that this provides as to the understanding and adoption of risk measures by management across and within the company. As an overarching risk forum, the conclusion of risk actions and the application of new actions to mitigate against repeat or duplicate incidents is an important role.

The risk committee should keep under review the effectiveness of the company's non-financial internal controls and risk management systems, including the risk systems applied to monitor internal financial controls. It should review and approve the statements to be included in the annual report concerning internal controls and risk management.

The committee should review the adequacy and security of the company's arrangements for its employees and contractors to raise concerns, in confidence, about possible wrongdoing in financial reporting or other matters. This may include the implementation of a whistleblowing policy, in which case the risk committee should ensure that it has been distributed to all staff to ensure they are aware of the processes they should follow. If appropriate, an external whistleblowing helpline should be set up. The committee should ensure that these arrangements allow proportionate and independent investigation of any such disclosed matters and that appropriate follow-up actions have been identified and undertaken.

In relation to financial risk and internal financial controls, the risk committee should liaise with the audit committee to ensure that appropriate review is undertaken without omission or duplication. The risk committee may want to take responsibility for the review of procedures in respect of the prevention of bribery and for detecting fraud, given the impact that any breach would have on the business both financially and reputationally. The chair of the risk and audit committees should agree the split of responsibilities and document and communicate these accordingly.

The risk committee should not be a point of escalation for the head of risk; however, they should review all reports that the risk function and the chief risk officer produce. The chief risk officer should be a member of the risk committee.

General

In general, the risk committee and its members should ensure that the chief risk officer is given unrestricted direct access to the chairman of the board and has the ability to approach the risk committee and its members whenever necessary. They should also liaise with other committees of the board, with a particular affinity with the audit committee given the high impact of any financial risks that may be uncovered. Within this, the risk committee and its members should be available for confidential discussion with individuals from other committees as well as from the wider business, to ensure that fear of disclosure does not discourage individuals from raising any risk-related concerns. Alongside this, the risk committee should ensure that the company has an effective and operative whistleblowing policy and system in place.

The three areas of advice, oversight and review should also be adapted to the specific needs of the company, adding specifics relevant to the company. Consideration should also be given to the maturity of the risk profile of the company. As businesses grow, move into new jurisdictions, sectors or contracts, the risk model will need to be tailored to the new environment. The risk committee should be mindful of this and take time to review both the remit of the committee and also the nature of the company in which they function.

Risk subcommittees

The risk committee of a large company may implement a matrix of risk committees across subsidiaries, divisions or geographical locations. Primarily these subcommittees would focus on the application of risk policies set by the risk function. This would be application of these policies from an operational perspective, with oversight of local application. They could be tasked with reviewing local risk adequacies, with limits set on the risks that can be managed locally and those that should be elevated to the main risk committee or risk function.

When creating a risk committee matrix, it should be made clear what the various committees have responsibility for and how they interact. Care should be given to setting limits on local responsibility with clarity on reporting both in terms of content and timing. Certain risks will require immediate escalation, others may be managed locally and reported as part of a standard reporting pack.

Examples of a subcommittee may be those acting in local countries, where the overall global risk framework is set centrally and then adopted and monitored locally by the local risk committee in the local jurisdiction.

It is unlikely that sub-risk committees would have independent members. Equally there may not be a member with a full-time role within the risk function or with an in-depth knowledge of risk, with committee members primarily being operationally focused. To ensure meetings focus purely on risk matters, the risk function or main risk committee should aim to attend each sub-risk committee meeting both to connect the global and local forum, as well as to contribute their risk expertise. Where this is impractical, occasional attendance should be implemented to align discussions to the overall risk framework. Regular reporting between sub-risk committees and the main risk committee should be created to ensure that risks are adequately tracked, mitigated and the framework applied effectively.

Another example of a sub-risk committee may be a risk committee that has a specific remit to review and approve all local new business contracts from a risk perspective. The ability to convene a sub-risk committee meeting quickly to opine on a new opportunity is invaluable. In this instance, it is important to have a standardised approach to, and framework for, approval of the new business so that it is consistent across the whole company. It is also key to have clearly defined parameters for when subcommittees can approve the new opportunity and when the decision should be escalated, either in totality or with a recommendation from the local committee.

Given the operational nature of a sub-risk committee, it is likely that it will meet more frequently than the risk committee itself. If the value of a sub-risk committee is seen, then the expectation is that risks should be monitored and reviewed more closely within that forum. As such, it would be expected that a sub-risk committee would meet formally at least four times per year. Potentially monthly meetings may be held during periods of heavy activity.

Sub-risk committees should also have an ability to meet ad hoc whenever a risk is required to be discussed urgently. In these cases, the specific topic should be the only agenda item, although all practical aspects of the meeting should apply equally, including quorum and minute taking. It is best practice to then include the minutes of this meeting at the next formal quarterly risk committee meeting to have these ratified, particularly if the ad hoc meeting was not a full meeting of the committee.

Whatever the stated purpose of a sub-risk committee, the same requirements apply in terms of formality of meeting, defined membership, quorum, minute taking and action lists. A standardised framework starting at the risk committee and cascading down through any other formalised risk committees should be applied.

Committee membership

The Walker Review states that the board risk committee should be a committee of the board comprising a majority of non-executive members and should be chaired by a non-executive director. The finance director should be a member or in attendance at meetings and the chief risk officer should, insofar as possible, be present at all meetings. The risk committee should have appropriate overlap with the audit committee, in particular involving the participation by the chair of the audit committee.

The Financial Stability Board member jurisdictions which includes G20 national supervisors and international standard setting bodies and other groupings, published their Periodic Peer Review Report on Risk Governance in February 2013 (the Risk Governance Report). Their recommendations are beneficial in relation to all companies and consideration should be given by those companies that it doesn't apply to as to whether the recommendation should be applied. Specifically, in terms of membership, the Risk Governance Report recommends that the risk committee:

(a) is required to be a stand-alone committee, distinct from the audit committee;
(b) has a chair who is an independent director and avoids 'dual-hatting' with the chair of the board, or any other committee;
(c) includes members who are independent; and
(d) includes members who have experience with regard to risk management issues and practices.

In general, the risk committee should comprise a majority of members with experience, knowledge and understanding of risk from different backgrounds and aspects, with expertise commensurate with the company to which they are appointed. There should also be a majority of independent members, which may be the independent directors that are appointed as directors of the board.

The chair should have a solid understanding of risk and its application within a business.

Interaction beyond the committee

Interaction beyond the risk committee is primarily internal to the company, other than through attendance at the AGM in order to answer any shareholder questions on the operations of the risk committee.

Internal company interactions clearly include that with the risk function and the individual that heads it. The relationship needs to balance the oversight role of the committee with support of the risk function in undertaking its role.

Interaction with other committees is clearly beneficial, including the audit committee in respect of financial risks as well as the future modelling of any activities and the impact that risk may have on such modelling.

Nomination committee interaction would primarily be in respect of the appointment of any executive or non-executive director appointments where there is a recognised requirement to add additional risk knowledge to the board or executive. There will clearly be input in the appointment of the chief risk officer or head of the risk function and there should be support for the nominations committee with technical knowledge and risk-related specifics required for the role. The chair of the risk committee should also discuss the composition and succession planning of the risk committee with the nominations committee as well as the chair of the board

The risk committee should support the remuneration committee in its role in defining executive remuneration policies. This support should take the form of providing qualitative and quantitative advice on risk weightings to be applied to performance objectives incorporated in executive remuneration.

Outside of other committees and the board, the risk committee should also liaise with any departments that are involved in risk mitigation in the company. An example would be the department responsible for ensuring that adequate insurance policies are in place for the day-to-day operations of the business as well as Director & Officer and key man insurance. The function responsible for obtaining adequate insurance is variously finance, legal, business support or another function. Its existence should be checked with regard to current and emerging risks as well as the board's risk appetite and should be reviewed on a regular basis, at least annually. It is not the responsibility of the risk committee to put insurance in place but, as a risk mitigation, they should be assured by evidence that it is in place.

Where risks are identified in relation to employees, the risk committee should liaise with the HR department to ensure that suitable policies are in place and that they are communicated and applied appropriately. These may include a whistle-blowing policy, data protection policy, anti-bribery policy and other people-related risk mitigation policies, procedures, guidance and training.

Where there has been a significant risk-related breach within a company, the risk committee should be confident that the risk function has liaised with the relevant offices, divisions or departments to ensure that mitigating actions have been put in place to ensure the issue does not re-occur. While driven by the risk function, the risk committee would be expected to have oversight and immediate knowledge of any significant breach or risk-related issue.

Given the increasing use of technology in all businesses, risk mitigation activities within the IT function of all business need to be appropriate, relevant and kept up-to-date. The risk committee should have the assurance that these are in place and adequately monitored. In addition, as new technology and systems are introduced into the business, a risk assessment should be undertaken for its implementation as well as its subsequent use. This is particularly important where private data is being obtained or held.

While the relationship with the chief risk officer is critical, risk committee members should also interact with members of the risk function to understand their roles, responsibilities and pinch points to validate and support the reporting of the head of the risk function.

Risk committee members should have access to the wider employee base of the company which may be facilitated through HR or company secretarial functions. It is important that risk committee members understand and can personally validate the risk culture prevalent throughout the company, rather than solely relying on the content of written reports. Frequently workshops or working groups are created to facilitate this wider company interaction and these can also be venues for risk committee members to share their expertise with a wider audience.

Reporting

As a delegated authority of the board with minimal ability to act independently, it is key that the risk committee ensures that the board is kept abreast of all their activities. This reporting should focus on the three areas of advice to the board, assurance that the oversight role of the committee is functioning effectively and updates on reviews undertaken.

As a minimum, the committee chairman should report to the board on its proceedings after each meeting on all matters within its duties and responsibilities. As part of this, they should make whatever recommendations to the board they deem appropriate on any area within its remit where action or improvement is needed.

The committee should also produce a report of its activities and the company's risk management and risk strategy to be included in the company's annual report. The report should present a meaningful description of the company and the risks it faces, why each risk is incurred and how the committee plays its part in managing them. The best reports offer great insight into the issues facing the company and give confidence that risk is well managed.

Frequently, and particularly where the risk committee may not be a separate forum, the annual report will incorporate the risks of the business in the main body of reporting as part of the directors' report. Specifically, this will identify the key risks of the company and how these are being monitored, addressed and mitigated.

Taking account of the company's current position and principal risks, the board should explain in the annual report how it has assessed the prospects of the company, over what period it has done so and why it considers that period to be appropriate. It should also include a description of what procedures are in place to identify emerging risks, and an explanation of how these are being managed or mitigated. The risk committee should be prepared to provide a report to support these explanations by the board or provide a risk report to be included directly in the annual report. This should specifically cover the company's risk management and risk strategy as well as the activities of the risk committee.

Where there is a dedicated risk committee, its focus for the forthcoming year should be included in the annual report reflecting the areas where the company, its board and the risk committee members recognise that further focus should be given.

> **EXAMPLE: Focus for Forthcoming Year**
>
> *Prudential plc, Annual Report 2018, Group Risk Committee report (extract)*
> - Building on strong progress made during 2018, the GRC will focus on a programme of continual improvement in the way the Group manages risk. The current interim Group CRO has agreed to remain in role until the end of the first Quarter 2019, by which time we expect to have progressed a new full-time appointment. This will ensure a continuing risk focus and also the opportunity to provide for effective handover of responsibilities.
> - To support the Board in developing its new customer centric approach and to help develop the target culture, supported by an appropriate risk infrastructure.
> - To on-board the new permanent Group CRO and ensure an effective handover from the current interim.
> - To review and consider the Group Risk operating model and determine where and how greater integration (subject to regulatory constraints) might provide opportunities to further enhance risk coverage, expertise and co-ordination.
> - To embed and enhance the risk frameworks and associated reporting.
> - To undertake reviews of key elements of our Group Risk Appetite and ensure these remain appropriate given a changing environment.
> - To complete the actions set out for the Group as part of the Conduct Risk Assessment.
> - To maintain a forward looking focus and ensure the Group is quick to identify emerging issues and address them with responsive action plans.

The board should state whether it has a reasonable expectation that the company will be able to continue in operation and meet its liabilities as they fall due over the period of assessment, drawing attention to any qualifications or assumptions as necessary. The directors' report in the annual report and accounts should set out risk management objectives and policies including, but not limited to, financial instruments.

Supporting the committee

The risk committee is independent of the organisation and, as such, does not benefit from having operational support on a daily basis. Hence the committee relies on the input and support of a wide range of functions in order to fulfil its obligations.

Those tasked with supporting or providing information to the risk committee should be mindful that the risk committee is a representative of the board of directors, their roles and responsibilities in advising, having oversight and reviewing risk and risk operations within the business are there to ensure that the business is robust and fit-for purpose.

When submitting papers to the risk committee for consideration at committee meetings, contributors should be mindful that the information submitted forms the basis of the discussion. Too much information can overwhelm the committee members and undermine the effectiveness of the meeting. Committee members need to be made aware of the critical issues that require their attention and discussion. Equally the committee should be clear on the information it expects to receive, the format and the timing. Checking for requirements before collating information or submitting papers and seeking feedback on their usefulness after meetings, are both ways of ensuring that submissions are useful. To enable effective and efficient data gathering, submissions and committee meetings, peripheral, non-useful information should be identified to avoid spending too much time on gathering and documenting it.

HR and risk members should be proactive in recommending forums where risk committee members can interact with the workforce at all levels to validate the culture of risk prevalent across the company.

Conclusion

One of the greatest risks of any company is to assume that the risks of the business are static and can be mitigated completely. Drawing on risk expertise through a dedicated risk committee or as part of another forum, will support board members in understanding how risks can be identified, addressed, mitigated and reported. Risks will emerge, increase and decrease; hence having clarity on the approach is highly beneficial.

As a minimum, the risk appetite and adoption of risk within the strategy of a company should be regularly reviewed by the board, preferably with the support of risk experts. Additionally, having risk understood at board level is not enough. The risk appetite of the company and the processes and controls in effecting this must be visible and communicated. Ensuring that all employees understand risk processes, risk appetite and the lines that cannot be crossed ensures that the company has a much more robust risk framework on which to build the company. Lack of focus on risk at all levels, is a catalyst for future risk failure.

With or without a dedicated risk committee, the oversight and review of risks is a key element to a business. A risk committee, or risk knowledgeable experts as advisers or non-executive directors, will support the board and its members in identifying and understanding risks, both present and potential.

8 – Remuneration committee

Introduction

'The [Remuneration] Committee ensures that executive pay arrangements remain appropriate when considering M&S's overall remuneration framework and external regulatory environment.'

Andrew Fisher, Chair of the remuneration committee,
Marks and Spencer Group plc

Of all committees of the board, the remuneration committee has three elements that are imperative in its successful functioning, namely, transparency, clarity and independence. Specifically, transparency of outcome, clarity of deliverables and independence of action from the board and other influencers. Throughout this chapter, these three elements will be reflected in how this committee functions, reports and delivers.

The remuneration committee is a required committee for all premium listed companies under the Code (Provision 32). In some cases, this committee is combined with the Nominations Committee given their shared roles on building effective leadership whether through appointments to the board or remunerating leaders and executives. This chapter will look at the role of the remuneration committee in isolation.

EXAMPLE: The role of the Remuneration Committee

BAE Systems Plc, Annual Report 2018, Responsibilities of the Remuneration Committee (extract)

The Committee remains responsible for the full spectrum of senior executive employment matters: recruiting, promoting and retaining the best top-level leaders, setting the incentives under which these leaders operate, and monitoring the results they produce and the manner in which they produce them. Our overall remuneration framework has a number of specific goals. It is designed to motivate our key talent to achieve the Company's strategic objectives, to deliver on customer commitments, to lead and inspire employees, and to drive value for our shareholders. It is also designed to be competitive in the various markets in which we operate and compete for talent.

Changes introduced by the 2018 UK Corporate Governance Code are applicable to all companies with a premium listing with effect from 1 January 2019 and include the actual setting of remuneration for senior management by the remuneration committee, in addition to Executive Directors (Provision 33). This is opposed to the previous recommending and monitoring by the remuneration committee under previous Codes. In addition, the remuneration committee now also has a responsibility to review workforce remuneration and related policies and for the alignment of incentives and rewards with culture, taking these into account when setting the policy for executive directors.

These guidelines for premium listed companies provide clear guidelines for the role of a remuneration committee. Given this, it is prudent for any large company or organisation to implement a remuneration committee to have clarity and transparency on remuneration at a senior level, as well as the inter-relation of this to the wider workforce.

Given the high profile of remuneration for directors, especially of executives in organisations providing services to the consumer market, the output and effectiveness of this committee are highly important for the public profile of the business and the knock-on effect this can have across the external marketplace. This is equally applicable to charities with a visible presence and significant member associations.

Public scrutiny of remuneration of senior executives of listed and public companies is high, and with every public fall in profits or failure of a business, the related focus on executive pay brings the work of this committee under considerable public scrutiny. As a result, transparent reporting is needed on the workings of the committee, the policies they are setting and their decision making noting that failures are often very public, such as Persimmon, while successes are usually kept confidential, such as Arup.

Role of the remuneration committee

There are three key roles that the remuneration committee fulfils, namely, to set the policy for board and senior management remuneration, to set or approve individual remuneration awards and to oversee company-wide remuneration policies.

Set the policy for senior remuneration

The main responsibility of the remuneration committee is to set the policy for board and senior management remuneration, aligning it to the strategy of the company as set by the board. This latter is key in ensuring that executives are remunerated aligned to the purpose of the company so driving executive engagement and delivers success for the business as well, keeping the two closely intertwined.

> **EXAMPLE: Linking Remuneration Policy to Strategy and the wider business**
>
> *SSE Plc, Annual Report 2019, Remuneration Committee report (extract)*
>
> **Linking Executive Directors' remuneration with SSE's purpose and strategy**
> Our remuneration policy is designed to be sustainable and simple and to facilitate diligent and effective stewardship that is vital to the delivery of SSE's core purpose of providing the energy needed today and building a better world of energy for tomorrow, and our strategy of creating value for shareholders and society.
>
> A sustainable approach to executive pay that is consistent with SSE's wider commitment to being a responsible employer is fundamental to the remuneration policy. Fairness is a central pillar of the policy – fairness to Executive Directors in recognition of the extent of their responsibilities, and fairness relative to the rest of the SSE team whose shared talent, skills and values are essential to SSE's success. The extent of their responsibilities means Executive Directors are well paid, but the remuneration policy is designed to, among other things, ensure they are not overpaid. Using reference points such as the ratio of the Chief Executive's pay to pay in SSE (which we have again chosen to disclose voluntarily) and wider workforce pay considerations are as important to us as the use of external benchmark data when setting executive pay levels.
>
> SSE is committed to being transparent in the way it does business. To this end, and mindful of the continuing public debate about executive pay, the Committee strives to keep remuneration arrangements clear, consistent and simple to enable effective stakeholder scrutiny. In part our decision to renew the Directors' Remuneration Policy on broadly the same basis as before, is based on the belief that the current arrangements are embedded into the business and well understood both internally and externally.
>
> The provision of energy needed today and building a better world of energy for tomorrow is, by definition, a long-term commitment that requires long-term stewardship. A remuneration policy that offers fair reward for the leadership, expertise and strategic decision making required in a challenging market is critical to SSE's future success. Our remuneration policy promotes sustainable performance over the longer term through significant deferral of remuneration and holding periods. Equally, Executive Directors are expected to demonstrate commitment by building and maintaining a substantial personal shareholding in the business.

The committee will also review the policy on a regular basis, ensuring it continues to adapt to changes in strategy, marketplace and direction. Within this, individual incentive plans would be addressed and reviewed, including where executives change responsibilities or roles.

When setting the policy, the committee should reflect on the balance between setting the policy for individuals versus the roles they perform.

Application in respect of individuals should reflect the actual contribution by that individual. The specific benefits that the individual has delivered due to their expertise and contribution. Aligned to the strategy of the company, reflection of this can also feed into the review of executive contribution and their annual appraisal, which may be picked up either by this committee or the nominations committee. Committee members should also be mindful of the attributes of each executive and their personal drivers. This may not always be financial so the incorporation of other drivers in remuneration packages is important. It should be remembered that the purpose of an executive remuneration policy is to encourage and motivate appointees to deliver the best they can in their role, aligned to them being appointed as, and continuing to be, the best candidate for the role.

Deliverables based on role are more generic and should be applicable for all incumbents of the role, thus being transferable when individuals change roles, join or leave the company. As an example, the remuneration of a sales director should clearly include metrics on new revenue generated, although this should be balanced with delivery of targeted new revenue aligned to the strategy of the company. If a company is moving towards online delivery of service, revenue metrics should be biased towards greater achievement in this segment, rather than other revenue forms.

The key is to ensure that the policy is aligned to strategy and corporate objectives, is effective in its aims and that management, at all levels, buys into it rather than seeking ways to work around it or manipulate it for personal benefit.

When setting the performance measures and targets for executive members, the committee should ensure that they are robust, meaningful and aligned to the strategy. The policy should be transparent to all shareholders and stakeholders. Hence, when documenting the policy, the committee should ensure that it is clear, concise and understandable. Complexity in policy will have a knock-on effect to complexity in its application with a resultant challenge in its application that would be difficult to explain.

Set the remuneration for senior management

As of January 2019, under the Code (Provision 33) the remuneration committee should also set the remuneration of senior management of the business, noting that prior to this the role of the remuneration committee was to approve individual rewards aligned to defined and documented guidelines, deliverables and policies. This change in approach reflects the importance of independent review and application of remuneration. As well as creating independence of application, it also separates the ability of senior management to influence metrics supporting remuneration setting to deliver greater personal benefit, i.e. to 'game' the process in their own favour.

Whether the committee's responsibility is to set or approve remuneration, the committee is the independent arbitrator of the application of the policy. During review, consideration should be given to the application of the set policy in respect of each individual award, as well as the impact of stakeholders and other third parties. While the committee could purely apply the policy and approve the award, circumstances may have changed between setting the policy and its application that should be taken into consideration. For example, one criterion may be market share by the company. At year-end the market share may meet the criteria. By the time the remuneration is applied, market share may have fallen considerably. If so, the committee should consider whether the market share fall is significant or consistent enough to be applied to the remuneration application, even though financial year-end numbers could support a full pay out.

When considering application of policy, committee members should also reflect on the adequacy of the metrics to which the remuneration is aligned. Could the numbers be manipulated? Should financial numbers be an average of previous months? Is there seasonality in metrics that are not obvious on the metrics underpinning the award?

A by-product of the review of executive remuneration may also include an annual appraisal of the Chief Executive, noting that the CEO will undertake the appraisal of the other board members themselves. Consistency in approach should be aimed for and the appraisal of the CEO may also form the framework for their appraisal of other board members. It is in this respect that the role of the remuneration committee may overlay with the nominations committee and, as such, these two committees are often combined into one forum.

Oversee the remuneration strategy of the company

Increasingly, the remuneration committee also oversees the remuneration strategy for the whole company and its effectiveness in delivering the required results. This is an additional responsibility that has been specifically applied by the updated Code. Oversight here is not just against the strategy of the company but, more particularly, in respect of diversity, inclusion and gender pay. Metrics on these latter points are required to be included in annual reports and publicly available, adding to the transparency required from the company and the remuneration committee on their behalf.

It should be remembered that the remuneration policy of the whole company is set, applied and reviewed by the HR department with the support of the board. The role of the remuneration committee is to review its application and the effectiveness of its desired results. For example, if a company-wide policy has an aim to retain staff, does the policy deliver this? Other aims may include support of professional development, inclusion and promotion of minorities, staff engagement in its widest sense or application of defined role deliverables.

In having oversight of the wider policy, remuneration committee members will need to understand the drivers beyond pure financials and will have to engage with people policies and development attributes. In the majority of companies, the cost of staff is the largest balance sheet cost as well as the greatest opportunity for success, so ensuring the people policy is effective and fully understood and supported by the executive is highly important.

Terms of reference

Standard terms of reference should be used for the remuneration committee (see Appendix 2), with some specific points to note.

The frequency with which the remuneration committee needs to meet will vary depending on the nature, scale and complexity of the business of the company which may change from time to time. It is clear, however, that its greatest impact is on the company when remuneration is discussed, reviewed, approved and applied with its resultant impact on the financials of the business. In addition, it must meet close to the year-end to review the directors' remuneration report which quoted companies must submit to shareholders for approval at the AGM.

It is recommended that the remuneration committee should meet at least twice a year in order to effectively discharge its responsibilities, although additional meetings may be considered to review the effectiveness of the company-wide employee strategy outside of the discussions on executive remuneration.

The chair of the remuneration committee should attend the AGM to be available to answer any questions about the workings of the committee.

The committee should also have the authority to appoint remuneration advisers or purchase information to support their discussions, without recourse or permission from the board. As long as they keep within any budgetary constraints or guidelines applicable within the company and as set by the board.

Duties, responsibilities and tasks

From the Code (Principle P), remuneration policies and practices should be designed to support strategy and promote long-term sustainable success. Executive remuneration should be aligned to company purpose and values and be clearly linked to the successful delivery of the company's long-term strategy.

However, it should be recognised that in all but extremely rare cases, remuneration committees are not creating a remuneration policy from the outset and are instead reviewing and revising existing policies for current suitability and application. Complete review of the policy, as if it was being implemented for the first time, should be undertaken at defined intervals and on significant change to the company or the composition of the executive team.

Significant changes that would impact on the remuneration policy could include a merger with, or acquisition of, another company. Remuneration policies would need to be reviewed, aligned and adjusted to ensure consistency across the business. In this instance the strategy of the newly combined business should also be taken into account. Acquisition of an online business by a company only previously focused on direct retail sales, would not only change the drivers but also the combined strategy of the business as well as the underlying metrics supporting the policy.

To be able to deliver in its role, the remuneration committee should have a clear understanding of the strategy of the business and its drivers. By understanding the strategy, suggested metrics and deliverables of the executive team can be proposed, discussed and agreed. As strategy is primarily a long-term view of the future of the business it can underpin long-term incentives within a remuneration policy. An understanding of the strategy, its focus and the future direction of the business is key to being able to align and adjust the policy.

With no member of the executive board being a member of the committee, the committee can have confidential and independent conversations regarding what the best metrics, drivers and deliverables by each executive should be.

Despite executive members not being members of the committee, having their input into the policy for executive remuneration is key. The deliverables, as well as being aligned to company strategy, must also be achievable and motivational for each executive. While considerable column inches is given in the press to the awards made to executives, little is given to the deliverables they have achieved that have ensured the success of the business.

Shareholder approval

Balancing business success with executive engagement is a priority to be balanced by the committee with the resultant policy and its application being one of the actions requiring approval by shareholders at the AGM. Shareholder activism has seen remuneration decisions increasingly being challenged at shareholder meetings.

The committee has a responsibility to establish a formal and transparent procedure for developing a policy on executive remuneration, as well as determining director and senior management remuneration on behalf of the board. This should also include an assessment of the company's performance against targets set within wider employee reward schemes.

Review of executive remuneration policies should be undertaken respective to the company's wider success, or failure, with the policy adapted to changes in circumstances of the company and its business environment. This latter is particularly important given an executive may continue to work effectively and successfully within their role and the organisation but the wider environment may have a negative effect on the business itself. Executive responsibility on adapting to these types of changes are inherent within their senior role, and both are intertwined when setting remuneration policies.

The interaction of the executive remuneration policy and employee policies should be monitored so neither works in isolation. Executives should not be benefiting through disadvantaging employees, while employees should be able to fully understand the added value that executives are bringing to the business and how this is reflected in their remuneration policy.

The financial interaction between executive and employee remuneration policies could include specific deliverables. For example, increasingly restrictions on executive bonus pay outs are aligned to employee bonuses; executive bonuses are not paid unless at least 75% of employees receive a bonus.

> **EXAMPLE: Aligning Executive Remuneration to Employee Remuneration**
>
> *Segro Plc, Annual Report 2018, Remuneration Committee report (extract)*
> The policy for the Executive Directors is designed with regard to the pay and benefits for employees across the Group. All employees are eligible for an annual Bonus on the same performance measures which are consistent with those of the Executive Directors save that those below Board level have a fourth target based on their personal performance. The maximum Bonus opportunity is fixed according to seniority banding across the Company.

Remuneration calculations

Specific details of how remuneration is calculated or the workings of the committee will not be covered here, and details, if such are needed, can be found in the NED Handbook published by The Chartered Governance Institute. However, as an overview, remuneration of executive management can be split into:

- salary, related pension contributions and other benefits packages such as healthcare, travel, insurance;
- short-term incentives such as bonuses, which are usually formula-driven related to defined performance criteria; and
- long-term incentives, with a measurement period of over one year, with three to five years being most common. These are often shares and share options which are almost always subject to restrictions.

Long-term incentives are often subject to restrictions on receipt, for example long-term bonuses, where they are not paid if the business does not continue to deliver growth. Equally, share incentives may include vesting criteria, restricting share transfers and realisation of value through sale, to specific time periods or over a set period of time.

Claw-back criteria are increasingly being discussed as a means to retrieve compensation payments if the initial criteria were subsequently seen to be ineffective. For example, new revenue sales may be subsequently found to be front-loaded to boost revenue numbers, without any follow-on revenue uplift or consistency in business revenue. The remuneration committee should review and update the remuneration policy in place in respect of changing opportunities and expectation on all aspects of the policy, including claw-back principles.

> **EXAMPLE – Updated Remuneration Policy provisions**
>
> *Greencore Plc, Annual Report 2019, Remuneration Committee report (extract)*
> The conclusion of the Committee's review was that our remuneration structure generally remained fit-for-purpose, particularly following the implementation of a number of changes to our current remuneration policy following the AGM in 2017, including:
>
> - the introduction, with effect from FY18, of malus and clawback provisions to both the Performance Share Plan ('PSP') and the Annual Bonus Plan ('ABP') during the vesting period and for two years post-vesting;
> - the introduction of Total Shareholder Return ('TSR') as an additional measure for our long-term PSP awards, to further augment alignment with shareholders and diversify the measures used under the PSP; and
> - the increase in shareholding guidelines, such that all Executive Directors must attain a shareholding of 200% of salary within five years of appointment to the Board.
>
> Following the aforementioned changes, as well as continuous shareholder engagement, the Committee was pleased with the high level of support for the FY18 Annual Report on Remuneration at the AGM in 2019, which received over 90% support. Notwithstanding the above, the Committee believes that certain amendments should be introduced to the 2020 Remuneration Policy to reflect our evolving strategy and shareholder expectations.

The aim of including vested shares, restricted stock, clawbacks and other similar remuneration criteria and restrictions is to ensure a direct link to long-term company success not short-term benefit. However, the implementation of these must be balanced with the need to motivate executives to deliver to the best of their ability.

General approach to determining a remuneration policy

When determining executive director remuneration policy and practices, the remuneration committee should address the following:

- Clarity – remuneration arrangements should be transparent and promote effective engagement with shareholders and the workforce.
- Simplicity – remuneration structures should avoid complexity and their rationale and operation should be easy to understand.
- Risk – remuneration arrangements should ensure reputational and other risks from excessive rewards, and behavioural risks that can arise from target-based incentive plans, are identified and mitigated.
- Predictability – the range of possible values of rewards to individual directors and any other limits or discretions should be identified and explained at the time of approving the policy.

- Proportionality – the link between individual awards, the delivery of strategy and the long-term performance of the company should be clear. Outcomes should not reward poor performance.
- Alignment to culture – incentive schemes should drive behaviours consistent with company purpose, values and strategy.

Policy specifics

The Code includes various provisions which provide a framework for an effective scheme. These include:

- under Provision 36, that remuneration schemes should promote long-term shareholdings by executive directors that support alignment with long-term shareholder interests. Share awards granted for this purpose should be released for sale on a phased basis and be subject to a total vesting and holding period of five years or more. The remuneration committee should develop a formal policy for post-employment shareholding requirements encompassing both unvested and vested shares; and
- under Provision 37, the importance of the committee being able to use discretion when applying the policy, recognising that formulaic outcomes or data-driven application needs judgement in its application to ensure it is effective. This should also include the ability to reduce payments or retrospectively recover cash or awards under specified circumstances, when it would be appropriate to do so.

Specific note is made that only basic salary should be pensionable. The pension contribution rates for executive directors, or payments in lieu, should be aligned with those available to the workforce. Market expectation is increasingly for executive pension contributions to be no greater than 25%, noting the additional expectation of it being aligned to company contributions to the wider workforce pensions. This should particularly be reviewed when executives are close to retirement thus requiring individual review as well as blanket policy application.

As previously noted, given the changing nature of the environment and the metrics used to underpin remuneration calculations, policies should also incorporate clauses to adjust packages based on significant changes in metrics or future significant shifts, such as a future significant dip in market share or change in share price. Specifically, bonus malus and clawback clauses should be carefully thought through, added to the policy and applied in practice. The aim is to incentivise for the long-term view thus seeking to discourage taking short-term risks that may yield short-term profits but be offset by long-term losses. Historically, traditional bonus calculations focused purely on short-term delivery with no long-term view. This change in approach is possibly the greatest impact on the requirement to implement a remuneration committee and ensure that its outcomes are practical and effective.

Committee membership

The Code (Provision 32) requires that the board should establish a remuneration committee of independent non-executive directors, with a minimum membership of three, or in the case of smaller companies, two.

In addition, the chair of the board can only be a member if they were independent on appointment and they cannot chair the remuneration committee.

Before appointment as chair of the remuneration committee, the appointee should have served on a remuneration committee for at least 12 months.

The input of information from other committees within the company may serve to form the core committee membership, noting the requirement for remuneration committee members to be non-executive and independent. Committee members from other committees may be invaluable members of the remuneration committee given, despite their independence from the operations of the company, by being a member of another committee of the company, they will have direct experience and understanding of the company, the executive and the strategy of the business.

Member characteristics

Independence of judgement and discretion when authorising or reviewing remuneration application is a core characteristic of all members of the remuneration committee. They must be able to balance the incentivisation of the individual versus the executive as a collective and the success and focus of the whole business. This includes independence from influence of board members, shareholders and other stakeholders. Taking evidence, advice or views from all relevant parties is highly important. The ability to assess and apply this feedback and use it as part of confidential and independent decision making is key.

Although an obvious conflict of interest, it should be stated in writing that no director may be involved in any decisions as to their own remuneration.

Key attributes of remuneration committee membership are:

- Knowledge – of HR processes and value drivers of people engagement through remuneration, whether at executive level or the wider workforce.
- Numeracy – technical financial knowledge is potentially greater than that for an audit committee member given it is the application of metrics that is key as much as trend identification and historical reporting.
- Diversity – of contributors to drive constructive discussion and debate to deliver meaningful and beneficial outcomes.
- Balance – opinions need to be fair, unbiased and balanced given this is the outcome required for remuneration policies and their application.
- Communication – outcomes need to be transparent while discussion needs to take into account views of, and input from, multiple shareholders and stakeholders. Receipt of information, its dissemination into discussions and

distribution via policies and reporting underpin the workings of this committee more than any other.
- Emotional Intelligence – members of the remuneration committee, require a high level of emotional intelligence to be able to balance the people element of their role alongside good governance and the application of decisions. It is this attribute that remuneration committee members identify as the distinguishing factor of a good remuneration committee member although it is intangible in its identification during interview stages for new committee members.

External advisers

Committee members can appoint an independent external remuneration consultant with this decision being independent of the board. The existence and identity of this consultant should be included in the annual report alongside a statement about any other connection it has with the company or individual directors.

> **EXAMPLE: Appointment of an External Adviser example**
>
> *Marks and Spencer Group plc, Annual Report 2019, Remuneration Committee (extract)*
>
> **Committee Advisers**
> In carrying out its responsibilities, the Committee is independently advised by external advisers. The Committee was advised by PwC during the year. PwC is a founding member of the Remuneration Consultants Group and voluntarily operates under the code of conduct in relation to executive remuneration consulting in the UK. The code of conduct can be found at remunerationconsultantsgroup.com
>
> The Committee has not explicitly considered the independence of the advice it receives, although it regularly reflects on the quality and objectivity of this advice. The Committee is satisfied that any conflicts are appropriately managed. PwC was appointed by the Committee as its independent advisers in 2014 following a rigorous and competitive tender process. PwC provides independent commentary on matters under consideration by the Committee and updates on legislative requirements, best practice and market practice. PwC's fees are typically charged on an hourly basis with costs for work agreed in advance. During the year, PwC charged £56,500 for Remuneration Committee matters. This is based on an agreed fee for business as usual support with additional work charged at hourly rates. PwC has provided tax, consultancy and risk consulting services to the Group in the financial year.
>
> The Committee also seeks internal support from the CEO, Group General Counsel and Company Secretary, HR Director and Head of Performance & Reward as necessary. All may attend the Committee meetings by invitation but are not present for any discussions that relate directly to their own remuneration. The Committee also

reviews external survey and bespoke benchmarking data including that published by New Bridge Street (the trading name of Aon Hewitt Limited), KPMG, PwC, FIT Remuneration Consultants, Korn Ferry Hay Group and Willis Towers Watson.

Independent judgement should be exercised when evaluating the advice of any external third parties and when receiving views from executive directors and senior management. Members should be mindful of the dynamics of executive relations and interactions when obtaining feedback, whether positive or negative, and care should be taken to obtain a full cross-section of input prior to any decision making.

External advisers may be particularly beneficial in providing reliable, up-to-date information about remuneration in other companies of comparable scale and complexity.

The remuneration committee should have the ability to appoint external remuneration consultants and commission or purchase any reports, surveys or information which it deems necessary to support its deliberations. The cost of such additional information should be borne by the company, with any budgetary constraints set by the board being applied to such purchase.

Interaction beyond the committee

Within the company

Of all the committees of the board, the remuneration committee has a connection with the widest internal audience reflecting its oversight role on all employee remuneration and incentive policies.

In light of this, the interaction with the HR team is critical, with members needing to have an understanding of the drivers and motivations of employees as well as the company itself. In the majority of companies, the costs of, and benefits from, employees are the highest when looking at cashflow and financials. Getting positive benefit from any incentive plan or spend by HR can underpin a successful business. The remuneration committee is there to challenge the incentive plans of the whole business aligned to the success of the company. Alongside this the remuneration of senior executives must not be seen in isolation and must drive individual success that derives benefit for the business, its shareholders and stakeholders.

Additionally, the remuneration committee will interact heavily with the finance team, ensuring that remuneration policies support the success of the business and do not have a negative impact financially. Stress-testing scenarios of policy application on the financial balance sheet will enable remuneration committee members to understand both the up-side and down-side potential that the policy may have. This stress testing should be undertaken outside of the policy application period to ensure that other calendar deliverables do not result in a rushed process that may deliver incomplete results.

Interaction with the wider employee community is most prevalent via publication of the expected deliverables under the executive remuneration policy. Metrics used to underpin the policy should be published to ensure visibility and clarity, while these same metrics should be applied from top to bottom so that people policies are fair from the bottom upwards. A general rule is that if deliverables are difficult to explain to all staff as stakeholders, then the policy does not work. This is particularly relevant when deliverables are aligned to behaviours rather than metrics. For example, if there is a company value on treating colleagues with respect, how is this translated into the actions of the executive and aligned to their remuneration?

Finally, the remuneration committee will interact with other committees instigated by the board. In particular, they have an affinity with the nominations committee, and these two committees are often combined. Input from other committees either directly or through their roles and responsibilities can also contribute to the remuneration policies being set. As an example, risk criteria, accountability, acceptability and mitigation may underpin specific deliverables thus understanding the workings of the risk committee is invaluable in aligning metrics, behaviours and expected outcomes. The terms of reference of the risk committee may specifically require this input particularly in providing qualitative and quantitative advice on risk weightings to be applied to performance objectives incorporated in executive remuneration.

Similarly, the output of the finance and audit committee will contribute to the remuneration policy related to the CEO and CFO, among others.

External to the company

Externally, remuneration committee members frequently interact with shareholders to gain their input into the remuneration policy. Shareholders will vote on remuneration policies and individual remuneration packages at the AGM, hence being able to understand concerns and, where relevant, adjust policies to reflect these concerns is beneficial. The remuneration committee chair should attend the AGM to be available to answer any questions on the operations of the committee.

In support of this, committee members should ensure that documented policies and their application are transparent and justified so that concerns of shareholders, including activists, can be addressed and responded to.

Remuneration committee members may meet shareholders formally as a committee seeking their input, or informally either individually or collectively. While shareholder views and opinions do not have to be followed, understanding their concerns, learning from these discussions and addressing any concerns would be prudent. Equally beneficial would be to address these concerns in any reporting if they have not been addressed in the remuneration policy. As an extreme example, if a major shareholder specifically wanted executive remuneration to be linked purely to one financial metric, such as sales growth, the remuneration committee may incorporate this as part of the policy balanced with other metrics but may want to address in their reporting the importance of the wider metrics and deliverables that have been included.

> **EXAMPLE: Shareholder Engagement**
>
> *Greencore Plc, Annual Report 2019, Remuneration Committee report (extract)*
>
> **Shareholder engagement**
> The Committee is very cognisant of the need to ensure that Executive Directors' and shareholders' interests are aligned and therefore, we consulted shareholders with a total holding of close to 70% of our issued share capital, as well as proxy advisors, on our initial proposals. Shareholder engagement in respect of the proposed 2020 Remuneration Policy was valuable with support evident for the strategic ambition and direction of the Company. While the feedback varied by investor, there was broad acceptance that the proposed 2020 Remuneration Policy was aligned with our strategic imperatives. ...
>
> The programme of engagement with shareholders and proxy advisors has provided valuable insights and important learnings for the Committee. The feedback received has been helpful in determining the remuneration structure and in building understanding on how best to communicate the decisions of the Committee. Our shareholder base is multi-jurisdictional and many of our shareholders have their own individual guidelines and policies as well as differing views on appropriate levels of remuneration and how best to incentivise management. While it is not always possible to reconcile views, which are sometimes diverging, we have taken all shareholder inputs into account and sought to reflect the balance of these views when applying appropriate judgement.
>
> The engagement exercise also provided us with the opportunity to understand the wider priorities for each shareholder we engaged with. The importance of the Committee promoting the long-term success of the Group in its remuneration decisions was a recurring message. Outside of discussions on the specific proposals, it was clear that environmental, social and governance ('ESG') matters are at the forefront of shareholders' agendas and, more specifically, how quantitative ESG related measures could be introduced to the remuneration framework. In this regard, this year the Committee reviewed the outcome of both the Group's financial and non-financial Key Performance Indicators ('KPIs'), ... when considering the outcome of the Executive Directors' personal and strategic objectives element of the ABP. Furthermore, the Group is currently progressing its sustainability agenda ... and the Committee will continue to consider how ESG measures might be incorporated in incentives in the future.

Under Provision 4 of the Code, when 20% or more of votes have been cast against a board recommendation for a resolution, the company should explain, when announcing voting results, what actions it intends to take to consult shareholders to understand the reasons behind the result.

In the UK, following their submission to a government review of corporate governance, the Investment Association was asked to develop and maintain a register of this shareholder dissent in companies listed on the UK FTSE All Share index. This register has been in operation since 2017 and includes details of opposition by shareholders, identifying the percentage of votes against a company resolution, or any resolution withdrawn prior to shareholder vote. The register can be found on the website of the Investment Association and includes:

- key details about the resolution (title, meeting date, etc.);
- results of the shareholder vote (percentage of votes cast for and against, number of votes withheld, and percentage of the issued share capital voted);
- a link to the AGM/GM results, including any statement made by the Board in response to the significant vote against at the time of the meeting; and
- a link to any further announcements by the company in response to the dissent, including shareholder views and what the company has done or plans to do.

The Code (under Provision 4) now requires an update statement within six months of the shareholder meeting with guidance on what these should contain being provided through the same source. To provide further information, companies who appear on the register for the same reason for two consecutive years are also identified and included in a repeat dissenter list. Given the increased focus on the remuneration of executives, dissent by shareholders on executive remuneration or the remuneration report is a frequent inclusion on the register.

As a visible committee of the company, activities of this committee may also be picked up by the press, whether local, national or international depending on the business. Members and those that support this committee should be mindful of the need for transparency in all reporting as well as confidentiality of discussions. Knee-jerk reactions in the press or on social media when a large company, especially a large employer, have financial issues can be particularly cutting and frequently centre on the remuneration of senior executives.

The public perception is that bonus-based remuneration is excessive and that executive pay ratios are unjustified and too high. The report of CEO remuneration packages by the CIPD and the High Pay Centre, found that the median CEO pay ratio to the mean employee pay was 114:1, down from 144:1 in 2017. From 2020, listed companies will need to specify this pay ratio in their annual reports so further discussion of the topic and the role of the remuneration committee can be expected.

Reporting

In the annual report

Best practice reports show how remuneration is considered alongside the long-term interests of shareowners and how effective the remuneration policy is in effecting positive change in organisational culture. Hence the operations of the committee should be reported in the annual report, mirroring the requirement of transparency and clarity in the remuneration policy itself. In general, the report should include details of:

- how the committee has delivered on its objectives;
- the meeting frequency and attendance by named members; and
- membership and any changes made during the year.

Under the Companies (Miscellaneous Reporting) Regulations 2018 for large and medium-sized companies under reg. 16 are required to include an annual statement from the chair of the remuneration committee in the annual report which should include a summary of any discretion exercised by the remuneration committee in relation to the award of directors' remuneration.

In addition, the report should include data provided by the company, specifically HR, on diversity, pay ratios and other people-specific metrics.

EXAMPLE: Remuneration Committee report incorporating diversity metrics

Marks and Spencer Group Plc, Annual Report 2019, Remuneration Committee report (extract)

GENDER PAY GAP

The M&S median gender pay gap for the year to April 2018 is 4.2%, compared to a national average of 17.9%. The M&S mean gap for the same period is 12.5%. In the last 12 months we've made several steps to further promote and enhance diversity and equality at M&S. This includes, but is by no means limited to, development of a formal female talent pipeline, ensuring gender balanced recruitment campaigns and building a clear diversity & inclusion strategy governed by an Inclusion Group made up of directors and our employee diversity network chairs. We're proud that 75% of our Customer Assistants are women but we need to do more to encourage diversity in senior roles.

Under FRC guidance, Provision 41, there should also be a description of the work undertaken by the remuneration committee in the annual report, including:

- an explanation of the strategic rationale for executive directors' remuneration policies, structures and any performance metrics;
- reasons why the remuneration is appropriate using internal and external measures, including pay ratios and pay gaps;
- a description, with examples, of how the remuneration committee has addressed the factors of clarity, simplicity, risk, predictability, proportionality and alignment to culture;
- whether the remuneration policy operated as intended in terms of company performance and quantum, and, if not, what changes are necessary;

- what engagement has taken place with shareholders and the impact this has had on remuneration policy and outcomes;
- what engagement with the workforce has taken place to explain how executive remuneration aligns with wider company pay policy; and
- to what extent discretion has been applied to remuneration outcomes and the reasons why.

Additional reporting requirements continue to be added as governance, diversity and alignment to company values and success are recognised as drivers for successful businesses and their environmental impact.

Small company reporting may not be as onerous; however, recommendations and requirements are provided under the Companies Act 2006, AIM rules for AIM-listed companies. In addition, the Quoted Companies Alliance provides guidance on the reporting requirements of small listed companies.

To the annual general meeting

The remuneration committee should be mindful of the high level of focus on their output which is frequently raised by shareholders, particularly at the AGM. While reporting at the AGM is led by the CEO and chairman, the chair of the remuneration committee should be in attendance to answer any questions on the operation of the committee and the application of its policy.

Dissent by shareholders of the remuneration report will be included in the register maintained by the Investment Association and is one of the areas where shareholder dissent is most frequently recorded. In the year to 17 October 2019, 51 companies were included in the register as seeing shareholder dissent of their remuneration report when presented to shareholders at the AGM, although only two of these had over 50% voting against the report. The prevalence of the dissent indicates the importance of this committee and having transparent and effective reporting of their activities.

Supporting the committee

Although not a provision in the Code, it is good practice for the company secretary (or their nominee) to act as secretary to the committee. The committee should also have access to the services of the company secretariat on all remuneration committee matters. The company secretary should ensure that the remuneration committee receives information and papers in a timely manner to enable full and proper consideration to be given to the issues.

When supporting a remuneration committee, HR, finance and other support teams should be mindful of the confidentiality of the discussions in these forums. Transparency of outcomes is important for shareholders and other stakeholders, including employees. Prior distribution of draft policies can have a significantly detrimental impact on the business.

It should also be noted that this committee does not have an executive board member represented, although the outcome of the discussions will invariably be discussed with the CEO, board chair or other senior executives to ensure alignment of thought. This lack of an executive member may put other internal information providers in a position of conflict and they may come under pressure to provide information or share knowledge of discussions. Most professional employees are mindful of these conflicts within their roles and can accommodate them; however, it is of particular note for any individual interacting with the remuneration committee.

When submitting financial or other metrics to the remuneration committee to support remuneration allocations aligned to the policy, staff members should ensure that the data is consistent with that submitted to other forums. Metrics, if they are different in content or show anomalies, should be clearly marked with any inconsistencies flagged and explained. For example, if employee numbers are a required metric, it should be clear if the employee numbers include all staff, exclude contracted staff, are pro-rata for part-time workers, reflect any zero-hour contracts appropriately, identify seasonal changes or whether any other adjustments are made to staff numbers.

Financial metrics often underpin remuneration deliverables, particularly those reflecting company growth, such as sales revenue, profit margins or excess cash. All financial metrics can be adapted to purpose with changes made depending on audience or need. When being used to support remuneration payments, those submitting the metrics should be as mindful of transparency and clarity as committee members themselves. If, once remuneration packages are disclosed, the underlying metrics are questioned, it will call into question the wider reporting of the business and its veracity.

EXAMPLE: Types of Measures and weighting when calculating Bonus Arrangements

Good Energy Plc, Annual Report 2018, Remuneration Committee report (abstract)

Measure	Strategic Objective	Weighting
Group profit before tax	Deliver profit growth	60%
Absolute net promoter score	Maintain customer satisfaction ratings	20%
Employee retention	Attract and retain employees with the right skills, knowledge and mind-set to help deliver the Company's growth plans	10%
Corporate CO_2 reduction	Help to reduce carbon emissions	10%

Conclusion

Transparency, clarity and independence are the three main features of the remuneration committee. Members and those supporting this committee should be mindful of these three elements in all interaction, written reporting, application of decisions and outcomes.

As can be seen throughout this chapter, in those organisations of sufficient size to justify the implementation of a remuneration committee, whether through applying specific guidelines or through a decision made by the board of directors themselves, this is a visible committee in respect of its actions. Executive members, shareholders, employees and other stakeholders are personally and professionally interested in outcomes and how they can affect the success of the business.

9 – Nomination committee

Introduction

'Effective **succession** planning is very important for the long-term success of a company. There is a clear link between succession planning, strategy and the culture of the company, and the nomination committee plays a vital role.'

Sir Win Bischoff, introduction to 'The Nomination Committee – Coming out of the shadows.' The Chartered Governance Institute and EY, 2014.

Despite this view, the function and benefit of the nomination committee can often be side-lined to the board itself, and membership often mirrors the composition of the board.

With this in mind, it should be noted that the role of the nomination committee straddles all committees of the board as well as the board itself. Its remit covers the current and future composition of all these forums, with the exception of the appointment of a new chairman of the board. This latter is most often led by the most senior independent director on the board unless they are a potential candidate in which case another non-executive board member would take the lead.

The committee does not work in isolation drawing on input from the existing board directors and committee members, as well as external experts, particularly on selection, evaluation and training. A topical area for nomination committees is that of boardroom dynamics and diversity within the boardroom and this chapter will touch on these matters alongside the specifics of the committee.

The nomination committee interacts closely with the remuneration committee and these two forums are frequently combined. In some companies, it is combined instead with a governance committee reflecting the importance of the governance framework and its members.

Within this chapter, we will consider the nomination committee as a stand-alone committee of the board. Where reference is made to the board, it should also be taken as reference to the board and its committees as the nomination committee has a remit for all governance forums within a company.

Nomination committees are a required committee of the board for large companies under the Code and are now a standard committee with a core focus on the current and future composition of the board as well as any committees of the board.

Throughout the guidance, there is an emphasis placed on having clear and defined processes, appointment of individuals through merit and relevant expertise and the importance of incorporating diversity within membership. Gone should be the days when appointments to large, listed or regulated companies were made purely through contacts to enhance the position of a single board member. The transparency of the process and shareholder and public approbation has driven an expectation of an open search and appointment process.

The best practice approach of bringing fresh ideas through the diversity of appointment can be used as a guideline for a robust governance framework. This is equally applicable and advantageous for non-listed and small owner-led companies as it is for premium listed organisations. Particularly where a company may be seeking new funding, a future sale or a move into public shareholding, gaining diversity of thought or experience can be an invaluable addition to the company.

The nomination committee sets the framework for the board itself through its recommendations for appointments, evaluations of composition and planning for future succession. It has a key role in identifying expertise that could add additional value to forums, whether in the near- or long-term.

Role of the nomination committee

In general terms, the nomination committee acts as an internal audit for the board and their committee in respect of their effectiveness. They have four key areas of focus in terms of planning, identifying, evaluating and training within which they either have oversight or delivery responsibilities.

In practice, the board establishes a nomination committee to:

1. Plan: ensure plans are in place for orderly succession to both the board and senior management positions. Within this they should oversee the development of a diverse pipeline for succession.
2. Identify: lead the process for determining board and executive appointments.
3. Evaluate: undertake or oversee regular evaluations of the board and its committees.
4. Train: ensure induction and ongoing training is in place for directors, executives and committee members.

What they are not usually responsible for is the practical process of appointment which is the responsibility of the head of HR working with the CEO. However, nomination committee members may be requested to be part of the interview panel or assessment processes.

> **EXAMPLE: The role of the nominations committee**
>
> *Legal and General Group Plc, Annual Report 2018, Nominations Committee report (extract)*
>
> **The role of the committee**
>
> The Committee has overall responsibility for leading the process for new appointments to the Board and ensuring that these appointments bring the required skills and experience to the Board to support the Board's role in development and oversight of the group's strategy. As part of this, the Committee reviews the structure, size and composition of the Board to ensure the Board is made up of the right people with the necessary skills and experience whilst striving to achieve a Board composition that promotes diversity of thought and approach.
>
> The Committee's key responsibilities are:
>
> - Regularly reassessing the structure, size and composition of the Board and recommending any suggested changes to the Board.
> - Reviewing the criteria for identifying and nominating candidates based on the specification for a prospective appointment including the required skills and capabilities.
> - Considering succession planning for directors and other senior executives, taking into account the promotion of diversity and inclusion, the challenges and opportunities facing the company, and what skills and expertise will be needed by the Board in future, ensuring the continued ability of the company to compete effectively in the market place.
> - Reviewing the time commitment required from Non-Executive Directors and assessing the Non-Executive Directors' other significant commitments to ensure that they continue to be able to fulfil their duties effectively.

FCA guidance for nomination committees

The UK Financial Conduct Authority ('FCA') guidance is specifically relevant to common platform firms (as defined therein, including banks, building societies and investment firms) regulated by the FCA. This guidance, while specific to these firms, is a useful framework for other firms seeking to implement a nominations committee.

Specifically, FCA guidance on the role of the nomination committee states (in SYSC 4.3A.8–10) that, when implemented, the nomination committee must:

(a) be composed of members of the management body who do not perform an executive function in the company;
(b) identify and recommend to the company persons to fill management body vacancies;

(c) at least annually assess the structure, size, composition and performance of the management body and make recommendations to the management body;
(d) at least annually assess the knowledge, skills and experience of individual members of the management body and of the management body collectively and report to the management body accordingly;
(e) periodically review the policy of the management body for the selection and appointment of senior management and make recommendations to the management body; and
(f) be able to use any forms of resource it deems appropriate, including external advice.

In addition, in performing its functions, the nomination committee must take account of the need to ensure that the management body's decision making is not dominated by either one individual or a group of individuals in a manner that is detrimental to the company as a whole.

When performing its function, the nomination committee must:

(a) evaluate the balance of knowledge, skills, diversity and experience of the management body;
(b) prepare a description of the roles, capabilities and expected time commitment for any particular appointment;
(c) decide on a target for the representation of the underrepresented gender in the management body and prepare a policy on how to meet that target; and
(d) engage a broad set of qualities and competencies, and for that purpose have a policy promoting diversity on the management body.

As noted, these guidelines, while specific for this regulated sector, are a beneficial reminder for any company seeking to implement a nomination committee to take ownership of board appointments or when appointing third-party providers to support or lead in the process, whether appointed by the company or the nomination committee.

Terms of reference

The terms of reference of the nomination committee, outside of their specific roles and responsibilities, follow standard content (see Appendix 3).

It should be noted that the role of the nomination committee is primarily to recommend, advise, plan and oversee. They do not usually have the specific authority to progress to the appointment of directors or committee members. If this is the case, it should be made clear in the terms of reference to what extent the committee has authority to appoint including any constraints, controls or guidance to be followed. Remuneration of directors and senior executives falls under the remit of the remuneration committee if there is one incorporated as a separate forum.

Meeting schedules for the nomination committee are generally only once or twice per year to cover the core functions of monitoring board and committee effectiveness, planning future succession and reviewing evaluations. However, terms of reference should allow for both scheduled meetings as well as the ability to call emergency meetings. These may be required for unexpected departures, unplanned resignations or changes in requirements. For example, a significant shift in strategic focus may require additional or changed board representation which the nomination committee should be heavily involved with. A planned acquisition would necessitate a board and committee review to assess the proposed future state of the governance framework as well as the deliverables and composition of the future board. In this latter scenario, consideration should be given to the forum for such discussion if both entities have nomination committees and the interaction or combination of the two.

Authority is given to the committee to appoint external providers for selection, evaluation and training, noting that budgetary constraints or related guidelines set by the board and the company should be adhered to.

Any external appointment would also be prior agreed with HR to align it to the wider organisational model and any areas where the company has specific requirements. For example, company-specific technical training may be better served through spending time with senior management or technical experts within the business instead of appointing external trainers. This has the dual advantage of tailoring the knowledge sharing to the specific company and giving employees exposure to senior independent committee and board members.

Any external appointment should also be disclosed in the annual report, reflecting the purpose of the appointment and any connections the appointee may have with the company.

Duties, responsibilities and tasks

The role of the nomination committee in its function to have oversight of the composition of the board and ensure its ongoing effectiveness must also give consideration to diversity, skills, experience and knowledge. Specifically, this should be in respect of individuals, individual roles, the board or committee as a whole and the interaction of appointed members when undertaking their roles.

This means that the committee has a dual focus on both the individual appointees as well as the board or committee as a collective. It is the composition and collection of knowledge and skills of the individuals that make up the effectiveness of each forum as a whole. As such, the appointment, retirement or removal of one individual must be considered against the impact on the wider group and not just in isolation. When considering the full composition, the committee should consider the dynamics of the board and the effectiveness of its current composition, as well as any areas where new members could enhance or improve the effectiveness of the board.

> **EXAMPLE: The role of the Nominations Committee**
>
> *Compass Group Plc, Annual Report 2018, Nominations Committee report (extract)*
> The Nomination Committee reviews the structure, size and composition of the Board and its committees and makes recommendations to the Board with regard to any changes considered necessary in the identification and nomination of new directors, the reappointment of existing directors and appointment of members to the Board's committees. It also assesses the roles of the existing directors in office to ensure that there continues to be a balanced Board in terms of skills, knowledge, experience and diversity. The Committee reviews the senior leadership needs of the Group to enable it to compete effectively in the marketplace and advises the Board on succession planning for executive director appointments, although the Board itself is responsible for succession generally.
>
> The Nomination Committee has standing items that it considers regularly under its terms of reference; for example, the Committee reviews its own terms of reference annually, or as required, to reflect changes to the Code or as a result of changes in regulations or best practice.

Plan

An effective succession plan should be maintained for board and senior management positions incorporating details on what objective criteria should be used for appointments and any specific objectives or deliverables of the roles. Within this, there is an expectation from governing bodies and stakeholders that this should promote diversity of gender, social and ethnic backgrounds, cognitive and personal strengths. Increasingly, the benefit of diversity is also underpinned by published results and academic research hence ignoring this would be detrimental for the success of the company itself.

The nomination committee should consider wider executive, leadership and senior management when looking at succession plans and future requirements for board and committee membership. Identifying internal candidates is as important as seeking potential external candidates for future roles. Working with the learning and development team within a company to develop and deliver training for future leaders can create a pool of candidates for future succession either in specific roles or to add diversity to a board. This is particularly beneficial when seeking to add younger or inexperienced candidates into governance roles.

> **EXAMPLE: Succession Planning for Executive Positions**
>
> *BAE Systems Plc, Annual Report 2018, Nominations Committee report (extract)*
> During the year, the Committee spent time with the Chief Executive and our Group Human Resources Director hearing about the work they have under way to ensure

> that we have effective executive succession planning processes in place. This included the presentation of data analysing all executive grade positions across the Group and the succession candidates for these roles. This analysis has been one of the key inputs to the work currently under way to actively manage our succession planning performance across all executive grades. The oversight of this work will remain a priority for the Committee in 2019.

The culture, vision and mission of the company should also be taken into consideration as well as the deliverables of each role. Co-ordination with the remuneration committee and the wider key performance indicators (KPIs) they use and the deliverables they define are a core part of the process. As an example, a homeless charity may have a KPI to increase access to homeless shelters as a year-on-year deliverable by the CEO. Identifying and including the skills necessary to accomplish this should be incorporated into the role description and candidate pack when re-appointing for the role.

From a wider perspective, the strategy of the business should be incorporated into the consideration of future succession plans. If a company is seeking to expand its services internationally, succession should include candidates with experience of working in an international market or with personal knowledge of the countries being targeted. If the operational strategy is to consolidate and outsource services, adding outsource experience and expertise to the board would be invaluable.

If the strategy is to refocus the customer profile to a younger demographic, identifying board or committee candidates with relevant expertise through personal profile or experience would be invaluable. Similarly, a shift to a technology-driven service solution would benefit from board candidates with technology experience and risk committee candidates with cyber knowledge.

Identify

While the committee does not have the responsibility for the practical appointment of board members, they do have oversight responsibilities with regard to the process of appointment and induction of new directors. The process should be clear and applied in all scenarios, no matter what the previous experience, or lack of, by individual appointees.

> **EXAMPLE: Actions taken by Nominations Committee**
>
> *Good Energy Plc, Annual Report 2018, Nominations Committee report (extract)*
> During the period, the Nominations Committee:
>
> - received and considered proposals to make redundant the role of Chief Financial Officer, including reviewing the resulting composition of the Board and the availability of a suitable mix of skills, experience and expertise;

> - oversaw the recruitment, appointment and induction of ... following its recommendation during 2017 that the Board appoint a senior independent director; and
> - conducted a market search for an additional independent non-executive director to succeed ... [the] chair of the Audit & Risk Management Committee, resulting in the appointment of ...

The appointment process will be led by the HR department, usually the head of HR given the seniority of the role. Appointment and induction processes may follow the standard process for all employees of the company but should have additional aspects reflecting the seniority of the role, the additional responsibilities and tone set as a leader of the company. This should incorporate the mission, vision and value statements of the company which should have formed part of the selection process.

Processes for the appointment of non-executive director and independent committee members should reflect the processes of employees where relevant; however, they should differentiate the external nature of their role. Employment legislation and guidelines should be applied effectively. In addition, induction and training should introduce the wider company and its organisational structure without the detail of application that would be necessary when working in an operational role.

The Code (under Provision 20) recommends the use of open advertising and/or an external search consultancy for the appointment of the chair and non-executive directors. The appointment of such external providers should include a recommendation by the nomination committee aligned to the size, sector and requirements of the company.

Evaluate

The nomination committee should review the structure, size, and composition of the board to ensure they remain appropriate. Within this there should be a formal evaluation process on at least an annual basis.

Specifically, the board and its committees should have a combination of skills, experience and knowledge reflective of the company, its industry or sector and the responsibilities of the relevant forum. Consideration should be given to the length of service of the board as a whole with membership being regularly refreshed to ensure that contribution does not become repetitive, the forum continues to be relevant and meetings are dynamic and results focused.

> **EXAMPLE: Review of Board Skills**
>
> *Hammerson Plc, Annual Report 2018, Nominations Committee report (extract)*
>
> **Board balance and skills**
>
> As it does annually, the Committee has also reviewed the composition and balance of the Board ... As part of this review the Committee considered:
>
> - Whether the balance between Executive and Non-Executive Directors was appropriate
> - The membership of the Committees
> - The tenure of Directors
> - A matrix of core skills and experience of the Board to ensure the right balance of relevant skills, experience and knowledge
> - Diversity on the Board
> - The independence of the Non-Executive Directors and confirmed that all remained independent.

Under the Code, an annual evaluation of the board should be undertaken to consider its composition, diversity and how effectively members work together to achieve objectives. Individual evaluation should demonstrate whether each director continues to contribute effectively and has relevant skills to contribute to the board at its current stage, as opposed to when they were appointed.

As part of the evaluation, the current stage of the company should be considered as a driver for board composition. Skills required when a company is in start-up or growth mode are different from those required when a company is static or its sector is declining. Companies expanding internationally will require a different skillset across its board members than one with a single country focus.

In large companies, under the Code, all directors should be subject to annual re-election. The board should set out in the papers accompanying the resolutions to elect each director, including the specific reasons why their contribution is and continues to be, important to the company's long-term sustainable success.

Annual evaluations of the board, its committees, the chair and individual directors should be formal and rigorous. The nomination committee should recommend to the chair of the board whether they believe this should be undertaken by an external expert to bring fresh and neutral expertise to the process. In FTSE 350 companies, this evaluation should happen at least every three years, while it should be annual for larger companies. Where external evaluation is not undertaken annually, the nomination committee should consider implementing an internal evaluation in years when formal external evaluators are not appointed.

Train

Any evaluation is only beneficial if the results are acted upon. The nomination committee should liaise with the chair in identifying and documenting an action plan to address the results. The nomination committee should oversee and monitor the implementation of the identified actions, which may include development plans, training, workshops or other formats either for individuals or the board as a group. When aligning the board to the deliverables of the business, actions may include strategy days that include the whole board plus additional executives and senior management.

Ongoing training for directors should include that specifically for their director role as well as wider training related to the company, whether technical or soft skills. Directors should also undertake all mandatory training, such as compliance training, setting an example to the wider workforce in their completion. Consideration should be given to inclusion of non-executive directors in executive training or training available elsewhere in the organisation. Most non-executive directors will maintain their own continuous professional development (CPD) which should be evidenced during the evaluation process.

Board or specific training may include sessions built within or around diarised meeting days or strategy away days. Online training is also often utilised as a flexible means to deliver knowledge.

> **EXAMPLE: Building Director Training around board meetings**
>
> *Taylor Wimpey Plc, Annual Report 2018, Nominations Committee report (extract)*
> All Directors visit Group operations on a regular basis, engaging with employees at all levels in order to foster and maintain an understanding of the business. Board visits are arranged each year to operations and at least one Board meeting per annum takes place either in, or at a nearby location with representatives from, a regional business over three days. In 2018, the Board visit, accompanied by the GMT, encompassed presentations on the Major Developments business; increasing use of direct labour; product and placemaking; large site strategy; building for the private rental and rent to buy markets; and on the performance of the South Thames business unit.

The on-boarding training maintained and used in the wider company should be utilised for executive directors and adapted appropriately for non-executive directors. In addition, it should include director induction on the requirements of acting as a director, sharing the existing strategy of the company and explaining the terms of reference of the relevant committee. Inductions should also include introductions to colleagues within the governance framework, both fellow committee members, the board and all other contacts that the committee will rely on.

> **EXAMPLE: Director Induction Process**
>
> *SSE Plc, Annual Report 2019 (extract)*
>
> **Board induction**
> Following appointment, all Directors engage in an induction process which has been designed to suit their individual needs. The tailored and comprehensive programme is agreed through discussion with the Chair and Company Secretary, and is reflective of existing knowledge and experience, and any agreed roles within the Board and its Committees. The meetings and activities are selected to ensure that any new Director is adequately informed and equipped to participate in Board discussions, with a sound understanding of long-term strategy, business operations, the sectoral context and Company culture. Engagements involve meetings with key personnel, technical briefings and site visits, which allow for conversations to take place with a representative cross-section of SSE's workforce. An appropriate time period is allowed in which to complete the agreed engagements, such that directorate knowledge can be built over time.

General

As the use and understanding of nomination committees develops, there has been a move to use the committee to dig further into the organisation to below executive level. The dual benefit of this is that the committee can use this as a means to identify future candidates for board-level roles in support of their succession planning. In addition, it embeds a consistent approach to evaluation through the business aligning board reviews to reviews undertaken throughout the company. The transparency that this provides can then further support the understanding of the board and its composition.

An alternative approach to connecting board-level evaluation and succession planning is for the nomination committee to receive information on the talent reviews undertaken by HR within the company. This can be in the form of a general report or through HR identifying talent early, which can then feed into succession planning considerations. The advantage this also gives is that nomination committee members then get an additional insight into the wider business. It can also be used as a means of identifying training or development needs to support future board talent that can be adopted in the learning and development plans of the business.

Any exposure that nomination committee members have with the wider company and its employees must recognise their role as an independent director, reflecting the confidentiality and sensitivity of the personal data that may be shared. There is also a risk that members of the nomination committee may stray into executive roles or overstep into the functions of the HR function, so this needs to be carefully managed and monitored.

Committee membership

There are no specific guidelines on the number of committee members that should be appointed or the specific skills they should have other than that those noted in relation to skills, experience and knowledge are equally relevant to nomination committee membership. As with the remuneration committee, a high degree of emotional intelligence and discretion is required when fulfilling the role.

The nomination committee has a duty to seek and consider a wider pool of candidate profiles when considering new board appointments. The impact of the board has wide-ranging consequences and, while diversity is often attributed to gender or race, consideration should extend to skills obtained in other sectors, countries or environments. Remember as well that the composition and attitudes of the board set the tone of the whole company from the top. Any aspiration to change the profile of a company's workforce should be started with a review of board composition. As an extreme example, having a strategic goal and aspiration to move into youth products would necessitate employee knowledge of the youth market. What better way to start to facilitate this than by appointing younger board members?

Broadening the candidate pool either for existing or future appointments necessitates seeking candidates from a new source. This may be through appointing an external search firm with a specific focus on recruitment of defined new attributes or skill sets.

Despite this, the appointment of known contacts of board members or other executives is still common and balancing this with candidates from a new pool can ensurethere is a balance between new experiences, skills and contribution to that of sector experts or known candidates. Hence neither one approach nor the other should be ruled out and consideration should be given to both approaches depending on the individual circumstances.

Noting this dual approach, a 2019 survey by InTouch noted that 70% of survey respondents found their non-executive director appointment through personal contacts, referrals or contact directly from the company. There may be a benefit to this approach as long as the candidate requirements are met and that executives recommending personal contacts do not take part in the interview process for their own contacts.

There is no restriction on the CEO being a member of the committee, although most include CEOs as an invited attendee rather than a formal committee member. In some cases, shareholders have expressed concern on the CEO being a member and heavily involved in such an influential forum.

Under the Code (Provision 17), a majority of members of the committee should be independent non-executive directors. The chair of the board should not chair the committee when it is dealing with the appointment of their successor.

Board appointments are approved by shareholders at the AGM with directors appointed before that time acting as a casual vacancy until their appointment is ratified at the AGM. It should be noted that casual appointments have all the benefits of being appointed as an appointed director from their date of appointment, including in respect of remuneration. Appointment of directors between AGMs should recognise the maximum membership numbers as well as the deliverables that are required. In some companies, board appointments may also require approval from regulators prior to formal ratification.

For listed companies, current board members can recommend new director appointments to shareholders but they cannot force their appointment and the decision of shareholders to approve, or not, should be accepted. As an aside, bond holders and other creditors do not have a vote on director appointments and cannot force a bond holder representative onto the board.

Board tenure

Under the Code, the chair of a large company should not remain in post beyond nine years from the date of their first appointment to the board. This can be extended for a limited time to facilitate effective succession planning and the development of a diverse board, as long as a clear explanation of the reason is communicated. This is particularly relevant in those cases where the chair was an existing non-executive director on original appointment, or their departure is part of a wider board review and staged development plan.

EXAMPLE: Extending a Director Appointment

BAE Systems Plc, Annual Report 2018 (extract)

In 2018, the Committee recognised the need to recruit up to two new non-executive directors, including a suitable candidate to join the Board and succeed ... as Chair of the Audit Committee. However, recognising that we have a new auditor this year and the level of geopolitical uncertainty facing the Company at present, the Board considered it was in the Company's and shareholders' best interests that we extend ...'s tenure as Senior Independent Director and Chair of the Audit Committee beyond the nine-year period to 31 December 2019.

I recognise that the provisions of the UK Corporate Governance Code state that a term of office in excess of nine years is one of the factors that is likely to impair, or could appear to impair, a non-executive director's independence. However, if a board believes that such an individual remains independent, the Code requires it to clearly explain why it takes that view. Having worked with him for some years, his fellow Board members and I certainly take the view that ... remains independent. He has been an excellent non-executive member of the Board, and our annual board evaluations evidence the quality of his contribution and the effective manner in which he discharges his responsibilities in chairing the Audit Committee and acting as our Senior Independent Director. I have also engaged with a number of our principal shareholders on this matter and they were very helpful in giving me the opportunity to explain the above and were supportive of the decision.

There are no guidelines for other board roles although the InTouch 2019 **NED Salary Survey** noted that most non-executive director board appointments were for two to four years. This links into an expectation that most board appointments should last for three years, with annual re-election.

Boardroom dynamics and diversity

Boardroom dynamics and the inclusion of diversity are intermingled within and across the role of the nomination committee. The former, when working well, creates a highly effective board or committee, focused on a joint purpose and delivering successful governance. Culture, tone and attitude filters from the top downwards in all organisations, so getting it right adds real value. Conversely, conflict in the boardroom is known of throughout a company, whether directors believe knowledge of it is kept within the boardroom or not. This negativity will have a detrimental effect on the company and will filter throughout the business.

Equally, diversity in the boardroom translates positively through a company and externally in its wider interactions and the perception of it. Diversity of attitude, background and thought shared in a positive board room environment can only be positive. Equally, by championing diversity and its benefits at board level, employees will recognise and see the equivalent permeating positively throughout the business.

This section will pick up on these two topics in isolation, recognising that they stem from the same area for any nomination committee.

Boardroom dynamics

Board and boardroom dynamics underpin the effective functioning of the board and, while considerable focus is given to the technical skills and experience of board members, the dynamic between individuals and the board as a group, often gives a better reflection of how effective the board will be.

Nomination committees should be mindful that the dynamics between individuals, especially the chair and other board members, are key drivers of success. The culture of a business starts at the top, and the dynamics in operation within the board context underpins this culture.

When reviewing the board, considering new appointments or planning for future succession plans, the dynamics of the board must be taken into consideration. These can be split into the more tangible technical capabilities of individuals and the board as a collective, and those that are more behavioural. No matter the type of company, the culture at the core of the business must be fit for purpose. While there is no one business culture type, there are certain behavioural characteristics that would be expected of board members, including, but not limited to, competence, respect, professionalism and emotional intelligence.

Diversity

Considerable attention has been given to the benefits of having diversity in business, and the added value that having diversity in the boardroom can deliver. The nomination committee has a duty to encourage diversity in all its forms when considering appointments to the existing board as well as planning for future succession.

When appointing external partners to work on succession planning or identifying candidates for the board, diversity should be included as a prerequisite. It should also be aligned to the existing board and any outcomes from board evaluations. However, boards should be cautious about appointing for diversity in isolation; they should ensure that the dynamics of the board embrace diversity and enable contributions to be made to their full effect and benefit. Rumours and tales abound of boards that have seemingly welcomed diversity, whether for gender, background, religion or other criteria, for the incumbent to then be silenced through the existing boardroom dynamics.

When undertaking or commissioning board reviews, the nomination committee should include diversity as a key point to evaluate, both in the current make-up of the board as well as their attitude to the inclusion of difference.

Recognising the benefits of diversity, the Code has developed its guidelines from its 2010 iteration where the recommendation was for 'due regard for the benefits of diversity on the board including gender'. In 2018 the Code was updated to include diversity beyond gender and stated that 'both appointments and succession plans should be based on merit and objective criteria and, within this context, should promote diversity of gender, social and ethnic backgrounds, cognitive and personal strengths.'

Nomination committees when reflecting the Code, should be able to evidence diversity inclusion in consideration beyond tick box exercises or adding one new candidate to meet criteria.

EXAMPLE: Diversity and the Nominations Committee

Segro Plc, Annual Report 2018, Nominations Committee report (extract)

DIVERSITY

The Directors are committed to having a balanced Board which recognises the benefits of diversity in its broadest sense and the value that this brings to the organisation in terms of skills, knowledge and experience. Our Board Diversity Policy is available at www.SEGRO.com.

With respect to gender specifically, the Board aspires to promote greater gender diversity. When running the process to appoint the Non-Executive Directors ... the Committee recognised that how it selected and briefed the executive search firms and, in particular, how it described the skills and experience needed for the roles were important elements in attracting as wide a pool of candidates as possible. The

> Committee will only use the services of executive search firms who have signed up to the Voluntary Code of Conduct for Executive Search Firms.
>
> In the final selection decision, all Board appointments are made on merit and relevant experience, against the criteria identified by the Committee with regard to the benefits of diversity, including gender.
>
> We are members of the 30% Club which aims to achieve of 30 per cent of women on FTSE 100 boards by 2020. As at 31 December 2018, there were two female and eight male Board members. By 1 March 2019, there will be three female Board members and eight male… We also support the aspirations of the Hampton Alexander review to identify and develop the next generation of female talent.

When appointing for diversity or challenging board room dynamics, potential candidates may be identified that bring great skills and experience but lack boardroom experience. Part of the role of the nomination committee is to ensure that individuals, when appointed do not feel that any lack of boardroom experience will hamper their contribution or, more concerningly, stop good candidates from applying in the first place.

As a final note, one key oversight and support for effective boardroom dynamics and diversity inclusion is in the monitoring of its effective impact on the board and its continuing benefit. Inclusion of any new members to a forum creates change and a period of adjustment. Both new and existing members will be affected by this, whether consciously or unconsciously, with individuals reacting differently. The aim of the board, and by default the nominations committee as its influencer, is to create and maintain the best forum for positive impact and future strategic delivery.

Interaction beyond the committee

The nomination committee and its members will have a core understanding of the board, its dynamic and each committee of the board. In order to deliver in their role, they must understand the deliverables of each forum and the interaction between them. They must appreciate the hierarchical nature of the governance structure and be able to work effectively within it.

The closest working relationship is with the chair of the board and the remuneration committee. If it is a separate forum, it is expected that the chair of the nomination committee will attend each remuneration committee meeting and may be a formal member. It may also be beneficial, where these two forums are not combined, for one individual to be the chair of both committees, albeit that the membership may be different.

By its nature, at least one of the nomination committee members will have interacted with directors and senior executives during their appointment process.

Given their intimate knowledge of each candidate, the role they have been appointed to and the deliverables that their unique experience will be able to deliver, members of the nomination committee have an in-depth insight into their colleagues. As such, their role in being able to support appointees during their initial appointment should not be underestimated. They can provide a support network to individuals to enable them to deliver successfully in as short a time period as possible.

Some larger companies pair their non-executive directors, whether members of the nomination committee or not, with senior executives and rising talent for mentoring purposes. As with any senior one-on-one mentoring programme this benefits both the identified individuals as well as the independent directors, giving the former access to senior executives with experience outside of their organisation and enabling the directors to gain a personal insight into the company through a different lens.

Shareholder approval of director appointments

For UK listed companies, director appointments and re-appointments must be approved by shareholders at the AGM. The Public Register, available on the website of the Investment Association, lists those companies where shareholder dissent has been registered, including in respect of director re-selection and the appointment of independent directors. Companies where dissent has been seen in consecutive years will also be included in the repeated dissent list. Post dissent, companies are required to provide an update statement within six months of the shareholder meeting.

By the end of October 2019, 53 companies had shareholder dissent registered against director appointments at their shareholder meeting, in some cases with multiple director appointments being challenged. To a lesser extent, the appointment of independent directors is challenged by shareholders with only six companies included in the register for 2019 to the end of October, although 50% of these had more than one independent director appointment being disputed.

It should also be countered that, on occasion, shareholder dissent is driven by alternative agendas although clearly the appointment of directors to the board of significant and listed companies is a difficult process that requires both transparency and clarity on the appointment process and the appointments themselves.

Reporting

Under the Code (Provision 23), the annual report should describe the work of the nomination committee, including:

- the process used in relation to appointments, its approach to succession planning and how both support developing a diverse pipeline;
- how the board evaluation has been conducted, the nature and extent of an external evaluator's contact with the board and individual directors, the

outcomes and actions taken, and how it has, or will, influence board composition;
- the policy on diversity and inclusion, its objectives and linkage to company strategy, how it has been implemented and progress on achieving the objectives; and
- the gender balance of those in the senior management and their direct reports.

Specific data included in the report, such as gender reporting, will be provided by the HR function. Otherwise, contents of nomination committee reports are often general in nature reflecting the overarching approach of the committee in terms of board evaluation, board member tenure or approaches to succession. Changes at board level are reported in hindsight stating facts about tenure and departure and appointment of replacements. Rarely is further insight provided either in the annual report or in other shared papers.

The challenge is to provide good reporting on the actions of the committee, how strategic goals are addressed in relation to future succession planning, board evaluation processes, recognising any talent identification processes and being open about skills analysis of current and future leaders.

Supporting the committee

Practical issues such as length of board meetings, agendas and content of board packs form one part of board evaluations. Ensuring receipt of advice and sharing best practice on these topics with committee members is a proactive way to support the nomination committee.

Some committees also proactively seek the input of company secretaries to provide best practice or knowledge from other boards that they may currently or previously have supported. As a professional contributor, company secretaries may have been involved in supporting a wider range of boards and committees through their careers than the committee members themselves may have attended. As such, the company secretary can provide knowledge and experience that can support the nomination committee in their deliberations.

EXAMPLE: Board Evaluation Facilitated by the Company Secretary

Marks and Spencer Group Plc, Annual Report 2019, Governance report (extract)
Our annual Board Evaluation gives us the opportunity to reflect on the effectiveness of our activities, the quality of our decisions and for board members to consider their performance and contribution.

This year, our evaluation was facilitated internally by our Group General Counsel and Company Secretary, who was considered by the Board to be a suitably independent sounding board for this process. In line with previous years, focused one-to-one discussions were held between the Company Secretary and each member of the Board. These covered a broad range of topics relating to the Board, its Committees and to the directors individually, including:

- What worked well during the year and where improvements could be made.
- Board culture, teamwork and relationships with management.
- Shareholders and stakeholders, including communication and relationships.
- Board composition and succession planning.
- Resourcing of meetings, agenda planning, quality of information.
- Strategic oversight and implementation.
- Corporate governance, regulatory compliance and associated support.
- Committee effectiveness and communications to the Board.

The Senior Independent Director also met with directors to review the Chairman's performance. This review was then shared with the Chairman.

All recommendations arising from the review are based on best practice as described in the UK Corporate Governance Code and other applicable guidelines.

Novices to board support can also bring knowledge through their formal training, professional contacts and their wider colleague interaction.

A good nomination committee will seek to obtain input from a wide range of contacts and those individuals supporting the committee can provide both their own feedback, if requested, as well as facilitate the contribution of other employees. This is particularly beneficial when the nomination committee is only composed of independent directors with limited connections to company employees outside of the executive team. The company secretary and HR representatives should also be prepared to enhance their contribution through sharing expertise and knowledge from their own wider external network.

In some cases, nomination committee members may seek input from the wider company or external contacts in relation to new board positions, whether in terms of potential candidates, role descriptions or external providers. Any contributor to the nomination committee, or any committee or the board itself, is in a unique position to be able to respond to such requests and should recognise this request as a means for the nomination committee to widen their knowledge and contacts. It should also be recognised that this input should primarily be on request from the committee or its members. The nomination committee has the responsibility and delegated authority to act in this regard. Any third party that they request input from, whether formally or informally, does not have this level of authority and has not been appointed to share their views or contribute directly to the discussions.

The HR function of a company has a considerable role in supporting and interacting with the nomination committee. This falls across training and development, identification of future leaders and proposing ways that the work of the nomination committee can be more effective through co-ordination with HR or interaction with the wider workforce. More obviously, the practical implementation of board appointments and new member on-boarding is likely to be driven by HR with the nomination committee having oversight of the process. HR members should ensure they are aware of the terms of reference of the nomination committee and identify any areas where they can be supportive or work in collaboration.

Conclusion

One concluding point is who appoints and evaluates the nomination committee itself? In practice, it is the board that has appointed them and whom the nomination committee reviews. This is a closed circle that could be abused. However, if clearly defined, appointed and applied appropriately, the benefits of an effective and, most importantly, independent nomination committee can be immense.

They have a significant role in shaping and modelling the board of a company which cascades into reflecting and influencing the culture of the company as a whole. By applying recommendations in a consistent and measured way, the nomination committee can support the chair, CEO and the wider business and can have an immensely positive impact on the success of a company. Conversely, poor recommendations, insubstantial board reviews, board evaluations findings that are not followed up and a lack of future succession plans are areas where the nomination committee can have a significantly negative impact.

While the workings of the nomination committee are often less contentious than the remuneration committee, the outcome of their actions underpins the company and can build a robust foundation for a company.

10 – Other committees

Introduction

This chapter will reflect on other committees that are set up, either through the needs of an individual company or sector. Also known as ad hoc committees, these are formed for a specific task, purpose or objective with clearly defined deliverables. Where they are related to a specific task or purpose, they are dissolved after the completion of the task, conclusion of the purpose or achievement of the objective. Membership may, or may not, include board members, depending on the purpose as well as the skills and experience required.

There are differing drivers for the creation of a committee which may be industry or purpose specific, with the two often interlinking. Clarity of purpose as documented by the terms of reference of the committee is an imperative that will ensure that committee members are clear on its purpose and focus on any defined deliverables. Where a committee is being set up for a specific purpose it is even more important that this purpose is clearly documented and agreed. Without this the committee may extend its remit beyond the expected purpose, may become less effective and as a result, will frustrate both the board members who saw value in its creation and members who are lacking direction.

Industry-driven committees are often, but not solely, driven by regulatory or sector-specific responsibilities that require technical knowledge to be fully compliant or successful. These may be delegated to a committee to deliver on behalf of the board, enabling these committees to gather the required expertise within its membership to oversee a specific area of responsibility. Examples would include financial markets committees within regulated banking and finance organisations, property market committees within property companies or environmental committees within energy production companies.

Purpose-specific committees are often, but not always, time-limited. These committees are implemented by the board to deliver on a specific project or purpose. In these instances, the terms of reference must be clear on the role and responsibilities, the authority of the committee to take decisions, the escalation points for referral to the board and the purpose of its creation. It should also detail any deliverable milestones and the timeline for the committee itself. Examples would include an HR organisational committee to lead a company re-organisation, an incident driven committee to follow up on a data security breach or a relocation committee if a company is moving to new premises or consolidating locations.

As with the five main committees already covered in more detail in specific chapters, these committees are constituted by the board under a sector-specific terms of reference. It should be noted that a board can constitute a committee for any purpose to act on their behalf, noting that the responsibility for delivery may be delegated but the ownership remains with the board. The board is not there solely to co-ordinate or manage a group of committees and should identify and, wherever possible, retain core responsibilities themselves.

Committee versus project

It is important to differentiate a formal committee constituted by a board of directors and a project team set up for a specific purpose.

Specifically, a committee of the board should have a board member taking responsibility for the committee, usually through being appointed the chair of the committee. By undertaking this role they are the interface between the two forums and are able to ensure that the committee maintains its focus on the defined deliverables. This board representative may be an executive or an independent director or a combination of the two if more than one individual is involved.

In general, a committee is implemented to oversee or progress a delegated responsibility of the board working under clear, documented terms of reference. Meetings are formally documented with progress reported back to the board on a regular basis. Committees frequently bring in members from across functions, departments and divisions of a company, as well as appointing external members. This ensures that the membership is broad in experience, knowledge and expertise.

A project board or team has a similar narrow focus but is usually set up for a single, time-limited purpose. It will primarily be composed of members from a specific function, division or geography with the deliverables centred within that area. It will have a project definition and project plan and may report progress to a member of the board or board contributor who, in turn, will include it within their wider board reporting.

In larger organisations, there may be a centralised project team providing support, frameworks, governance, reporting and project expertise. The focus will be on delivery of the defined purpose with milestones tracked and regular project updates communicated to stakeholders. Unlike a committee, project meetings will focus on the delivery of the project rather than discussion of the purpose, the wider topic itself or the sharing of knowledge.

From a career perspective, the experience of working within a project-based environment is a positive grounding for future committee membership given their similarities related to defined purpose and structure.

When setting up a committee the board should first consider whether a project team would be better placed to deliver on the requirements. Is the purpose narrow in focus and only related to one geography, function or division? Will it only be composed of internal members? Will it be time-limited? Does it have sufficient breadth of purpose to warrant direct reporting to the full board of directors or should it be a subset of the responsibilities of one executive director? These and other questions may assist the board in deciding on the format of the requirement.

Operational practicalities

The terms of reference of a committee would mirror those of the standard five committees defining purpose, responsibilities, authority, membership, quorum and other practical aspects. The terms of reference in the Appendices can be used as a framework when creating a new committee with a new terms of reference. Standard administrative terms should mirror that of the board, including support of the committee. By reviewing and documenting the duties of the proposed committee the board will be able to agree a clear purpose that can be monitored for delivery. It also gives a written framework for discussions with potential committee members, as well as supporting the appointment of candidates with suitable experience and recognising why this expertise is required.

If a board meets quarterly, a committee with a specific purpose may meet more frequently. As such, when setting the terms of reference, it should be clear how board input between formal board meetings can be obtained.

- What decisions can the committee make without board consent?
- If board consent is required, is there a subset of the board that is required for a quorum to be met?
- Has the board delegated decision making to the chair of the committee if they are also a board member?

If a committee is scheduled to meet frequently, careful consideration should also be given to attendance and the quorum for each meeting:

- Can subsets of the committee meet to discuss specific items?
- Does the chair always have to be in attendance and, if not, who is the role of chair delegated to?
- If the role of the chair is delegated, does this delegated person have the same decision-making authority as the committee chair?
- Alternatively, if the chair of the committee is the only representative of the board on the committee do they, as an individual, hold the sole authority to make decisions?
- If so, should any absence by this individual be covered by an alternative member of the board instead of a member of the committee?

Ongoing monitoring

As with all committees, it is important that the board continues to monitor the effectiveness of the committee in its actions as well as its relevance of purpose. Often the purpose of the committee, once constituted, will change as factors influence and develop. The committee itself should monitor its purpose and contribution, formally documenting, at least annually, that this has been done and that the terms of reference are still appropriate. They should inform the board as to their considerations and the outcome. This is particularly important where the committee believes that their terms of reference should be adjusted or extended to meet updated focus. By undertaking this, they will ensure that their contribution and discussions are recognised and accepted by the board as providing valuable support.

The board itself should also consider the contribution of each committee, their interrelations on topics and the purpose of their implementation. Should the committee remain in place or should the board resume direct ownership of the topic? Should the remit of the committee be extended to incorporate other areas of consideration? Would part of the focus of one committee be better covered by an alternate committee as the topic changes in direction and deliverables?

> **EXAMPLE: Reviewing and terminating a committee**
>
> *Cairn Energy Plc, Annual Report 2018, Governance Committee (extract)*
> The Governance Committee met twice in 2018 and was comprised of a majority of Non-Executive Directors. The ongoing role of the governance committee was reviewed in late 2018 and, in view of the infrequency of its meetings and the importance of full Board oversight of the Company's corporate governance activities, it was decided this Committee should be abolished with effect from 31 December 2018. The responsibilities of the governance committee have subsequently been assumed by the Board and/or other Board committees as appropriate.

The board should also review committees aligned to board membership and attendance at committees. For example, if board membership changes, new appointees may not necessarily have the same skills as the board member they are replacing. Where the retiring board member is also a committee member, the board should consider if the newly appointed board member should act in the committee role as well or whether an alternative board member should be appointed. This inter-relation between board changes and committee membership should be incorporated in the considerations undertaken by the nomination committee.

Examples of other committees

Larger companies often combine the focus of their committees into a single forum, ensuring that the various topics receive sufficient time spent on their discussion that would not be possible if they were a standing agenda item for the board. By creating a committee, the board can ensure that focused attention is given by knowledgeable committee members to these key areas, without distracting the board from their core responsibilities or losing their importance in what is often a long boardroom agenda.

Where topics are combined in a committee, it is key that the role of the combined committee is clearly documented and is clear on its deliverables. It should also be regularly reviewed to ensure that topic creep is not seen in discussions or that the topic has grown significantly or reduced over time. The composition of the committee should also be monitored given the changing focus of these types of broad-ranging committees.

Here various committees and their topics will be introduced. Examples will also be used to showcase how these can be combined, how their focus is transparent and clear and how they are reported in the annual report.

Future activities of these committees also give an indication of the direction that the company and the board believe the company is moving in terms of strategy, the sector in which they function and the markets in which they operate. For instance, Smith and Nephew Plc's compliance and culture committee, showcased here as an example, includes corporate culture and sustainability as two areas where the committee will focus in the subsequent year.

Compliance committee

Companies with a high level of regulatory oversight or compliance related to authorisations often see the benefit of implementing a compliance committee to focus on any changes to their regulatory framework, be aware of potential developments, oversee any compliance-related internal projects and contribute to external forums.

These are often combined with other remits aligned to compliance depending on the nature of the company and the sector in which they work. Examples could be legal committees, ethics or governance.

EXAMPLE: Compliance and Culture Committee

Smith & Nephew Plc, Annual Report 2018 (extract)

Compliance and culture committee (formerly the ethics and compliance committee) with a broad remit of ethics, compliance, quality assurance and regulatory affairs. From the report in the annual report, 2018, it is evident the areas in which the committee acts and the focus that they have:

At each meeting we noted and considered the activities of compliance and enforcement agencies and investigation of possible improprieties. At every meeting a report on the Quality Assurance Regulatory Affairs (QARA) function was provided along with updates of product complaint trends. We also reviewed a report on the activities of the Group's Ethics & Compliance Committee and reviewed the progress of the Global Compliance Programme.

OVERSIGHT OF QUALITY & REGULATORY

Product safety is at the heart of our business. Regulatory authorities across the world enforce a complex series of laws and regulations that govern the design, development, approval, manufacture, labelling, marketing and sale of healthcare products. During the year, we oversaw the quality and regulatory activities of our business. At each meeting, we received a report on quality and regulatory matters from the Chief Quality and Regulatory Affairs Officer, or the SVP Quality Assurance.

We reviewed the results of inspections carried out by the FDA and other regulators and monitored the progress of improvements following some of these inspections. We also monitored the work being undertaken to help our manufacturing sites to prepare for future inspections.

We reviewed the results of quality audits undertaken during the year, noted follow up actions and monitored progress made to address these actions.

OVERSIGHT OF ETHICS & COMPLIANCE

'Doing the right thing' is part of our licence to operate. During the year, we oversaw the ethics and compliance activities of our business. At each meeting we received a report on ethics and compliance matters from the Chief Legal and Compliance Officer.

We regularly review our compliance programme as it relates to healthcare professionals and third party sellers (such as distributors and sales agents), particularly in higher risk markets. For healthcare professionals, this includes policies, training and certification for employees and sales agents, as well as pre-approval of consulting services and grants and fellowships. For third parties, our programme includes due diligence, contracts with compliance terms, compliance training and certification, and site assessments to check compliance controls and monitoring visits to review books and records.

We ensure that comprehensive due diligence is carried out prior to an acquisition and we ensure that following acquisitions new businesses are integrated rapidly into the Smith & Nephew compliance programme.

We oversee the employee compliance training programme, ensuring that all new employees are trained on our Code of Conduct, which sets out our basic legal and ethical principles for conducting business. We are updated on significant calls made to our whistle-blower line, which enables employees and members of the public to contact us anonymously through an independent provider (where allowed by local law) and are updated on allegations of potentially significant improprieties and the Company's response. During the year, we expanded our remit and reviewed the policies and procedures we have in place to handle claims of sexual harassment.

Safety, health and environment committees

Many companies implement a health, safety and environment ('HSE') committee reflecting the importance of this within their organisation, across their workforce and in the communities in which they operate. Their terms of reference would be company-specific but are generally consistent in their focus on both complying with legislation but also ensuring that this is embedded in the culture of the business and the way that the workforce operates.

The implementation of, and support to, this committee, as well as the strength of its members and the additional experience and expertise they bring to a company, also serves as evidence to regulators and authorities of the commitment that a company has within this area of responsibility. Nomination committees, when looking to add or replace members to this committee, will have a requirement to appoint a combined membership that understands the legislative deliverables of the company, the application of the legislation, the oversight of the implementation and delivery, as well as workforce engagement in this topic.

EXAMPLE: Safety, Health and Environment Committee

SSE Plc, Annual Report 2018 (extract)

Role

The SHEAC advises the Board on matters relating to safety, health and the environment. The remit of the SHEAC is set out in its Terms of Reference which were reviewed by the SHEAC in November 2017 and were approved by the Board in January 2018. The SHEAC is responsible for:

- overseeing relevant Group Policies, namely: the Safety Health and Environment Policy; the Environment and Climate Change Policy and the Corporate Responsibility and Sustainability Policy;
- monitoring the level of resource, competence and commitment applied to the management of safety, health and the environment issues, to ensure that a culture of continuous improvement is embedded across the Group;
- reviewing feedback from a range of stakeholder engagement activities on matters relating to safety, health and the environment;
- receiving reports on the safety, health and environment audits planned for the forthcoming year, and periodic updates on any significant matters arising from the audits carried out across the Group;
- reviewing the effectiveness of the Group's strategy, initiatives, training and targets in relation to the environment, the safety of employees and contractors, and also the occupational health and well-being of employees and contractors;
- reviewing reports on environmental, occupational health and safety performance, which cover performance against targets; incident trends; high potential incidents;

significant risks; mitigations and plans; and other key emerging issues arising from operations and projects across the Group; and
- supporting SSE's general commitment to being a responsible company that makes a positive contribution to the communities and societies of which it is part.

Case study: reframing the safety family

Recognising the static nature of SSE's safety performance in recent years, a comprehensive review was undertaken of all safety communications across the SSE Group in 2017/18. Detailed focus groups were held with front line employees with a clear communications strategy emerging. The re-focused tone centres on straightforward messages, positive story-telling, and avoiding language around rules or procedures. The core of this safety message is SSE's safety licence: If it's not safe, we don't do it.

Underpinning this licence are four guiding principles of SSE's Safety Family culture:

1. We take care of ourselves and each other.
2. We take pride in our work and our workplace.
3. We plan, scan and adapt.
4. We see it, sort it, report it.

With the starting point of the Safety Family being the SSE licence: If it's not safe, we don't do it, the end point is: We all get home safe.

Environmental, social and governance committee

Historically, environmental and social impact of a company has been delegated to a secondary discussion or raised to primary discussion on the back of an incident or concern raised that impacts on the profitability of a company. Increasingly, this topic is moving centre stage as environmental impact is a core topic for most organisations while social media pressure and focus has raised attention to how individual companies act and react. Research is also now available that aligns business profitability and growth to implementation of better social and environmental practices and bringing these to the centre of an organisation.

Recognition of this changed environment and the governance required to bring this to the centre of decision making and strategy initiatives is a board topic that can no longer be side-lined or ignored. It is also a very wide topic with various strands dependent on the company and the markets and environments in which it operates. Critically it can include the impact on the environment, climate change, legal changes, consumer drivers, supply chain sustainability and corporate social responsibility (CSR), as well as health and society impacts, depending on the sector.

Environment, Social and Governance ('ESG') committees, or committees covering this area under a different title, are also being implemented by companies to act on issues but also as a means to demonstrate to investors and other stakeholders how they oversee strategic and operational decisions in relation to ESG. Reporting in the annual report evidences the work of this committee, while changing vision, mission and strategy statements reflect company engagement, or lack of, in this key area.

> **EXAMPLE: Environmental, Social and Governance as part of a wider governance framework**
>
> Rolls-Royce Holdings plc has an executive-level focus on the environment and sustainability, as well as a safety and ethics committee which has a wide ranging remit including product safety, HSE, sustainability, ethics, compliance and principal risks.
>
> *Rolls-Royce Holdings plc, Annual Report 2018 (extracts)*
>
> **Strategic Report – Sustainability – Environment**
> As a leading industrial technology company we have an irrefutable role in enabling the transition to a low carbon global economy. We are committed to utilising our engineering skills and technology capabilities to enable and accelerate this.
>
> **Our Approach**
> We believe that the successful management of climate change will depend upon a structured transition to a low carbon economy, driven by the development of sustainable power solutions.
>
> During 2018, our executive-level environment & sustainability committee reviewed our governance, strategy and policies in relation to our environmental impacts. Our environmental commitments are embedded within our governance framework and operational procedures, including Our Code and associated Group policies. We have also begun developing dedicated scenarios to understand the potential opportunities and risks associated with climate change.
>
> *Safety and Ethics Committee report*
>
> **Sustainability**
> We were briefed in July about the work across the Group on sustainability topics, focused through the executive-level environment & sustainability committee (E&SC).
>
> At the Safety & Ethics Committee in December 2017 (as reported in the previous Annual Report), we agreed that the pre-existing sustainability strategy would be reconsidered. This has enabled the Group to concentrate on developing position statements on material issues. This includes developing a single environmental position statement that crystallises operational and longer-term strategic commitments. It also sets out the Company's commitment through investment to the decarbonisation of its product portfolio and supporting the global transition to a low carbon economy. Through reports from the E&SC and the Science & Technology Committee, this Committee will oversee how this position statement is applied across

> the Group and summarise in future annual reports sustainability progress across all activities in the Group.
>
> We were briefed on the Company's approach to the management of the risk of 'conflict minerals' being potentially used in our supply chain; the review of a sustainable alternative fuels strategy; and a review of the approach to investor engagement in sustainability topics. This resulted in the development of the Group's first environmental, social and governance (ESG) newsletter, which was sent to investors and other external stakeholders in July this year. The newsletter highlighted progress made against the commitments set out in our previous annual report and demonstrates commitment to increasing our external engagement on these important topics.
>
> The Company has maintained its listing in the Dow Jones Sustainability Index (DJSI), one of only five aerospace and defence companies to achieve this. Overall, our score improved slightly from 2017 and we achieved industry leading scores for the social dimension of the assessment, including top scores for the environmental reporting and corporate citizenship and philanthropy question sets.

Within particular sectors this is a priority in addressing current concerns and is becoming a core focus of business in general, aligning corporate goals to social and environmental issues. Large manufacturers heavily utilising plastics in their packaging, energy providers utilising natural resources and food distributors fuelling concerns on health issues are among other visible sectors where social and environmental impact is clearly visible and can heavily impact the success of a company. Addressing these matters in a committee aligning considerations, decisions and actions to the purpose of the company and its strategy can be a means to demonstrate that addressing concerns is a core part of the business rather than lip-service to maintain existing operations. Board acceptance, acknowledgement, discussion and action resulting from reporting of this committee is an imperative if the company wants to develop or maintain their commitment in this space.

Corporate social responsibility committee

In many companies, corporate social responsibility ('CSR') is a relatively new topic for the board to consider in isolation and as a key topic when historically it may have fallen within wider topics such as community matters, charity, employee and social engagement. More forward-looking companies or those with a strong connection to the community or their impact on the environment, have had this as a core topic for many years, often incorporating a committee with this as a focus, albeit that the purpose may have evolved over the years. The updated Code brought this more into focus with the principle that a successful company should contribute to the wider society.

Terms of reference of this committee usually focus on the broad approach to corporate responsibility aligned to the purpose of the company, its strategy and its values. They should also reflect that application of these discussions and the KPIs aligned to these that reflect the success, or otherwise, of their implementation. Here a company has a direct connection to the community, their impact on the community and their support therein should also be addressed and monitored as should stakeholder engagement in its widest sense, from employees to shareholders and suppliers to communities.

As with other non-standard committees, this committee can evolve to having a broad and wide-ranging focus. At its core would be the environment and the community, which may include the impact of the company on the environment in terms of its use of materials, particularly man-made materials or those that directly negatively impact the environment. Where natural materials are used within the company or are sourced in some way, it is clear that the use of this type of committee would be beneficial, for example oil and gas or mining companies.

Community aspects that may be covered by this committee could include the social impact of services provided, the ability of the company to support the local community or charities, support of individuals, particularly vulnerable customers. This may also include the development of apprenticeships, training or career development programmes. Particularly where the company is a primary or significant employer within an area, the impact of the company on the community, both directly and indirectly, should be recognised, valued and supported. In these circumstances, the implementation of a committee to have oversight of community impact benefits the board in ensuring that this has focus and can be monitored with any arising issues flagged back to the board.

EXAMPLE: Corporate Social Committee

The United Utilities Group Plc corporate responsibility committee has existed for over eleven years with three members, two of whom are independent. There is also a large cohort of attendees at each meeting ensuring that the broad role of the committee can be effectively discussed. These attendees include senior representatives from all the relevant areas of the company, from corporate affairs, customer services, the people director and operational directors.

The committee's agenda during the year ending March 2019 included the following areas within environment and social (see committee report below from the annual report) as well as a broader focus on governance, reputation, engagement and cross company issues, such as social media.

United Utilities Group Plc, Annual Report 2019, Corporate Responsibility committee (abstracts)

ENVIRONMENTAL

Climate change mitigation
With the current carbon strategy coming to an end in 2020, the committee was updated on proposed priorities up to 2025. This included the company's intention to

set a new science-based emissions target and to evolve its reporting in line with expectations to achieve net zero emissions. In addition, the strategy will include continued focus on delivering solutions to reduce operational carbon emissions, enhancing climate-related disclosure and, as a last resort, purchasing green credits to achieve emissions targets. It was particularly impressed with work to develop an organisational capability matrix for carbon, which incorporates components from existing frameworks such as HM Treasury Infrastructure Carbon Review and the Task Force on Climate-related Financial Disclosure recommendations. The updated carbon strategy, objectives and targets will be finalised later in 2019.

Climate change adaptation

The committee welcomed the instigation of an independent review of the company's approach to climate change adaptation whose scope includes a critique of the approach taken to assess the risk for drought, peak demand, sewer flooding and pollution and flooding of assets; a review of other potential approaches to better assess the risk, incorporating the findings of UKCP18; and a recommendation of which method should be adopted for each risk. The findings of this study will feed into the third round climate adaptation report to be submitted to Defra in the autumn of 2020.

Valuing natural capital

Some of the steps necessary to adapt to climate change were covered as part of discussions examining how to better value the services provided by nature. The committee was presented with an overview of how the company is developing a strategic plan to implement a natural capital approach. This takes into account the identification of specific organisational barriers and challenges in implementing a natural capital approach, such as explaining the relevance of natural capital; an action plan to address these challenges, including how natural capital is measured and adopted through policies and projects, such as the company's approach to catchment management; and the identification of external factors and changes.

Approach to plastics

The committee reviewed the steps being taken by the company to tackle this high profile issue. It heard how a multi-functional 'task and finish' group has been established to assess the company's touchpoints with plastic, creating a 'water-cycle map' of potential impacts. The committee supported the review of the existing evidence base and the company's research project with the University of Manchester to understand how plastics interact with the wastewater treatment process. It was explained that single use plastic had been removed from the company's catering outlets and that dialogue was under way with suppliers to examine how plastic use could be reduced, in particular for delivery of materials, water sample bottles and bottled water used in emergency response. The company was actively supporting the refill campaign, focusing to begin with in Greater Manchester.

SOCIAL

Affordability and vulnerability
The committee covered this topic extensively in 2018/19, reviewing performance against 22 measures used to track progress in assisting lower income groups. It welcomed an update on the second North West affordability summit, where the North West hardship hub was officially launched. Delegates were updated on the company's new payment break scheme where bill payments can be delayed for a set period of time under specific circumstances, such as a temporary drop in income, to help customers avoid falling into debt.

Diversity and inclusion, including gender pay
It was reported to the committee that there had been good progress implementing the company's gender plan, part of its diversity and inclusion action plan. The committee shared the company's ambition to increase diversity of thought and to build a diverse workforce representative of all the communities served. In its review of the company's second gender pay gap report, the committee commented that the report would benefit from a clearer explanation that the gap will close through the successful implementation of the company's diversity and inclusion strategy.

Update on community strategy
The committee was briefed on the company's intention to revisit its community strategy in the context of, among other issues, what the 25-year natural environment plan means for access and recreation; the impact of the PR19 business plan and its emphasis on building a positive connection with the communities of the North West; and that opportunities exist to enhance reputation through more targeted and effective engagement on current activities.

Early careers and developing young people
The committee was updated on the positive impact of current initiatives such as the graduate and apprentice programmes, youth employment programme and focus on STEM subjects. Because of the demands, skills and diversity gaps of the company, coupled with the expectations from a future workforce, the company's review had prompted several new initiatives including degree apprentices, a partnership with Teach First to gain access to talented young people from diverse communities across the region and the launch of an engineering master class with high schools in Warrington.

IT and technology committee

IT and technology is at the heart of many companies and its security and development is often a key driver to the success of the company. Given the speed of development and technical knowledge that is often required to fully benefit from focus, this may be a topic considered for delegation from the board to a committee composed of knowledgeable experts.

It may also be part of a wider committee responsibility, such as the risk committee. In technology driven companies or systems as a service ('SAAS') companies, it may be constituted as part of a markets committee looking at the wider sector and market environment, competitor analysis and product development given this is the core of the company.

Wherever the topic is captured, clarity should be given to the focus of the relevant committee whether use of technology, its development or its security.

EXAMPLE: Technology focused committee

Legal and General Group Plc, Annual Report 2018, Letter from the Chairman (extract)

IT and Cyber Issues
It is vital that we do all we can as a business to mitigate potential risks, especially with the continued rise in cybercrime. Technology is increasingly fast-paced and we need to ensure we stay ahead of the curve to ensure we are delivering the best service for our customers and providing the best support for our employees. In order to ensure sufficient focus on this critical area for the business, a Group Information Technology Committee of the Board was established at the beginning of 2018. The Committee enables the Board to have greater oversight of the company's IT programmes and the implementation of improvements during 2018 to ensure the group is operating within its targeted access management, information security and cyber risk appetite. This Committee has met regularly throughout the year and has proven to be a successful forum in which progress on IT and cyber projects and strategy can be properly tracked and management can be held to account against tangible deliverables. Recognising the critical importance of IT and cyber security on our business, we have made this Committee a full committee of the Group Board, covering a broad remit of IT and cyber security issues across the group.

On occasion an incident may be so significant that it requires immediate, specific and focused attention in order to address the situation or scenario. In these cases, the board may not have the capacity or time availability to give sufficient focus or may not have the technical expertise, knowledge or experience to undertake a deep dive into a specific issue. In such cases, the board may decide to set up a committee with relevant members to consider the topic on their behalf.

An example of such a committee would be a committee set up following a hacking incident affecting the company that is set up to specifically review security. This committee may be set up as a subcommittee of the risk committee, if there is one in place, or may be a direct committee of the board.

The remit of the committee would be to ensure that all necessary steps are identified and taken to ensure company security and minimise the possibility of future reoccurrence. Specifically, the terms of reference may define the roles and responsibilities of this committee to identify and understand why the hacking was possible, identify mitigating actions that should be implemented to reduce the future potential of this happening again and oversee the implementation of agreed mitigants and actions by the wider company.

Given the seriousness of a subsequent data security breach and the recent hacking incident to use as a working example, the committee should be formed quickly, would meet regularly and would report back to the board frequently. Where the data breach impacts on regulatory responsibilities, reporting from the committee may also underpin reporting to the relevant regulator with the identified mitigating actions and their successful implementation being part of the resolution agreed with the regulator.

On conclusion of the process, the security committee may then become an agenda item for the board and the risk committee to ensure continued focus on future security breaches. If such occurred, the security committee could be quickly reinstituted utilising the same terms of reference updated for the specific incident.

Markets committees

Businesses in a rapidly developing marketplace, such as technology reliant firms, or those with a wide number of services or products, may implement a committee to keep abreast of market developments. Often a specific department within a business, such as a product development team, the advantage of a committee with this remit is that there is no conflict with the operational development and delivery of new products so the collation of market intelligence and the discussion thereof can be aligned to strategic growth rather than operational capability.

A markets committee will often be tasked with keeping abreast of market developments whether legislative, environmental, regulatory or sector-specific. They are able to focus entirely on this remit and can provide invaluable input to the board for strategy discussions on growth opportunities, risks related to market initiatives and changes, or competitor analysis. In smaller businesses the expectation is that the CEO and senior managers would have at least a watching eye on their own markets and competitors, however, the time available to commit to this is often lost to operational delivery or pure revenue generation.

With a clear remit for being knowledgeable about the market and its environment in which a company acts, having a balanced markets committee would enable individuals to keep abreast of changes in their area of knowledge with the combination of this knowledge becoming a powerful tool for the board in setting future strategy, both near- and long-term. For example, committee composition could include members who are tasked with legal developments, regulatory changes, competitors, product developments, technological advances. There could also be representatives of the wider community, perhaps an external contributor from a research institute or market association, although conflicts of interest and sensitivity of data would have to be noted and resolved.

> **EXAMPLE: Industry specific committee**
>
> *Astra Zeneca Plc, Annual Report 2018, Energy Committee (extract)*
>
> **Role of the Committee**
> The Science Committee's core role is to provide assurance to the Board regarding the quality, competitiveness and integrity of the Group's R&D activities. This is done by way of meetings and dialogue with our R&D leaders and other scientist employees, visits to our R&D sites throughout the world, and review and assessment of:
>
> - the approaches we adopt in respect of our chosen therapy areas
> - the scientific technology and R&D capabilities we deploy
> - the decision-making processes for R&D projects and programmes
> - the quality of our scientists and their career opportunities and talent development
> - benchmarking against industry and scientific best practice, where appropriate.
>
> The Science Committee periodically reviews important bioethical issues that we face and assists in the formulation of, and agrees on behalf of the Board, appropriate policies in relation to such issues. It may also consider, from time-to-time, future trends in medical science and technology. The Science Committee does not review individual R&D projects but does review, on behalf of the Board, the R&D aspects of specific business development or acquisition proposals and advises the Board on its conclusions.
>
> **Our focus during 2018**
> - AI, automation, digital technologies and analytics
> - In vivo biologics; personalised immunotherapy; and biologics device differentiation
> - Achieve Scientific Leadership targets
> - Scientific competitive intelligence

This committee may also be tasked with creating and maintaining links to relevant external communities, research establishments or professional associations. Internal committee members may also be appointed to committees of these external associations as a means to develop their governance expertise but also to support their technical knowledge and development through knowledge sharing.

Where product or service development is a key part of keeping a business successful in rapidly expanding market sectors, the markets committee may also be tasked with oversight of product development projects, ensuring they have clear deliverables, timetables for launch and resources to develop. By having this in a clear forum for all developments, prioritisation of development can be clear while resource allocation across and between projects can be monitored and directed.

In larger organisations where products are segregated into different divisions of the company, this committee could be used as a facilitator between and across these divisions and their respective teams. Specifically, the committee could have oversight of the timing of product launches to ensure they are co-ordinated; review market trends for the market as a whole and its impact on the company in totality; ensure legislative changes impacting the company are identified and shared with the various divisions; ratify IP and other licences across products, divisions and geographies; and implement or oversee standardisation of product launch processes and procedures

Investment committee

Where a company has significant or active investments the oversight and monitoring of these investments may be delegated to an investment committee on behalf of the board. Escalation of significant shifts of investment value, changes in investment activity or significant divestments or additions would be reported to the board either for pre-approval or ratification depending on the terms of reference of the committee.

EXAMPLE: Investment Committee

Biffa plc, Annual Report 2019 (extract)

Investment Committee
Reviews all significant capital expenditure, potential acquisitions and disposals, major contracts, tenders and property transactions.

Relocation committee

Where a business is seeking to consolidate its property footprint and merge offices into a single location, it may be beneficial to implement a relocation committee. The board should consider at what stage they delegate this to a standalone committee. For example, should the committee be constituted initially to evaluate the business benefit of consolidation, the alignment of this to the overall company strategy and the impact on the operational effectiveness of the company and its workforce? Should it additionally be tasked with identifying suitable locations or working with an external consultant to provide the expertise needed?

In this scenario, the committee may then be split into two, the first to agree the strategic plans, identify the new location and agree resource allocation and timeline. A second constituted committee, or a second phase of the same committee, may be constituted to facilitate the implementation of the office move, or may be a subcommittee of the original committee implemented to oversee the approach.

The terms of reference for the implementation of the relocation could cover:

- existing property departure(s);
- new property plans including floorplans, fit-outs;
- departure/moving date effectiveness;
- legal negotiations of lease/purchase agreements, exit and dilapidations;
- internal communications, to employees; and
- external communications, to suppliers, customers, regulators and other third parties

Each subset topic of the committee may be delegated to a project team with specific deliverables and a defined time scale for such delivery. The committee then acts as an oversight to ensure that deliverables and timescales are met. The benefit of the committee is that it will also have full oversight of all sub-projects and can ensure their effective interaction.

If projects are delayed or require additional resourcing, the committee can discuss and confirm additional resources and/or changes to the timeline with knowledge of the other project plans.

Committee members for a relocation committee are likely to be the project managers of each of the individual projects identified by the committee as well as a project manager to oversee all the projects. Given the importance of the alignment to strategy, the resource cost and the impact on the business, its financials and the workforce, at least one board member should be a member of the oversight committee or be a designated point of contact for escalation of significant matters.

Employment committee

If a business is going through a defined period of change applicable to all, or a majority of, its staff it may be beneficial for the board to constitute a specific committee rather than relying solely on the HR department who may not have the time to deliver this without it impacting on their other roles and responsibilities. An example could include where a business is seeking to reduce its workforce considerably through a period of planned retirements, redeployment and redundancies necessitating clear employee communication, employee and/or union consultation and legislative regulations to be followed.

The employment committee would require the contribution of HR professionals from within the business. Depending on the remit and requirements, additional internal and external attendees may be co-opted on to the committee or asked to submit knowledge.

External contributors, either as committee members or advisers to the committee, could include lawyers, HR advisers with specific experience in the sector or process, pensions consultants or other required specific experts. Where the business has a union or workers' body in place, the inclusion of these representatives should be discussed and agreed so that their input can be effective.

It should be noted that the committee is constituted to consult on, and contribute to, the implementation of the decision as made at board level. This committee would be focused on the processes for implementation not as a means to change the decision already made and documented. Despite this, the committee will report into the board and this reporting may include proposed adjustments, updates or clarifications on the original decision to ensure that it can be effectively implemented.

Authorities of this committee may include that of appointing external advisers within specific resource and cost guidelines.

The committee may also be tasked with identifying, adopting and implementing a communications plan to cover the process. Authority over this plan and related communication should be clear, including when authority by the board is required. It may also include authority to communicate to the workforce within agreed guidelines which may also need to align to legislative requirements. Such communications may require sign off at board level with the quorum for such approval being agreed to ensure approval is timely. The board, particularly its executive members, should not use this committee to lead on the communication of the message or ownership of the decision. Hence the connection to the board and its responsibilities requires particularly strong and clear interaction and differentiation.

Social committee

Given the impact that employees have on a company, the engagement, development and support of the workforce is key to company success. This workforce engagement, while clearly a company imperative for any company with employees, may, or may not, be best served by the implementation of a social committee. If a social committee is implemented, given the potential negative cost of employee disengagement, board acknowledgement and contribution of financial, administrative or other support to a social committee has its advantages.

This could be focused on generating employee engagement within the company, could align the company to the local community through creating a corporate social responsibility programme linked to working with local charities nominated by employees, may initiate sports teams and competitions or could be as simple as creating social events such as summer or year-end social events.

Whatever the format, the creation of a social committee often does not follow the standard format of having a terms of reference signed off by the board. More frequently, it is a gathering that is created by the workforce themselves to generate engagement across, between and throughout the workforce. The larger and more disparate the workforce, the more beneficial an engaged social committee would be.

By encouraging and supporting its events and efforts the board will enable a forum that could also be an indicator of the engagement of staff members that is separate from the formal reporting provided by the HR department or the negotiations that may be undertaken with union representatives.

Niche examples of committees

Each company can, through its own discussion and decision making, implement a committee that adds value to the effectiveness of the board. Aligned to their company purpose or to bring expertise from outside contributors as members, these rarely report within the annual report and, while the terms of reference may be standard in format, their content is often confidential or company-specific.

Companies often implement narrowly focused committees to ensure key actions and requirements are met on behalf of the board. For example, Biffa plc has a Disclosure Committee that reviews all material Regulatory News Service (RNS) announcements required under the Listing Rules.

BT Group Plc alongside its audit and risk, nominations and remuneration committees has also implemented additional committees:

- Digital Impact & Sustainability Committee: the Digital Impact & Sustainability Committee provides oversight and direction to bring BT's purpose to life through the digital impact and sustainability strategy.
- Investigatory Powers Governance Committee: the Investigatory Powers Governance Committee oversees BT's role in the use of official investigatory powers.

Many other examples can be seen within companies where their specific requirements, whether regulatory, legal, geographical or purpose-driven, are best served by having a committee implemented with a delegated and focused agenda drawing on expertise relevant to the specific needs of the company.

EXAMPLE: Globally focused committee

Given its global footprint and the countries in which it invests, BP has constituted a committee with a specific remit on behalf of the board.

BP, Annual Report 2018, Report of the Geopolitical Committee (extract)

Role of the committee

The committee monitors the company's identification and management of geopolitical risk.

Key responsibilities

- Monitor the company's identification and management of major and correlated geopolitical risk and consider reputational as well as financial consequences:
  - Major geopolitical risks are those brought about by social, economic or political events that occur in countries where BP has material investments.

- Correlated geopolitical risks are those brought about by social, economic or political events that occur in countries where BP may or may not have a presence but that can lead to global political instability.
■ Review BP's activities in the context of political and economic developments on a regional basis and advise the board on these elements in its consideration of BP's strategy and the annual plan.

External committees to the company

Committees created by professional bodies or associations as cross-industry forums draw their committee members from expertise within and across their member firms. As with any committee they are set up with specific terms of reference, often focused on the technical expertise or legislative market in which the professional body works. Often their primary focus is on governmental advice or lobbying in respect of their industry, presenting feedback from the sector to support and influence legislative change. Their positive impact is based on their cross-market constituents being able to represent multiple firms.

EXAMPLE: The Personal Investment Management and Financial Advice Association (PIMFA)

PIMFA is the trade association for firms that provide investment management and financial advice to help individuals and families plan for their financial life journeys.

They have a number of committees including an operations committee, private investor indices committee, strategic markets oversight committee as well as a number of forums related to their industry and the clients they serve. Committee members are representatives of member firms and the association itself. As an example of one of their committees:

Financial Crime Committee

The Financial Crime Committee aims to discuss all financial crime matters of significance, such as anti-money laundering measures, serious organised crime, terrorist financing, share fraud, identity theft, and boiler rooms, with a view to ensuring members are kept fully informed of relevant legislative and regulatory developments and can pick up on the latest approaches to combating financial crime.

Where a company is a member of such forums, membership of the committee by individual employees benefits the individual through their ability to work in a governance environment understanding the roles and responsibilities of a committee outside the in-house specifics. It creates an environment where they can interact with knowledgeable experts in their specific industry, building a personal network on which to draw for their own, and their employer's benefit.

From a company perspective, having a place on the committee provides the opportunity to contribute to the development of the sector while also gaining knowledge of the opinions of individuals working in competitor organisations.

Administratively, these committees and forums are either supported from the association or organisation itself or by member firms providing support, depending on the size and funding of the organisation.

Committees of wider membership organisations or professional bodies, not aligned to corporate members, also benefit from having committees to drive activities, social engagement, government initiatives or act as a core body to further the interests of their members.

EXAMPLE: The British Dental Association

The British Dental Association is both a trade union and the representative body of all fields of dentistry including general practice, community dental services, the armed forces, hospitals, academia, public health and research. As an association, it is owned by its members who in turn elect those who make decisions on strategy and policy. There are also a number of committees set up to cover a variety of purposes, of which the following is one example:

General Dental Practice Committee

The General Dental Practice Committee (GDPC) represents all general dental practitioners in the UK and aims to reflect the mixed economy of dental practice.

The GDPC is the official representative body for GDPs – it negotiates with government and other stakeholders on behalf of dentists working in general practice across the UK and is recognised by Government, as the official representative body in negotiations and consultations.

Membership

There are 72 directly elected members of the Committee, three members from LDC Conference, a representative of the Conference of Vocational Training Advisers and there are a number of seats for other organisations.

The Chair and Vice-Chair of the BDA's Principal Executive Committee are also members of the Committee.

Members are elected for three-year terms.

The full GDPC usually meets three times a year in London.

What issues does the GDPC work on?

The GDPC Remuneration Subcommittee deals with aspects of dental remuneration for both NHS and private practitioners.

It prepares the GDP element of evidence to the Review Body on Doctors' and Dentists' Remuneration and contributes to reports and policy papers on general practice finance and business expenses.

The BDA hosts meetings of the Local Dental Committees (LDCs) regional representatives and oversees a GDPC-LDC liaison group, to ensure that both groups share information and work together to achieve common aims.

Meetings are invariably held in confidence with any company-specific knowledge shared not being shared outside of the committee room. Meeting minutes need to be carefully written to ensure that the confidential nature of any contribution is maintained, otherwise the goodwill of member firms will be lost.

Members are not paid for their attendance at committee meetings and attendance is usually funded by the member firm rather than the association.

Subcommittees

In larger companies or those with multi-locations and geographical spread, it is common for subcommittees to be implemented to have oversight and responsibility of a specific division or geography. These subcommittees are subsets of the main committee, the latter being constituted by the board. Their purpose is to have a local smaller oversight based on the same framework as the main committee.

In the same way that the main committee would have a representative of the board as a member, these subcommittees would have a member of the main committee as a member or, as a minimum, an attendee. Their constitution and focus would mirror that of the main committee, reflecting the core terms of reference.

Subcommittees may be implemented for a variety of purposes, including:

- to take a specific project, task or responsibility of the main committee and provide more in-depth focus on behalf of the main committee. In this way they are acting in the same way as an ad hoc committee of the board; or
- to take ownership for the responsibilities of the main committee in respect of a particular division or geographical region.

Best practice for the implementation of a subcommittee is to ensure that the roles, responsibilities and delegated authorities from the main committee are clearly documented and agreed by each forum. This enables the subcommittee to be effective in its actions and provides clarity on the division of responsibilities between the two forums. In effect the terms of reference of a subcommittee are those of the main committee with removal of any specifics that remain at the main committee level.

Membership of the subcommittee may, or may not, include representation from the main committee to which it is a sub-part. Where there is main committee representation, this individual is able to ensure that the differentiation between the two forums is maintained with no duplication or overlooked areas for consideration. An alternative is for a main committee member to be included by invitation as an observer and/or contributor without the responsibility of being a full subcommittee member. This may be most useful for subcommittees implemented across geographical regions enabling the contributor to attend when in the location or alternatively by telephone.

The subcommittee should report into the main committee as part of their meeting reports, escalating any matters that require further input from the main board or greater resources. The main board should also cascade knowledge, actions and guidance on a regular basis to ensure both forums remain current and aligned.

General

As with all committees, it is imperative that the purpose of the committee and its deliverables are clearly explained and documented. It is not the committee's responsibility to agree the purpose of the committee or change a decision made by the board. For example, if the board has decided that it is in the company's best interests to reduce the workforce considerably, an HR Committee can be instigated to implement the decision, not to renegotiate it. Similarly, if the board has decided and agreed to consolidate offices, the decision itself is not a discussion for the committee.

When setting out the terms of reference for a subject-specific or time-limited committee, it is important that the ability for the committee to make decisions is clear and when further approval is required from the board. The chair of the committee should be mindful of this at all times and will function as the intermediary between the two. This is particularly important if an ad hoc board meeting is required to give approval for an urgent action to be taken by a committee.

Conclusion

As can be seen throughout this chapter, there is a breadth of differing committees implemented by companies depending on the requirements of the board. These may be short-lived or permanent committees. The over-riding requirement is that the purpose of the committee is clearly documented and understood both by the board and the committee itself.

When effectively governed, a committee of the board can add enormous value to the ability of the board to discharge its duties bringing added expertise and time to commit to the topic identified. However, if not carefully constituted and governed, a complex or wide-ranging committee structure can have a detrimental impact on the board and the company delegating too widely and resulting in the board struggling to have clear oversight. The key is to ensure that a committee structure continues to add value, has robust governance and develops with the needs of the board and the company as a whole.

Smaller companies may also benefit from considering the implementation of a committee to take pressure from the board. As can be seen, committees can be implemented for any purpose decided by the board, as long as they are governed effectively and add value. Where there may be limited resource available to implement or maintain a full committee, the use of term-limited committees can provide short-term relief for the board, as well as gaining broader input into a specific topic from the wider business. The board of smaller companies should not shy away from considering implementing a committee if it adds value to themselves or the company. As long as the implementation is efficient and the remit is clear, the benefit can often be seen relatively quickly.

11 – Subsidiary boards

Introduction

A subsidiary board will be present where a company has a number of legal entities sitting underneath the primary parent company or a holding company. Their formal status is diverse, varying from dormant companies, non-operational asset holding companies to operational entities aligned to product, service or location.

They are obviously prevalent in large organisations and can be seen in both expanding and contracting companies. Companies expanding through acquisition may take time to merge legal entities, and historic companies may continue to exist, often in name only as dormant companies, way beyond when the merger has been completed and superseded. In some cases, these dormant companies are maintained to protect the use of the name so that it cannot be used by another company or for the continuation of existing contracts to ensure their continuation of legality.

Contracting companies, where the organisation itself is reducing in size or the range of products and services is being scaled back, may merge their workforce and product placement into fewer legal entities. The companies no longer required may remain as dormant companies protecting the name from use by other parties, or may, over time, be liquidated.

Legal standing

While created as part of the organisation structure of a company; subsidiaries are full legal entities in their own right. As such, they are set up with Memorandum & Articles of Association. Although these are anecdotally likely to be standard form, with little adjustment to reflect the purpose of the company, unless it is an operating company requiring specific incorporation documents.

No matter their purpose or status, all companies, including dormant companies, must have a named director and must continue to file relevant documentation with the relevant registration body, for example, Companies House in England and Wales.

While often administrative housekeeping, the maintenance of these entities is an ongoing obligation and their monitoring can be an ongoing project for the company secretariat in a large organisation.

Subsidiary board members have the same legal standing, responsibilities and obligations as those appointed at parent board level, albeit that they often have limited ability to make decisions or influence strategy.

Similarities to committees

Unlike committees, subsidiary boards rarely have a formal documented terms of reference. Roles and responsibilities are often defined through line management of subsidiary board members. For example, the line manager of the subsidiary managing director may set their personal objectives and deliverables with the formal, or informal, expectation these will be delivered through both personal responsibility and through the collective activities of subsidiary board members and their teams.

Subsidiary board members may also have a matrix reporting line through to both the subsidiary managing director and the function at the parent company level, for example a subsidiary finance director will have a dual reporting line to the group finance director and the subsidiary managing director. The dominant reporting line between these will be defined by the organisation, although practical management housekeeping and administration is primarily undertaken by the subsidiary managing director based on proximity and day-to-day connectivity. It is important for this individual to have clarity of reporting between the two line managers to ensure that they focus on priority deliverables, report effectively to each party and avoid prioritising one over the other. Their success is based on delivering within the role as a whole not to one party. Where there is a lack of clarity between the two line managers, or in extreme cases, conflict of interests, deliverables from the individual will necessarily be lessened and will be less beneficial to the organisation.

While a subsidiary board is unlikely to have a formal terms of reference, it does remain a delegated authority of the parent company board. As such there are expectations for reporting to the board, usually as part of a combined functional report, for example as part of the financial reporting, risk committee reports or governance updates. If the subsidiary is significant in terms of responsibility, location, visibility or is a larger representative percentage of the group as a whole, there may be a requirement for direct reporting.

Attendance at the main group board meeting by representatives of subsidiary companies is usually by invitation, with it being rare for a subsidiary board member to also be a main board member unless they have additional wider responsibilities. However, subsidiary board members should be prepared to attend main board meetings or relevant committee meetings as and when requested to provide input into specific topics.

Subsidiary board reporting flows through to the parent company and group functions, either through independent reporting such as monthly financial reporting or as a collective through board meeting minutes.

Operations of subsidiary boards

In effect, the operations of a subsidiary board are downwards to the delivery of the specific service or product ensuring its continued successful delivery. The functions are largely operational incorporating resource management, client interaction and process flow. They may also be responsible for local growth through sales or product development.

Despite this, parent companies have performance and delivery expectations of their subsidiary companies and will hold the local executive management responsible for its delivery. Even with some semblance of independence provided to some subsidiaries, policies and procedures are likely to be centralised as are systems and procedures for all financial matters as well as large-scale spend, joint ventures or significant contracts.

EXAMPLE: Subsidiary governance structure

Legal and General Plc, Annual Report 2018, Letter from the Chairman

Subsidiary Boards
Guiding principles are in place for the relationship between the Group Board and the Board of the group's principal subsidiaries. This framework promotes full and effective interaction across all levels of the group to support the delivery of strategy and business objectives within a framework of best corporate governance practice.

Local budgets may be set including for below limit spend, as well as centralised third-party support services, such as banking, to benefit from the greater opportunity from allocating the full group to a provider.

Policy implementation at a subsidiary level is most frequently through adoption of parent company policies, with minor adjustments to meet local requirements while maintaining the core purpose of the policy. Care needs to be taken on the application to ensure that local adjustments meet both the group requirements and local legislation. Equally, the local subsidiary should be tasked with flagging any local legislation that should be implemented, especially where this may not have a multi-jurisdictional requirement or may not have reached the radar or the parent company or centralised functions.

Setting strategy

One of the primary responsibilities of any board is to set the strategy for the company of which they are a board member. As a subsidiary, this primarily falls under the strategy of the whole group set at the parent level and incorporating the strategy of all subsidiaries. Additional strategic focus or subsidiary level nuances may be delegated to the subsidiary board from the parent. As a board member of a subsidiary, it is important to clarify, understand and adopt the remit of the subsidiary with reference to its strategic independence, or not, as the case may be. This subsidiary independence and flexibility will be different in its remit and application and will vary between companies under the same group structure. For example, an overseas subsidiary may have more flexibility to adopt certain strategic actions cascaded from the board to ensure that they meet local legislation, requirements or culture. Equally single geography subsidiaries may adopt and have the ability to adapt strategic actions differently depending on the purpose of the subsidiary company.

Operating companies are most frequently challenged by parent company boards to deliver against a financial budget with a focus purely on its achievement. Limited freedom may be given to actions beyond the support of its delivery and, where this freedom is present, it will be within the framework of the company's wider guidelines.

Subsidiary board members

When appointing to the board of a subsidiary company, the parent company will usually set the standards and approach to take. Key questions to be asked include: Should the parent company have representation on all operating subsidiary boards? Will non-executive directors be appointed to any subsidiary boards? If there is a different approach to more significant subsidiary boards, how is significant defined, by size, group contribution, location or otherwise?

For overseas subsidiary boards, local legislation may prohibit the group company having a common approach. For example, certain countries exclude the appointment of directors located overseas. Others require that all board meetings are physically held in the relevant country. In these cases, would the representative of the parent company have the time and resource to attend all meetings in person?

For operating subsidiary companies, will the relevant managing director be the primary driver to appointing an effective and balanced board? If so, are there any group guidelines that should be followed. Equally, is the purpose of the board purely operational, in which case local operational requirements should be accommodated. Could these requirements be implemented without creating a large subsidiary board that brings more individuals into personal director responsibilities? For example, could a reduced board be more effective in an operating company, with the use of delegated authorities?

When looking for consistency of approach, this may be better serviced by having an effective and consistent approach to the practicalities of the board meetings themselves, perhaps having them supported in a consistent manner by a single team. Where digital tools are used to support all governance meetings, this is easier to adopt, maintain and audit. Where a consistent approach to board membership is preferred, there may be an option to incorporate consistent training for all subsidiary board members to reflect common core approaches and values.

Where non-executive directors are to be appointed to a subsidiary board, are these appointed by the parent group on behalf of the subsidiary or does the subsidiary itself appoint based on local requirements?

Where a group has grown considerably and has multiple dormant subsidiary companies in their legal entity model, there may be a centrally taken decision to have a consistent approach to the boards of these types of subsidiaries. For example, could the appointment of a director to these legal entities be outsourced to a third-party provider of services? Alternatively, where legally possible, should a representative of a centralised function, such as the legal or finance team, be appointed on the board of dormant companies to ensure consistency and centralised control?

When appointing to subsidiary boards, care should initially be taken to understand the purpose of the subsidiary board, whether it is operational or dormant and what the practical requirements for board members will be in terms of the legal entity and the jurisdiction in which it is registered.

Finally, parent companies should also consider the board composition of any joint venture subsidiaries where the parent company may not hold 100% of the shares of the subsidiary. In these circumstances, greater consideration needs to be given to the purpose of the company, the controlling influence that may, or may not, be required. Equally, who holds the remaining shares? If it is a joint venture with a single counterparty, will both shareholders appoint a representative to the board? If the remaining shares are held by members of the subsidiary board itself, should there be a shareholder representative on the board as a non-executive? If so, how will they report to the shareholder and how will they effectively interact with the executive directors?

The role of a subsidiary board member

A board member at the subsidiary level has the same legal standing as all other board members. In the UK, this includes applying the same principles of acting as a director and as defined in the Code. Specifically, this requires the director to have particular regard to the general duties of directors as set out in Part 10, Chapter 2 of the Companies Act 2006, including the duty to promote the success of the company to which they are appointed, namely the subsidiary company. Specifically, this states that:

> 'A director of a company must act in the way he considers, in good faith, would be most likely to promote the success of the company for the benefit of its members as a whole, and in doing so have regard (amongst other matters) to:
> (a) the likely consequences of any decision in the long term,
> (b) the interests of the company's employees,
> (c) the need to foster the company's business relationships with suppliers, customers and others,

(d) the impact of the company's operations on the community and the environment,
(e) the desirability of the company maintaining a reputation for high standards of business conduct, and
(f) the need to act fairly as between members of the company.'

As such, each director will be required to exercise relevant powers under, and abide by, the company's articles of association and in accordance with the company's policies and procedures.

Being appointed to a subsidiary board is an opportunity for senior employees with a local business to have their first opportunity to contribute at board level. It is often a beneficial way to introduce senior individuals to governance frameworks, senior decision making and leadership. While the main board sets the tone for the company as a whole from the top, board members at a subsidiary level have the same position of responsibility in their local environment. Moving from local line management to board membership gives individuals an insight into leadership. As such, it can also be a source of committee members for the wider company given its similarity in terms of structure, practicalities, reporting and professionalism.

Overseas subsidiaries

The governance of overseas subsidiaries is different from domestic subsidiaries due to differences in language, culture, legal environment and tax laws. In overseas boards, the role will include understanding and applying any local jurisdiction specifics in terms of regulation and legislation. In significant global organisations, the breadth of their global footprint may mean that this matrix of regulatory and legislative requirements is extensive and complex. As a result, greater reliance on the local subsidiary board and their expertise in governance matters may be expected.

Parent companies also need to give due recognition to local culture and values when incorporating overseas subsidiaries into a global organisation. While the parent board and central functions may view the company as a single entity, those in local jurisdictions may not view the organisation in the same way.

Local nuances and cultural expectations will be applied. Local employment laws may mean that consistent application of HR policies, procedures and benefits is not possible. Whereas in some countries there is minimal government reporting on personnel matters, often limited to that related to tax collection, in other countries, there is a raft of reporting that all companies are required to complete. Adopting a 'one size fits all' approach for all locations may not be practically possible in all matters.

Conflicts may arise where parent company policies are cascaded to all subsidiaries with significant adaption required to meet local laws. For example, while US and European legislation is often similar in intent; the application of it can vary considerably. In these instances, it is important for both the parent to recognise that local differences may be required to meet local laws, while the subsidiary board recognises the intent of the policy and adopts the framework and purpose with local adjustments. It is not the purpose of the subsidiary board to identify and implement policies in isolation. Where a local policy is required to meet local laws, this should be implemented within the policy framework of the company with reference and notification to the parent company, legal function or company secretariat.

Internal non-operating subsidiaries

Non-operating, dormant or asset-holding companies, the latter often referred to as Special Purpose Vehicles (SPVs) or Special Purpose Companies (SPCs) have the same legal standing as all other constituted companies. Their terms of reference are included in the corporate documents of the company while their named directors will act as a director of the company alongside other operational roles. Usually, their meetings are rare and for a specific purpose, such as to approve their annual accounts or a transactional approval, their governance and company secretarial requirements are light touch and largely administrative. Despite this, they have the same external reporting standards and submission deadlines as other operating companies.

To offset internal risk or for ease of oversight and management, services provided to these types of companies may be outsourced to corporate service providers who will manage the company and provide directors, often as part of a portfolio of companies.

Accounting records

Subsidiary companies will often have their accounting records consolidated within the parent company. Where they are not, the subsidiary may also be able to benefit from audit exemptions as long as the parent company is their guarantor, and there are no shareholder requirements for audited accounts.

Where the parent company has an audit committee, audit function and centralised finance teams, the subsidiary would usually utilise these resources to support the subsidiary.

Subsidiary governance

Creating consistency in approach to the governance of subsidiaries, once implemented, will enable simpler oversight and greater control to be gained, without restricting the subsidiaries in delivering against their purpose.

The Chartered Governance Institute has produced a subsidiary governance framework to create sound governance practices and promote best practice in companies with a subsidiary matrix within their organisation. It also acts as useful guidance for those new to working within a large matrix organisation or who are appointed to a subsidiary board and are feeling exposed to their legal responsibilities without the ability to address their roles and responsibilities as a director directly.

The Chartered Governance Institute subsidiary governance framework

The following is The Chartered Governance Institute subsidiary governance framework checklist at a glance:

Initial steps:

- Obtain holding company board and subsidiary boards 'buy-in'; set the tone from the top.
- Audit/diligence subsidiaries in the group and collate key information/documents on them.
- Establish/resource the team for the project.
- Set priorities, key goals and timeframes for the project.
- Clearly communicate the rationale for the project with the key people to be involved in setting up the subsidiary governance framework.

Key considerations:

- Implement best practice corporate governance throughout the group where possible, bearing in mind the key local legal, regulatory and best practice sources impacting on corporate governance.
- Be mindful of local laws, regulation and also local customs.
- Consider whether prescription or flexibility or a balance between the two is desirable in terms of, for example, policies and procedures; a 'one size fits all' approach may not be suitable.
- Involve and encourage subsidiary boards and management.

Key issues – subsidiary boards:

- Consider the composition and effectiveness of subsidiary boards; regularly review this including after key events such as acquisitions or substantial expansion.
- Review director's service contracts at the subsidiary level to ensure they include appropriate protections.
- When reviewing remuneration policies and practices in general, consider what is appropriate for staff (particularly senior executives) of subsidiaries.

Key issues – documents, policies and procedures:

- Draft or refresh group-wide policies, statements and procedures (e.g. anti-bribery; ethics; health and safety; human rights; whistleblowing and more) and make them easily accessible.

- Consider overarching subsidiary board guidance or terms of reference for what is expected of subsidiary boards. This could encompass their general duties vis-à-vis the subsidiary company, their interaction with the holding company, and other matters.
- Ensure delegated authorities and decision-making procedures are carefully defined in the board guidance/terms of reference and that local constitutional documents are catered for.
- Establish clear reporting lines to the parent company and put in place measures for encouraging communication and engagement. Consider creating a communications guide.
- Draft and implement board meeting procedures guidance on matters such as the circulation and form of agendas and board papers and how meetings should be minuted and who minutes should be circulated to.
- Draft and implement a conflict of interest policy if considered necessary and, if desired and relevant, ensure that the constitutional documents of each subsidiary company permit independent directors to authorise any conflicts.

Implementing the framework and ongoing steps:

- Communicate clearly to subsidiaries and their staff the rationale and aims of best practice subsidiary corporate governance and what is expected of them.
- Consider appointing corporate governance champions at subsidiaries.
- Put in place a programme of regular training for subsidiary directors, including an induction programme at the time of their appointment.
- Advertise, and if necessary train, subsidiary personnel on, the new/refreshed subsidiary governance framework.
- Maintain close relationships with subsidiary boards and management and regularly review, and encourage regular feedback on, the operation of the subsidiary governance framework.

Subsidiary oversight

Effective oversight of all subsidiaries by the parent company is key to ensuring that the health of the group as a whole remains robust. This is of particular importance where the subsidiary is significant, either through size, location or potential impact on the group due to their actions. In these cases, parent companies will often pay closer attention to the governance and decision making within these subsidiaries, creating a clear framework for authorisations as well as reporting to the parent company.

Where there is no clear definition of reporting requirement or authorisation levels between the two levels, a considerable amount of time and resource can be spent in both entities understanding the issues and duplicating allocation of resources. Hence there is a clear need to document the critical escalation points, the local ownership actions and any grey areas between them. For example, there may be an approval limit for financial spend by the subsidiary company, above which parent company approval is required. Conversely, the subsidiary board may be able to allocate financial spend within a set of financial guidelines. An example could be the allocation among subsidiary staff of a local bonus pot being allocated by the local board without further input from the parent company.

Irrespective of where the lines are drawn between central and subsidiary authority, it is critical that these are recognised, documented and audited for adherence to provide assurance to the parent company that the subsidiary is meeting all relevant processes and controls. The level of control maintained by the parent company over subsidiaries is often aligned to the culture of the company as a whole, whether tightly held at the centre or delegated through the organisation.

There is no one perfect model for subsidiary oversight, although clear, transparent communications of expectations and deliverables can play an important role in it being effective.

Subsidiary risks

Managing risk in subsidiaries presents an interesting corporate governance challenge, especially given the high potential impact of a downstream governance failure on the group as a whole. Legally separated, subsidiaries have their own boards and management teams and are often answerable to regulators in different parts of the world. Yet with companies facing ever-increasing domestic and international regulatory and legal pressures, companies cannot afford to underestimate the reputational and financial risks that subsidiaries can bring.

Robust governance frameworks for subsidiary structures creates an opportunity to limit the risk of operating across multiple locations through multiple legal entities. The implementation of local sub-risk committees is a benefit in most large organisations and will enable risk in the subsidiary to utilise the risk framework of the wider group risk function and group risk committee.

Despite creating better local oversight, the creation of a sub-risk committee at a subsidiary level will not remove the local risk entirely. Oversight of the local risk framework should be monitored at parent group level through the centralised risk function and the over-arching risk committee. Further detail on this can be found in Chapter 7, Risk Committee.

The conflict between personal responsibility as a subsidiary director and reliance on parent company actions, can cause issues and increase the levels of risk at both parent and subsidiary level. Having clearly defined differentiation and documented responsibilities between the two forums can give certainty as to deliverables and also provide a clear audit trail of what and where in the organisation the authorisations are given, and decisions are made. This doesn't stop a maverick acting in isolation or stop a group board making decisions that are against local legislation, but it does create clear responsibilities and a framework for operations.

The content of these documented responsibilities should be regularly reviewed and maintained in an accessible place.

Conclusion

Subsidiaries pose a particular issue to large companies, and there is no single framework for their oversight and governance. Being mindful of the differences between the various types of subsidiaries as well as the influences on each of these is a starting point to having better control.

As large companies continue to expand globally, these issues will grow exponentially, and the governance framework will grow in complexity. Indeed, legal entity management has become a career in itself and an industry for third-party providers. Whether fully managed internally, or outsourced in some way, as with committees, transparency and clarity are key to having some semblance of consistency and effectiveness in managing subsidiary frameworks and the subsidiaries themselves.

12 – Other boards as formal forums

Introduction

There are many other formal forums within a company that may not be constituted as a committee or may not have responsibilities delegated from the board. Often these are driven by regulatory or legislative requirements or through the constitutional format of the legal entity of the company.

Examples of these have been grouped within this chapter through their commonality of being independent forums of an organisation with either a direct or indirect connection to the main board of the company. While having a link to, or reporting requirement into, the board, they are not a delegated forum or under the control of the board and have independent judgement. Their constituent members may or may not be board members or elected representatives of the shareholders, employees or other stakeholders.

Examples include pension trustee boards, employee ownership trust boards, employee representative forums, including but not limited to trade union representative forums.

This chapter introduces the concept of a shadow board as a forum to introduce a wider group of employees to the expectation of board membership, strategy setting and business oversight. Similarly, it will introduce advisory boards as a means to support main boards through a formal channel to extend knowledge, skills and contacts without widening board membership.

Advisory boards

Advisory boards are often implemented as a means to support main boards through a formal channel to extend knowledge, skills and contacts without widening board membership.

Advisory boards supporting the main board are frequently seen in start-ups or where new markets or developments are being tried and tested. Similar to a committee, they are an extension of the board bringing expertise that isn't otherwise present in the board. Often members are appointed for a specific skill or network to support the board for a period of time, for example, the first two years of business growth. Similar to a committee they do not have the legal responsibility of being a main board director but do bring specific expertise and knowledge to widen that of the board.

By their nature, members of advisory boards are experts in their fields with wide-ranging knowledge and experience. As such, it's key that their remit, role and responsibilities are clear and distinct from the board otherwise they may stray into oversight of the business or operational roles. Experienced or knowledgeable advisory board members will recognise the value that they bring in their role and will themselves be able to measure their input and when the value of their contribution is complete.

Advisory board members may also be investors in a business, supporting its development and future success through both their financial investment and the knowledge, expertise, and often most importantly, contacts.

When creating an advisory board, consideration should be given to whether a group of individual advisors whose expertise could be accessed on an ad hoc basis would be preferable. By appointing members formally to an advisory board, they are accepting a legally responsible role with the related personal risks and liabilities. Identifying and accommodating individuals as an unofficial non-appointed advisor to the board can still enable skills and expertise to be accessed without the formal director level legal connotations. In contrast to this, individuals or organisations investing in a business may have a board role as a prerequisite to their investment, with this director representing the investors' interest on the board. In these cases, their role as a board member, whether on the advisory board or main operating board, will be aligned to the success of the company with additional oversight on behalf of the investor.

Creation of an advisory board may be the preferred option where the company is seeking to have a formal forum to draw on and the individual members recognise the benefit of formal appointment.

Advisory boards made up of experts in their field, could be compared to the supervisory boards of the two-tier management structure prevalent in Europe. Here a management board is responsible for the day-to-day operations of the company, reporting into a supervisory board who have oversight and strategic responsibilities.

Shadow boards

A shadow board is a forum that meets separately to the main board of a company with members drawn from across a company, particularly focused on those individuals who may not yet be board-ready but whose contribution and knowledge is invaluable to the support of the success of the company.

Members
Membership gives individuals an opportunity to experience the formal process of acting at a senior level, providing practical skills in contributing to a senior forum.

With the right terms of reference, guidance, planning, commitment and support, a shadow board can introduce a wider group of employees to board responsibilities in terms of strategy setting and business oversight. Practically, meetings enable members to implement and embed their learning in a mutually beneficial forum where they can gain experience of what it is like to be a board member, without the legal liabilities that being an appointed board member brings.

It is not training or role play. This is a formally adopted forum tasked with achieving results and sharing knowledge that supports the board in its considerations. A shadow board can often identify areas of interest or opportunity that the board, or executive committee, may have overlooked or been unaware of. Having a shadow board may also enable broader contribution by a much more diverse group of individuals that may not otherwise have an opportunity to share their experience, knowledge and expertise.

Through being a shadow board member, individuals will start to understand the nuances of acting at a senior level and the power and influence and dynamics in play at the executive level. They will also learn to benefit from others' shared knowledge and experience while participating in and often leading, discussion on a wide range of topics. It supports the development of aspirant leaders and directors in understanding the difference to and transition from being a functional specialist to that of executive-level leader. It also enables individuals to recognise the roles and responsibilities of the board and board implemented committees thereby helping them support their leaders more effectively.

Company benefit

Implementation of a shadow board provides an organisation with the opportunity to bring together a diverse group of individuals to discuss company matters, particularly company strategy and culture, outside of the formally appointed board. Through the nature of its membership, it increases the diversity of thought on senior-level discussion topics, offering the opportunity to become more representative of the stakeholders that the company services, whether employees or customers.

It also provides an invaluable opportunity to identify and nurture the leaders of the future and build succession plans into the board and other governance forums, such as committees. Too frequently, the move into a leadership position and appointment to a board or committee is the first step for an individual. There is little lead up to the challenges they will face or the significant shift in mindset that is required when moving beyond a purely operational role. By providing identified talent with exposure to the governance framework and opportunities to contribute as part of a formal forum, the company can gain invaluable insights while also providing on-the-job training for individuals.

Shadow boards have the same organisational and administrative framework as the main board or a committee, without the full board reporting pack. Meetings should have a standard agenda and minutes taken, as well as administrative support provided. They may also have a representative of the main board in attendance or as a full member depending on the purpose and focus of the forum.

Pension trustee boards

Where an employer has their own pension scheme in place, instead of relying on multi-platform or government-provided umbrella schemes, a board of pension trustees will be appointed to oversee the scheme on behalf of the scheme members, whether they are current employees or previous employees who are still members of the scheme. This board is usually made up of a group of trustees who between them represent the pension scheme members and they work closely with the pension scheme advisors and administrators in undertaking their responsibilities.

Most large pension schemes also appoint an independent pension trustee to their pension trustee board given their pension-specific knowledge and ability to bring wider sector knowledge to discussions alongside the company knowledge brought by other board members.

Increasingly pension schemes and the contributions provided to them by the company are having a significant impact on the financial health of companies. Significant company failures have often seen a detrimental impact on their financial state through pension scheme contributions. Add to this financial burden the increasingly frequent changes in legislation surrounding pension schemes, and the composition of the pension trustee board can be seen to be a critical decision.

Given the impact that the pensions scheme can have it is unsurprising that corporate stakeholders are taking a greater interest in the management of pension schemes and its effective management. In addition, the Pension Protection Fund, the statutory fund in the UK that was set up to protect scheme members if their defined pension fund becomes insolvent, is increasingly emphasising the need for more and stronger professional trusteeship as a means to seeking alternatives to their services when companies become insolvent and their schemes see the resultant impact.

Pension trustee responsibilities

The responsibilities of the pension trustee board, and how they are carried out, will depend on whether it is managing a defined benefit or defined contribution scheme, or a scheme that offers both. The trust deed and rules, together with pensions legislation, define the powers of the pension trustee board and the procedures that must be followed.

The trust deed and rules give the trustee board certain powers, some of which will be discretionary. Trustees' powers differ from scheme to scheme, but usually, the trust deed includes the power to:

- accept contributions into the scheme;
- decide the investment strategy;

- invest the scheme's assets;
- amend the rules of the scheme;
- admit members on special terms;
- increase (or 'augment') members' benefits;
- deal with a funding surplus (defined benefit only); and
- wind up a scheme.

In some cases the trust deed or rules may state that the company has to agree to the use of a particular power by the pension trustee board, or that it may only use the power if the company asks them to do so.

The pension trustee board is also responsible for

- pension scheme contributions;
- financial records and requirements;
- investment;
- any professional advisers and service providers;
- pension scheme records;
- members; and
- registration, scheme return and collecting levy.

They also have a responsibility to report certain matters to the pensions regulator.

Given the extent of the roles and responsibilities of a pension trustee board as well as its necessary autonomy, the composition of the pension trustee board should reflect its significance. Independent trustees with solid knowledge of pension regulations and their application are an imperative appointment for any large pension scheme.

The pension board will be supported either by the internal company secretariat or, as an alternative, by pension scheme administrators with specific knowledge of the pensions market. No matter the source of the administrative support, the focus on risk mitigation, maintaining scheme success, asset investment oversight and member communications are core areas of responsibility for this board. As part of this, they will need to understand the current and future business of the company and the effect that this will have on the pension scheme.

This board is independent of the company main board with reporting responsibilities primarily to the scheme members but also to the funding company.

Charity funding boards

Large charities, or those with a particular requirement to generate funding through alternative sources, may set up a subset of the main board to focus on this area. While this may also be constituted as a committee, as a forum, it takes specific responsibility for generating new revenue flows, often from corporate sponsors. Where constituted as a board in their own right, these are primarily subsidiary boards of the main charity and, as such, act in the same manner as a subsidiary board with specific roles and responsibilities on behalf of the charity. With a single specific purpose, they have limited, if any, operational responsibilities for the day-to-day workings of the charity. Their specific goal is to ensure the continued generation of revenue to support the aims and objectives of the charity. Board members are often representatives of the main corporate sponsors, with this often an opportunity for these corporates to provide senior staff members with their first experience of acting on a board in an environment that is external to their business or function. The chair or deputy chair of a funding board is often a member of the board of the charity and can act as a conduit between the two forums.

Funding boards are particularly effective where the aims of the charity are clear and the responsibility for identifying funding is a primary deliverable. In general, their responsibility does not extend to sourcing day-to-day financing of operations and they are instead promoting charitable contributions through sharing the aims and objectives of the charity with a wider audience. The added benefit they may bring is sharing back to the main charity board, the perception of the charity in the wider community and how it is perceived. As such, they can be an invaluable source of intelligence for the charity in positioning their proposition in the marketplace.

Employee ownership trust board

There are an increasing number of businesses where ownership has been transferred from their private owners to the employees themselves. Often structured through an employee ownership trust, these companies have all, or a majority of, their shares owned under a trust structure on behalf of the current employees. In the UK, the trust itself is structured as a separate legal entity with the board of directors being the trustees appointed to represent the interests of the employee shareholders. As a legal entity, this board has the same responsibilities for reporting to Companies House, including submission of annual financial statements and confirmation statements.

These boards predominantly have a combination of employee and management representatives, an independent trustee and, on occasion, the departing shareholder.

This board is fully independent of the main company board, sitting independently as the shareholder. In effect, the main company board is the equivalent of the operational executive committee. The employee ownership trust board has oversight responsibility to ensure that the strategy is in place and being implemented. With members that are intimately involved with the business at different levels, their ability to represent the shareholders and their wide-ranging views can be highly beneficial. The inclusion of an independent trustee director, often acting as the chair, can bring independent thought and external knowledge to the discussions.

Where a company has implemented an employee ownership trust, the benefit of having a proactive, supportive, but challenging, trustee board is invaluable in aiding the newly structured company in its future success.

Support of this forum is often the same as that provided to the company board in terms of practical administration. Meetings would be less frequent than board or management meetings, with quarterly being the norm. Board packs are largely the management reports that are circulated in the business while input from the management board in sharing the long-term strategy and near-term business plan supports the discussion.

It should be noted that, while this board represents the employees, it is their role as shareholder, not as employees, that is being represented. This forum does not negate the need for employee engagement, whether formal or informal.

Conclusion

There are a wide variety of additional forums and boards prevalent within and alongside companies that are accommodated either directly or indirectly. Some are implemented by the main board in the same way that a committee is implemented with clear terms of reference and documented authorisations and deliverables.

Others have a requirement to be independent of the board and sit outside of the core governance framework of the company. These independent forums are primarily focused on a particular subject-matter or legal requirements, often ensuring that the operations of the company comply with legislative or regulatory requirements.

Alternative boards constituted as independent forums benefit both from having a clear and transparent terms of reference, as well as a governance framework that is robust and documented. This is particularly important in areas where multiple forums may interact or overlap. Those supporting these different forums often have a dual requirement to support company forums as well and will need to be able to personally differentiate between the two.

13 – Conclusion

Committees are implemented to support the board in being more effective, not to create a complex governance structure. Correctly implemented with clear roles and responsibilities documented in a terms of reference enables the board, committee members themselves and those supporting and contributing to the committee to be confident in the deliverables. When this is effective, a committee can be a powerful tool in the armoury of a company and its board in discharging their duties and maintaining a robust governance structure.

Many may discard these foundations as purely administrative or legal without adding tangible value to a business. But this is not just about having a transparent governance framework. The benefits can be much more advantageous to the day-to-day workings of a company. By focusing requirements in committees containing the best skills and knowledge to perform, resources can be aligned for positive delivery. Centring discussions in formal meetings creates an audit trail for decisions, action plans for delivery and an ability to progress forwards. Without the framework, objectives and deliverables may drift or lack clarity. Without committees, boards with a wide remit may struggle to prioritise or may rely too heavily on external advisers and consultants.

Where there are committees in place, regular review of their deliverables and effectiveness will ensure that they remain beneficial. It will also ensure that committee members have their work recognised for the value that it provides and that their contribution remains effective and beneficial. Particularly where there are multiple committees or a complex governance framework, having a comprehensive review covering the interaction of each of these forums as well as individual committee reviews will ensure that the greatest benefit is achieved. It may also enable best practice to be shared across and between committees.

As a conclusion, it is worth revisiting the benefits of implementing a committee structure, either through one committee or many.

- Expertise: being able to draw on experts on the topic of the committee, thus drilling down into the detail which the board wouldn't have the time and expertise to undertake.
- Time: delegating topic-specific discussions and oversight to a separate forum thus enabling the board to focus its time on other priorities.

- Breadth: enables the company to undertake a detailed review and wider oversight than would be possible through the board in isolation.
- Succession: provides forums that challenge and engage senior employees, thus creating a pool of individuals who are closer to being board ready when the opportunity arises.

Committees can add real benefit and value to a company but only if they are carefully constituted, effectively overseen and have their purpose reviewed to ensure they remain fit for purpose. Hence there are two final questions:

- If you already have a committee(s) are they effective? If not, why not?
- If you don't have any committees, can you afford not to?

Appendices

The standard form terms of reference can be used as the basis for drafting a terms of reference for any committee of the board. Administratively, each committee of the board should benefit from the same support and framework as the board itself to ensure consistency as well as effective and efficient processes. Care should specifically be taken when discussing and agreeing the duties (Section 8), reporting responsibilities (Section 9) and authority (Section 11) to ensure that the committee has clear guidance in their expected actions, their reporting thereon and their authority to act independently.

To download the latest versions of The Chartered Governance Institute's terms of reference, please visit: https://www.icsa.org.uk/knowledge.

Appendix 1 – Terms of reference for the audit committee

Introduction

This guidance note proposes model terms of reference for the audit committee of a company seeking to comply fully with the requirements of the UK Corporate Governance Code, published in July 2018 (the Code) and reflects the FRC Guidance on Audit Committees (FRC Guidance), published in April 2016. It draws on the experience of company secretaries and is based on good practice as carried out in some of the UK's largest listed companies. The Code and the FRC Guidance are available at www.frc.org.uk.

The model terms of reference are intended as a guide for companies to adapt to their needs. In particular

- Companies with additional primary listing(s) may need to amend the terms of reference in light of additional requirements in the relevant country, in particular the US Sarbanes-Oxley Act 2002.
- Some responsibilities that are relevant to certain companies or sectors only are shown in square brackets.
- There are a number of responsibilities that may be carried out by the audit committee which, alternatively, may be carried out by another board committee or at board level and these have been mentioned in footnotes.

The guidance notes on terms of reference for all board committees should be read together when allocating responsibilities to the committees. It is important to recognise the links and overlap between the responsibilities of board committees and consequently the need for each board committee to have full knowledge of the deliberations of other committees through reports to the board and, if possible, by appointing at least one member of a committee to each of the other committees.

The UK Corporate Governance Code

The Code states that

'The board should establish formal and transparent policies and procedures to ensure the independence and effectiveness of internal and external audit functions and satisfy itself on the integrity of financial and narrative statements.'[1]

It also provides that

'The board should establish an audit committee'.[2]

As with most aspects of corporate governance, the company must be seen to be doing all these things in a fair and thorough manner. The responsibilities of the audit committee and the authority delegated to it by the board should be set out in terms of reference and published on the company website.[3]

The audit committee should report to the board on the nature and content of discussion, on recommendations, and on actions to be taken, and adequate time should be made available for discussion when necessary.[4]

The Code clearly sets out the responsibilities that should be included in the role of the audit committee[5] and it is, therefore, essential that the audit committee is properly constituted with a clear remit and identified authority.

Notes on the terms of reference

The list of duties we have proposed is based on existing good practice from a number of sources. Some companies may wish to add to this list and some companies may need to modify it in other ways.[6] The audit committee should take the initiative in deciding the key matters it should consider and what information and assurance it needs to carry out its functions.[7]

The FRC Guidance is designed to assist company boards in making suitable arrangements for their audit committees and provides recommendations on the conduct of the audit committee's relationship with the board, executive management and internal and external auditors. Audit committees are not required to follow the FRC Guidance but it provides a useful framework when implementing the provisions of the Code. It recognises that audit committee arrangements need

---

1   Code Principle M
2   Code Provision 24 and Financial Conduct Authority (FCA) Disclosure and Transparency Rules (DTRs) 7.1.1R
3   FRC Guidance on Board Effectiveness 2018, paragraph 63
4   FRC Guidance on Board Effectiveness, paragraph 62
5   Code Provision 25
6   For example, some companies also require the committee to monitor/make recommendations on the potential implications of legal actions being taken against the company, the adequacy of arrangements for managing conflicts of interest, the expenses incurred by the chair, treasury management policies, monitoring the company's supply chain and processes/procedures for compliance with the Modern Slavery Act 2015, and gender pay gap reporting.
7   FRC Guidance, paragraphs 31, 41 and 42

to be proportionate to the task, and will vary according to the size, complexity and risk profile of the company.[8]

The Code states that the audit committee should comprise a minimum of three independent non-executive directors or, for smaller companies, a minimum of two.[9] The board should satisfy itself that at least one member of the committee has recent and relevant financial experience and that the audit committee as a whole has competence relevant to the sector in which the company operates.[10]

The audit committee should be provided with sufficient resources to undertake its duties.[11] The company secretary is responsible for helping the board and its committees to function effectively[12] and the company secretary (or their nominee) should act as secretary to the committee. The committee should have access to the services of the company secretariat on all audit committee matters including assisting the chair in planning the committee's work, drawing up meeting agendas, maintenance of minutes, drafting of material about its activities for the annual report, collection and distribution of information and provision of any necessary practical support. The company secretary should ensure that the audit committee receives information and papers in a timely manner to enable full and proper consideration to be given to the issues.[13]

The frequency with which the audit committee needs to meet will vary depending on the nature, scale and complexity of the business of a company and external regulatory requirements, which may change from time to time. The FRC Guidance states that it is for the audit committee chair, in consultation with the company secretary, to decide the frequency of meetings. There should be as many meetings as the audit committee's role and responsibilities require and the FRC Guidance recommends there should be no fewer than three meetings each year.[14] When scheduling meetings, there should be a sufficient interval between audit committee meetings and board meetings to allow for work arising from the audit committee to be carried out and reported to the board.[15]

Model terms of reference

Note: square brackets contain recommendations which are in line with best practice but which may need to be changed to suit the circumstances of the particular

---

8   FRC Guidance, paragraph 2
9   A smaller company is one that has been below the FTSE 350 throughout the year immediately prior to the reporting year (see the Code footnote 8)
10 Code Provision 24, FRC Guidance, paragraph 15 and also FCA Rule DTR 7.1.1A R
11 FRC Guidance, paragraph 23
12 FRC Guidance on Board Effectiveness, paragraph 79
13 FRC Guidance, paragraph 25
14 FRC Guidance, paragraph 18
15 FRC Guidance, paragraph 19

organisation, or excluded where not relevant to the company or if the company has a separate risk committee.

1. Membership

1.1 The committee shall comprise at least [three][16] members, all of whom shall be independent non-executive directors. [The committee shall include at least one member of the risk committee.[17]] At least one member shall have recent and relevant financial experience and the committee as a whole shall have competence relevant to the sector in which the company operates.[18] The chair of the board shall not be a member of the committee.[19]

1.2 Members of the committee shall be appointed by the board, on the recommendation of the nomination committee in consultation with the chair of the audit committee.[20] Appointments shall be for a period of up to three years which may be extended for up to two additional three-year periods, provided members continue to be independent.

1.3 Only members of the committee have the right to attend committee meetings. However, the finance director, head of internal audit and external audit lead partner will be invited to attend meetings of the committee on a regular basis and other individuals may be invited to attend all or part of any meeting as and when appropriate.[21]

1.4 The board shall appoint the committee chair. In the absence of the committee chair and/or an appointed deputy at a committee meeting, the remaining members present shall elect one of themselves to chair the meeting.

2. Secretary

The company secretary, or their nominee, shall act as the secretary of the committee and will ensure that the committee receives information and papers in a timely manner to enable full and proper consideration to be given to issues.[22]

---

16 Or in the case of smaller companies (companies below the FTSE 350 index) two members. Code Provision 24 and FRC Guidance, paragraph 9
17 If the board has a separate risk committee
18 Code Provision 24 and FRC Guidance, paragraph 15
19 Code Provision 24
20 FRC Guidance, paragraph 13
21 FRC Guidance on Board Effectiveness 2018, paragraph 64 and FRC Guidance, paragraph 20
22 FRC Guidance, paragraph 25

3. Quorum
The quorum necessary for the transaction of business shall be [two] members.[23]

4. Frequency of meetings
4.1 The committee shall meet at least [three] times a year at appropriate intervals in the financial reporting and audit cycle and otherwise as required.[24]

4.2 Outside of the formal meeting programme, the committee chair will maintain a dialogue with key individuals involved in the company's governance, including the board chair, the chief executive, the finance director, the external audit lead partner and the head of internal audit.[25]

5. Notice of meetings
5.1 Meetings of the committee shall be called by the secretary of the committee at the request of the committee chair or any of its members, or at the request of the external audit lead partner or head of internal audit if they consider it necessary.

5.2 Unless otherwise agreed, notice of each meeting confirming the venue, time and date together with an agenda of items to be discussed, shall be forwarded to each member of the committee and any other person required to attend no later than [five] working days before the date of the meeting. Supporting papers shall be sent to committee members and to other attendees, as appropriate, at the same time.

6. Minutes of meetings
6.1 The secretary shall minute the proceedings and decisions of all committee meetings, including recording the names of those present and in attendance.

6.2 Draft minutes of committee meetings shall be circulated to all members of the committee. Once approved, minutes should be circulated to all other members of the board and the company secretary unless, exceptionally, it would be inappropriate to do so.[26]

---

23 Code Provision 24 requires that at least one member of the committee has recent and relevant financial experience and DTR 7.1.1A R states that one committee member must have competence in accounting and/or auditing. It would therefore be preferable for any quorum to include such a member whenever possible.

24 FRC Guidance, paragraph 18. The frequency and timing of meetings will differ according to the needs of the company and meetings should be organised so that attendance is maximised. The FRC Guidance suggests key dates within the financial reporting and audit cycle might include: when the audit plans (internal and external) are available for review and when interim statements, preliminary announcements and the full annual report are near completion.

25 FRC Guidance, paragraph 22

26 FRC Guidance on Board Effectiveness 2018, paragraph 65

7. Engagement with shareholders

The committee chair should attend the annual general meeting to answer any shareholder questions on the committee's activities.[27] In addition the committee chair should seek engagement with shareholders on significant matters related to the committee's areas of responsibility.[28]

8. Duties[29]

The committee should have oversight of the group as a whole and, unless required otherwise by regulation, carry out the duties below for the parent company, major subsidiary undertakings and the group as a whole, as appropriate.[30]

8.1 Financial reporting

    8.1.1 The committee shall monitor the integrity of the financial statements of the company, including its annual and half-yearly reports, preliminary announcements and any other formal statements relating to its financial performance, and review and report to the board on significant financial reporting issues and judgements which those statements contain having regard to matters communicated to it by the auditor.[31]

    8.1.2 In particular, the committee shall review and challenge where necessary[32]

        8.1.2.1 the application of significant accounting policies and any changes to them

        8.1.2.2 the methods used to account for significant or unusual transactions where different approaches are possible

        8.1.2.3 whether the company has adopted appropriate accounting policies and made appropriate estimates and judgements, taking into account the external auditor's views on the financial statements

        8.1.2.4 the clarity and completeness of disclosures in the financial statements and the context in which statements are made

        8.1.2.5 all material information presented with the financial statements, including the strategic report and the

---

27 FRC Guidance, paragraph 85 and FRC Guidance on Board Effectiveness 2018, paragraph 38
28 Code Provision 3 and FRC Guidance on Board Effectiveness 2018, paragraph 38
29 Code requirements on the main roles and responsibilities of the audit committee can be found at Provision 25
30 FRC Guidance, paragraph 7
31 FRC Guidance, paragraph 32. See also FRC Guidance, paragraph 83 which clarifies that the audit committee would not be expected to disclose information that would be prejudicial to the interests of the company
32 FRC Guidance, paragraphs 32 to 38

corporate governance statements relating to the audit and to risk management.

8.1.3 The committee shall review any other statements requiring board approval which contain financial information first, where to carry out a review prior to board approval would be practicable and consistent with any prompt reporting requirements under any law or regulation including the Listing Rules, Prospectus Rules and Disclosure Guidance and Transparency Rules sourcebook.

8.1.4 Where the committee is not satisfied with any aspect of the proposed financial reporting by the company, it shall report its views to the board.

8.2 Narrative reporting

Where requested by the board, the committee should review the content of the annual report and accounts and advise the board on whether, taken as a whole, it is fair, balanced and understandable and provides the information necessary for shareholders to assess the company's performance, business model and strategy[33] and whether it informs the board's statement in the annual report on these matters that is required under the Code.[34]

8.3 Internal controls and risk management systems[35]

The committee shall

8.3.1 keep under review the company's internal financial controls systems that identify, assess, manage and monitor financial risks, and other internal control and risk management systems[36]

8.3.2 review and approve the statements to be included in the annual report concerning internal control, risk management, including the assessment of principal risks and emerging risks, and the viability statement.[37]

8.4 Compliance, speaking-up and fraud[38]

The committee shall

---

33 Code Provision 25 and FRC Guidance, paragraph 37
34 Code Principle N and Code Provision 27
35 Code Provision 25 See also FRC Guidance, paragraph 41. If the board has a separate board risk committee with responsibility for the review of internal controls and risk management systems, or the board itself has this responsibility under the matters reserved for the decision of the board, the audit committee's responsibilities would be confined to internal financial controls.
36 Code Provision 25. See also FRC Guidance, paragraphs 40 and 41
37 Unless this is carried out by the board or risk committee. Code Provision 28 and FRC Guidance, paragraph 44
38 If the board has a separate risk committee the duties of that committee could include speaking-up, fraud, the prevention of bribery, and procedures for compliance with the Modern Slavery Act 2015. Where the company is required by regulation to have in place a designated non-executive director as 'speaking-up champion', the interaction of their responsibility with the committee's will need to be considered and suitable arrangements put in place.

- 8.4.1 review the adequacy and security of the company's arrangements for its employees, contractors and external parties to raise concerns, in confidence, about possible wrongdoing in financial reporting or other matters. The committee shall ensure that these arrangements allow proportionate and independent investigation of such matters and appropriate follow up action[39]
- 8.4.2 review the company's procedures for detecting fraud
- 8.4.3 review the company's systems and controls for the prevention of bribery and receive reports on non-compliance
- 8.4.4 [review regular reports from the Money Laundering Reporting Officer and the adequacy and effectiveness of the company's anti-money laundering systems and controls]; and
- 8.4.5 [review regular reports from the Compliance Officer and keep under review the adequacy and effectiveness of the company's compliance function].

8.5 Internal audit[40]

The committee shall

- 8.5.1 approve the appointment or termination of appointment of the head of internal audit[41]
- 8.5.2 review and approve the role and mandate of internal audit, monitor and review the effectiveness of its work, and annually approve the internal audit charter ensuring it is appropriate for the current needs of the organisation[42]
- 8.5.3 review and approve the annual internal audit plan to ensure it is aligned to the key risks of the business,[43] and receive regular reports on work carried out
- 8.5.4 ensure internal audit has unrestricted scope, the necessary resources and access to information to enable it to fulfil its mandate, ensure there is open communication between different functions and that the internal audit function evaluates the effectiveness of these functions as part of its internal audit plan, and ensure that the internal audit function is equipped to perform in accordance with appropriate professional standards for internal auditors[44]

---

39 FRC Guidance on Board Effectiveness 2018, paragraphs 57-59
40 If the company does not have an internal audit function, the committee should consider annually whether there should be one and make a recommendation to the board accordingly; the absence of such a function should be explained in the annual report: Code Provision 26 and FRC Guidance, paragraph 46. See also FRC Guidance, paragraphs 45, 47 and 56
41 FRC Guidance, paragraph 52
42 FRC Guidance, paragraph 48
43 FRC Guidance, paragraph 49
44 FRC Guidance, paragraphs 50 and 51. Guidance about the standards can be found in the Chartered Institute of Internal Auditors' Code of Ethics and International Standards for the Professional Practice of Internal Auditing.

- 8.5.5 ensure the internal auditor has direct access to the board chair and to the committee chair, providing independence from the executive and accountability to the committee[45]
- 8.5.6 carry out an annual assessment of the effectiveness of the internal audit function[46] and as part of this assessment
  - 8.5.6.1 meet with the head of internal audit without the presence of management to discuss the effectiveness of the function
  - 8.5.6.2 review and assess the annual internal audit work plan
  - 8.5.6.3 receive a report on the results of the internal auditor's work[47]
  - 8.5.6.4 determine whether it is satisfied that the quality, experience and expertise of internal audit is appropriate for the business[48]
  - 8.5.6.5 review the actions taken by management to implement the recommendations of internal audit and to support the effective working of the internal audit function[49]
- 8.5.7 monitor and assess the role and effectiveness of the internal audit function in the overall context of the company's risk management system and the work of compliance, finance and the external auditor[50]
- 8.5.8 consider whether an independent, third party review of processes is appropriate.[51]

8.6 External Audit

The committee shall
- 8.6.1 consider and make recommendations to the board, to be put to shareholders for approval at the AGM, in relation to the appointment, re-appointment and removal of the company's external auditor[52]
- 8.6.2 develop and oversee the selection procedure for the appointment of the audit firm in accordance with applicable Code and regulatory requirements, ensuring that all tendering firms have access to all

---

45 FRC Guidance, paragraph 52
46 FRC Guidance, paragraph 53
47 FRC Guidance, paragraph 54
48 FRC Guidance, paragraph 53
49 FRC Guidance, paragraph 53
50 FRC Guidance, paragraph 49. If the board has a separate risk committee, the duties of that committee could include review of the company's internal control and risk management systems
51 FRC Guidance, paragraph 55
52 Code Provision 25 and FRC Guidance, paragraphs 58 and 60

necessary information and individuals during the tendering process[53]

8.6.3 if an external auditor resigns, investigate the issues leading to this and decide whether any action is required[54]

8.6.4 oversee the relationship with the external auditor. In this context the committee shall

    8.6.4.1 approve their remuneration, including both fees for audit and non-audit services, and ensure that the level of fees is appropriate to enable an effective and high-quality audit to be conducted[55]

    8.6.4.2 approve their terms of engagement, including any engagement letter issued at the start of each audit and the scope of the audit[56]

8.6.5 assess annually the external auditor's independence and objectivity[57] taking into account relevant law, regulation, the Ethical Standard[58] and other professional requirements and the group's relationship with the auditor as a whole, including any threats to the auditor's independence and the safeguards applied to mitigate those threats[59] including the provision of any non-audit services

8.6.6 satisfy itself that there are no relationships between the auditor and the company (other than in the ordinary course of business) which could adversely affect the auditor's independence and objectivity[60]

8.6.7 agree with the board a policy on the employment of former employees of the company's auditor, taking into account the Ethical Standard[61] and legal requirements, and monitor the application of this policy[62]

8.6.8 monitor the auditor's processes for maintaining independence, its compliance with relevant law, regulation, other professional requirements and the Ethical Standard,[63] including the guidance on the rotation of audit partner and staff[64]

---

53 FRC Guidance, paragraph 59. For additional guidance see FRC Audit Tenders Notes on Best Practice February 2017
54 FRC Guidance, paragraph 61
55 Code Provision 25 and FRC Guidance, paragraphs 63 and 65
56 Code Provision 25 and FRC Guidance, paragraphs 63 and 64
57 Code Provision 25
58 FRC Revised Ethical Standard December 2019
59 FRC Guidance, paragraph 66
60 FRC Guidance, paragraph 66
61 FRC Revised Ethical Standard December 2019, section 2
62 FRC Guidance, paragraph 69
63 FRC Revised Ethical Standard December 2019
64 FRC Guidance, paragraphs 66, 67, 68 and 70

8.6.9 monitor the level of fees paid by the company to the external auditor compared to the overall fee income of the firm, office and partner and assess these in the context of relevant legal, professional and regulatory requirements, guidance and the Ethical Standard[65]

8.6.10 assess annually the qualifications, expertise and resources, and independence of the external auditor and the effectiveness of the external audit process, which shall include a report from the external auditor on their own internal quality procedures[66]

8.6.11 seek to ensure coordination of the external audit with the activities of the internal audit function

8.6.12 evaluate the risks to the quality and effectiveness of the financial reporting process in the light of the external auditor's communications with the committee[67]

8.6.13 develop and recommend to the board the company's formal policy on the provision of non-audit services by the auditor, including prior approval of non-audit services by the committee and specifying the types of non-audit service to be pre-approved, and assessment of whether non-audit services have a direct or material effect on the audited financial statements.[68] The policy should include consideration of the following matters

    8.6.13.1 threats to the independence and objectivity of the external auditor and any safeguards in place

    8.6.13.2 the nature of the non-audit services

    8.6.13.3 whether the external audit firm is the most suitable supplier of the non-audit service

    8.6.13.4 the fees for the non-audit services, both individually and in aggregate, relative to the audit fee

    8.6.13.5 the criteria governing compensation.[69]

8.6.14 meet regularly with the external auditor (including once at the planning stage before the audit and once after the audit at the reporting stage) and, at least once a year, meet with the external auditor without management being present, to discuss the auditor's remit and any issues arising from the audit[70]

8.6.15 discuss with the external auditor the factors that could affect audit quality and review and approve the annual audit plan, ensuring it is

---

65 FRC Guidance, paragraph 67 See also FRC Revised Ethical Standard December 2019, section 4
66 FRC Guidance, paragraph 60
67 FRC Guidance, paragraph 62
68 Code Provision 25 and FRC Guidance, paragraphs 71 to 74
69 Code Provision 25 and FRC Guidance, paragraph 72
70 FRC Guidance, paragraph 21

consistent with the scope of the audit engagement, having regard to the seniority, expertise and experience of the audit team[71]

8.6.16 review the findings of the audit with the external auditor. This shall include but not be limited to, the following

8.6.16.1 a discussion of any major issues which arose during the audit

8.6.16.2 the auditor's explanation of how the risks to audit quality were addressed

8.6.16.3 key accounting and audit judgements

8.6.16.4 the auditor's view of their interactions with senior management

8.6.16.5 levels of errors identified during the audit[72]

8.6.17 review any representation letter(s) requested by the external auditor before it is (they are) signed by management[73]

8.6.18 review the management letter and management's response to the auditor's findings and recommendations[74]

8.6.19 review the effectiveness of the audit process, including an assessment of the quality of the audit, the handling of key judgements by the auditor, and the auditor's response to questions from the committee[75]

9. Reporting responsibilities

9.1 The committee chair shall report formally to the board on its proceedings after each meeting on all matters within its duties and responsibilities and shall also formally report to the board on how it has discharged its responsibilities.[76] This report shall include

9.1.1 the significant issues that it considered in relation to the financial statements (required under paragraph 8.1.1) and how these were addressed

9.1.2 its assessment of the effectiveness of the external audit process (required under paragraph 8.6.10), the approach taken to the appointment or reappointment of the external auditor, length of tenure of audit firm, when a tender was last conducted and advance notice of any retendering plans

9.1.3 any other issues on which the board has requested the committee's opinion[77]

---

71 FRC Guidance, paragraph 75
72 FRC Guidance, paragraph 76
73 FRC Guidance, paragraph 77
74 FRC Guidance, paragraph 77
75 FRC Guidance, paragraphs 78 and 79
76 Code Provision 25
77 FRC Guidance, paragraph 29

9.2 The committee shall make whatever recommendations to the board it deems appropriate on any area within its remit where action or improvement is needed.

9.3 The committee shall compile a report on its activities to be included in the company's annual report.[78] The report should describe the work of the audit committee, including

9.3.1 the significant issues that the committee considered in relation to the financial statements and how these issues were addressed

9.3.2 an explanation of how the committee has assessed the independence and effectiveness of the external audit process and the approach taken to the appointment or reappointment of the external auditor, information on the length of tenure of the current audit firm, when a tender was last conducted and advance notice of any retendering plans

9.3.3 an explanation of how auditor independence and objectivity are safeguarded if the external auditor provides non-audit services, having regard to matters communicated to it by the auditor and all other information requirements set out in the Code.

9.4 In compiling the reports referred to in 9.1 and 9.3, the committee should exercise judgement in deciding which of the issues it considers in relation to the financial statements are significant, but should include at least those matters that have informed the board's assessment of whether the company is a going concern and the inputs to the board's viability statement.[79] The report to shareholders need not repeat information disclosed elsewhere in the annual report and accounts but could provide cross-references to that information.[80]

10 Other matters

The committee shall

10.1 Have access to sufficient resources in order to carry out its duties, including access to the company secretariat for advice and assistance as required.[81]

10.2 Be provided with appropriate and timely training, both in the form of an induction programme for new members and on an ongoing basis for all members.[82]

10.3 Give due consideration to all relevant laws and regulations, the provisions of the Code and published guidance, the requirements of the FCA's Listing

---

78 Code Provision 26
79 FRC Guidance, paragraphs 44 and 82
80 FRC Guidance, paragraph 84
81 Code Provision 16, FRC Guidance on Board Effectiveness 2018, paragraphs 79-85 and FRC Guidance, paragraph 23
82 FRC Guidance on Board Effectiveness, paragraph 81

Rules, Prospectus Rules and Disclosure Guidance and Transparency Rules sourcebook and any other applicable rules, as appropriate.

10.4 Be responsible for oversight of the coordination of the internal and external auditors.[83]

10.5 Oversee any investigation of activities which are within its terms of reference.

10.6 Work and liaise as necessary with all other board committees ensuring interaction between committees and with the board is reviewed regularly, taking particular account of the impact of risk management and internal controls being delegated to different committees.[84]

10.7 Ensure that a periodic evaluation of the committee's performance is carried out.

10.8 At least annually, review its constitution and terms of reference to ensure it is operating at maximum effectiveness and recommend any changes it considers necessary to the board for approval.[85]

11. Authority

The committee is authorised to

11.1 Seek any information it requires from any employee of the company in order to perform its duties.

11.2 Obtain, at the company's expense, independent legal, accounting or other professional advice on any matter if it believes it necessary to do so.[86]

11.3 Call any employee to be questioned at a meeting of the committee as and when required.

11.4 Have the right to publish in the company's annual report, details of any issues that cannot be resolved between the committee and the board.[87] If the board has not accepted the committee's recommendation on the external auditor appointment, reappointment or removal, the annual report should include a statement explaining the committee's recommendation and the reasons why the board has taken a different position.[88]

---

83 FRC Guidance, paragraph 49
84 FRC Guidance on Board Effectiveness paragraph 65 and FRC Guidance, paragraph 43
85 FRC Guidance on Board Effectiveness, paragraph 63
86 FRC Guidance on Board Effectiveness 2018 paragraph 83 and FRC Guidance, paragraph 26
87 FRC Guidance, paragraph 30
88 Code Provision 26

Appendix 2 – Terms of reference for the remuneration committee

Introduction

This guidance note proposes model terms of reference for the remuneration committee of a company seeking to comply fully with the requirements of the UK Corporate Governance Code, published in July 2018 (the Code). It draws on the experience of company secretaries and is based on good practice as carried out in some of the UK's largest listed companies. The Code is available at www.frc.org.uk.

The model terms of reference are intended as a guide for companies to adapt to their needs. In particular

- Companies with additional primary listing(s) may need to amend the terms of reference in light of additional requirements in the relevant country, in particular the US Sarbanes-Oxley Act 2002.
- Some responsibilities that are relevant to certain companies or sectors only are shown in square brackets.

The guidance notes on terms of reference for all board committees should be read together when allocating responsibilities to the committees. It is important to recognise the links and overlap between the responsibilities of board committees and consequently the need for each board committee to have full knowledge of the deliberations of other committees through reports to the board and, if possible, by appointing at least one member of a committee to each of the other committees.

The UK Corporate Governance Code

The Code states that

'A formal and transparent procedure for developing policy on executive remuneration and determining director and senior management[1] remuneration should be established.'[2]

---

1 Footnote 4 to the Code defines 'senior management' for these purposes as the executive committee or the first layer of management below board level, including the company secretary
2 Code Principle Q

It also provides that

> 'The board should establish a remuneration committee[3] ... with appropriate terms of reference, which should be published on the company website.'[4]

As with most aspects of corporate governance, the company must be seen to be doing all these things in a fair and thorough manner. The Code requires companies to go through a formal process of considering executive remuneration. It is essential that the remuneration committee be properly constituted with a clear remit and identified authority.

Notes on the terms of reference

The list of duties of the remuneration committee is based on existing best practice from a number of sources. Some companies may wish to add to this list and some companies may need to modify it in other ways.

The Code states that the remuneration committee should comprise at least three independent non-executive directors (or in the case of smaller companies,[5] two). In addition to the independent non-executives, the chair of the board may also be a member of the remuneration committee if they were considered independent on appointment as chair of the board, but may not chair the committee.[6]

The company secretary is responsible for helping the board and its committees to function effectively.[7] The company secretary (or their nominee) should act as secretary to the committee. The committee should also have access to the services of the company secretariat on all remuneration committee matters, including assisting the chair in planning the committee's work, drawing up meeting agendas, maintenance of minutes, drafting of material about its activities for the annual report, collection and distribution of information and provision of any necessary practical support. The company secretary should ensure that the remuneration committee receives information and papers in a timely manner to enable full and proper consideration to be given to the issues.

The frequency with which the remuneration committee needs to meet will vary depending on the nature, scale and complexity of the business of a company and external regulatory requirements, which may change from time to time. It is clear, however, that it must meet close to the year end to review the executive directors' remuneration policy and the directors' remuneration report which quoted companies must submit to shareholders for approval at the AGM. It is

---

3   Code Provision 32
4   FRC Guidance on Board Effectiveness 2018, paragraph 63
5   A smaller company is defined in footnote 8 to the Code as one which is below the FTSE 350 throughout the year immediately prior to the reporting year
6   Code Provision 32
7   FRC Guidance on Board Effectiveness 2018, paragraph 79

recommended that the remuneration committee should meet at least twice a year in order to effectively discharge its responsibilities.

Model terms of reference

Note: square brackets contain recommendations which are in line with best practice but which may need to be changed to suit the circumstances of the particular organisation.

1. Membership

1.1 The committee shall comprise at least [three] members, all of whom shall be independent non-executive directors. The chair of the board may also serve on the committee as an additional member if they were considered independent on appointment as chair.[8]

1.2 Appointments to the committee are made by the board on the recommendation of the nomination committee and in consultation with the chair of the remuneration committee and shall be for a period of up to three years which may be extended for up to two additional three-year periods, provided members (other than the chair of the board, if they are a member of the committee) continue to be independent.

1.3 Only members of the committee have the right to attend committee meetings. However, other individuals such as the chief executive, the head of human resources and external advisers may be invited to attend for all or part of any meeting, as and when appropriate.[9]

1.4 The board shall appoint the committee chair who shall be an independent non-executive director who should have served on a remuneration committee for at least 12 months.[10] In the absence of the committee chair and/or an appointed deputy, the remaining members present shall elect one of themselves to chair the meeting who would qualify under these terms of reference to be appointed to that position by the board. The chair of the board shall not be chair of the committee.

2. Secretary

The company secretary or their nominee shall act as the secretary of the committee and will ensure that the committee receives information and papers in a timely manner to enable full and proper consideration to be given to the issues.

3. Quorum

The quorum necessary for the transaction of business shall be [two].

---

8 Code Provision 32
9 FRC Guidance on Board Effectiveness 2018, paragraph 64
10 Code Provision 32

4. Frequency of meetings

The committee shall meet at least [twice] a year and otherwise as required.[11]

5. Notice of meetings

5.1 Meetings of the committee shall be called by the secretary of the committee at the request of the committee chair or any of its members.

5.2 Unless otherwise agreed, notice of each meeting confirming the venue, time and date together with an agenda of items to be discussed, shall be forwarded to each member of the committee and any other person required to attend no later than [five] working days before the date of the meeting. Supporting papers shall be sent to committee members and to other attendees, as appropriate, at the same time.

6. Minutes of meetings

6.1 The secretary shall minute the proceedings and resolutions of all committee meetings, including the names of those present and in attendance.

6.2 Draft minutes of committee meetings shall be circulated to all members of the committee. Once approved, minutes should be circulated to all other members of the board and the company secretary unless, exceptionally, it would be inappropriate to do so.[12]

7. Engagement with shareholders

The committee chair should attend the annual general meeting to answer any shareholder questions on the committee's activities.[13] In addition, the committee chair should seek engagement with shareholders on significant matters related to the committee's areas of responsibility.[14]

8. Duties

The committee should carry out the duties detailed below for the parent company, major subsidiary undertakings and the group as a whole, as appropriate.

The committee shall

8.1 Have delegated responsibility for determining the policy for directors' remuneration and setting remuneration for the company's chair and executive

---

11 The frequency and timing of meetings will differ according to the needs of the company and external regulatory requirements. Meetings should be organised so that attendance is maximised.
12 FRC Guidance on Board Effectiveness 2018, paragraph 65
13 FRC Guidance on Board Effectiveness 2018, paragraph 38
14 Code Provision 3 and FRC Guidance on Board Effectiveness 2018, paragraph 136

directors and senior management, including the company secretary[15], in accordance with the Principles and Provisions of the Code.[16]

8.2 Establish remuneration schemes that promote long-term shareholding by executive directors that support alignment with long-term shareholder interests, with share awards subject to a total vesting and holding period of at least five years, and a formal policy for post-employment shareholding requirements encompassing both unvested and vested shares.[17]

8.3 Design remuneration policies and practices to support strategy and promote long-term sustainable success, with executive remuneration aligned to company purpose and values, clearly linked to the successful delivery of the company's long-term strategy, and that enable the use of discretion to override formulaic outcomes and to recover and/or withhold sums or share awards under appropriate specified circumstances.[18]

8.4 When determining executive director remuneration policy and practices, consider the Code requirements for clarity, simplicity, risk mitigation, predictability, proportionality and alignment to culture.[19]

8.5 No director or senior manager shall be involved in any decisions as to their own remuneration outcome.[20] The board itself or, where required by the Articles of Association, the shareholders should determine the remuneration of the non-executive directors within the limits set in the Articles of Association.[21]

8.6 In determining remuneration policy, take into account all other factors which it deems necessary including relevant legal and regulatory requirements, the provisions and recommendations of the Code and associated guidance. The objective of such policy shall be to attract, retain and motivate executive management of the quality required to run the company successfully without paying more than is necessary, having regard to views of shareholders and other stakeholders.

8.7 Review the ongoing appropriateness and relevance of the remuneration policy.

8.8 Within the terms of the agreed policy and in consultation with the chair and/or chief executive, as appropriate, determine the total individual remuneration package of each executive director, the company chair and senior

---

15 Code Provision 33. Footnote 4 to the Code defines 'senior management' for these purposes as the executive committee or the first layer of management below board level, including the company secretary. See also FRC Guidance on Board Effectiveness, paragraph 80.
16 See Code Principle P and Code Provisions 33 and 38 to 40. See also FRC Guidance on Board Effectiveness 2018, paragraphs 130-135.
17 Code Provision 36
18 Code Principle P and Provision 37. See also FRC Guidance on Board Effectiveness 2018, paragraphs 133-135
19 Code Provision 40
20 Code Principle Q
21 Code Provision 34

managers including bonuses, incentive payments and share options or other share awards. The choice of financial, non-financial and strategic measures is important[22], as is the exercise of independent judgement and discretion when determining remuneration awards, taking account of company and individual performance, and wider circumstances.[23]

8.9 Have full authority to appoint remuneration consultants[24] and to commission or purchase any reports, surveys or information which it deems necessary at the expense of the company. However the committee should avoid designing pay structures based solely on benchmarking to the market or on the advice of remuneration consultants.[25]

8.10 Review the design of all share incentive plans for approval by the board and, where required, shareholders. For any such plans, determine each year whether awards will be made, and if so, the overall amount of such awards, the individual awards for executive directors and senior managers, and the performance targets to be used.[26]

8.11 Review workforce remuneration and related policies.[27]

8.12 Work and liaise as necessary with other board committees, ensuring the interaction between committees and with the board is reviewed regularly.[28]

9. Reporting responsibilities

9.1 The committee chair shall report to the board after each meeting on the nature and content of its discussion, recommendations and action to be taken.[29]

9.2 The committee shall make whatever recommendations to the board it deems appropriate on any area within its remit where action or improvement is needed, and adequate time should be available for board discussion when necessary.[30]

9.3 The committee shall provide a description of its work in the annual report in line with the requirements of the UK Corporate Governance Code.[31]

9.4 The committee shall also ensure that provisions regarding disclosure of information as set out in The Companies (Directors' Remuneration Policy and Directors' Remuneration Report) Regulations 2019[32] and the Code are

---

22 FRC Guidance on Board Effectiveness 2018, paragraph 137
23 Code Principle R and FRC Guidance on Board Effectiveness 2018, paragraph 138
24 Code Provision 35
25 FRC Guidance on Board Effectiveness 2018, paragraph 134
26 FRC Guidance on Board Effectiveness 2018, paragraphs 135 and 137
27 Code Provision 33 and FRC Guidance on Board Effectiveness 2018, paragraph 130
28 FRC Guidance on Board Effectiveness 2018, paragraph 65
29 FRC Guidance on Board Effectiveness 2018, paragraph 62
30 FRC Guidance on Board Effectiveness 2018, paragraph 62
31 See Code Provision 41
32 For detailed guidance on the reporting requirements see GC100 and Investor Group: Directors' Remuneration Reporting Guidance 2019

fulfilled, and that a report on the directors' remuneration policy and practices is included in the company's annual report and put to shareholders for approval at the AGM as necessary.

9.5 If the committee has appointed remuneration consultants, the consultant should be identified in the annual report alongside a statement about any other connection it has with the company or individual directors.[33]

10. Other matters

The committee shall

10.1 Have access to sufficient resources in order to carry out its duties, including access to the company secretariat for advice and assistance as required.[34]

10.2 Be provided with appropriate an timely training, both in the form of an induction programme for new members and on an ongoing basis for all members.[35]

10.3 Give due consideration to all relevant laws and regulations, the provisions of the Code and published guidelines or recommendations regarding the remuneration of company directors and the formation and operation of share incentive plans, the requirements of the FCA's Listing Rules, Prospectus Rules, Disclosure Guidance and Transparency Rules sourcebook, and any other applicable rules, as appropriate.

10.4 Ensure that a periodic evaluation of the committee's own performance is carried out.

10.5 At least annually, review its constitution and terms of reference to ensure it is operating at maximum effectiveness and recommend any changes it considers necessary to the board for approval.[36]

11. Authority

The committee is authorised by the board to obtain, at the company's expense, outside legal or other professional advice on any matters within its terms of reference.[37]

---

33 Code Provision 35
34 Code Provision 16 and FRC Guidance on Board Effectiveness 2018, paragraphs 79-85
35 FRC Guidance on Board Effectiveness 2018, paragraph 81
36 See FRC Guidance on Board Effectiveness 2018, paragraph 63
37 FRC Guidance on Board Effectiveness 2018, paragraph 83

Appendix 3 – Terms of reference for the nomination committee

Introduction

This guidance note proposes model terms of reference for the nomination committee of a company seeking to comply fully with the requirements of the UK Corporate Governance Code, published July 2018 (the Code). It draws on the experience of company secretaries and is based on good practice as carried out in some of the UK's largest listed companies. The Code is available at www.frc.org.uk.

The model terms of reference are intended as a guide for companies to adapt to their needs. In particular

- Companies with additional primary listing(s) may need to amend the terms of reference in light of additional requirements in the relevant country.
- Some responsibilities that are relevant to certain companies or sectors only are shown in square brackets.

The guidance notes on terms of reference for all board committees should be read together when allocating responsibilities to the committees. It is important to recognise the links and overlap between the responsibilities of board committees and consequently the need for each board committee to have full knowledge of the deliberations of other committees through reports to the board and, if possible, by appointing at least one member of a committee to each of the other committees.

The UK Corporate Governance Code

The Code states that

> 'Appointments to the board should be subject to a formal, rigorous and transparent procedure and an effective succession plan should be maintained for board and senior management.'[1]

---

1 Code Principle J

It also provides that

> 'The board should establish a nomination committee to lead the process for appointments, ensure plans are in place for orderly succession to both the board and senior management positions, and oversee the development of a diverse pipeline for succession.'[2]

The Code also states that 'a successful company is led by an effective and entrepreneurial board, whose role is to promote the long-term sustainable success of the company.'[3]

The board and its committees should have a combination of skills, experience and knowledge. Its membership should be regularly refreshed and non-executive directors should have sufficient time to meet their board responsibilities.[4]

As with most aspects of corporate governance, the company must be seen to be doing all these things in a fair and thorough manner. The terms of reference of the nomination committee, explaining its role and the authority delegated to it by the board, should be published on the company's website.[5] It is, therefore, essential that the nomination committee be properly constituted with a clear remit and identified authority.

Notes on the terms of reference

The list of duties of the nomination committee is based on existing best practice from a number of sources. Some companies may wish to add to this list and some companies may need to modify it in other ways.

The Code states that the majority of members serving on the nomination committee should be independent non-executive directors although it gives no guidance on the overall size of the committee.[6] We have recommended a committee of at least three but companies with larger boards may wish to consider increasing this number. Unlike other board committees, the chair of the board can be chair of the nomination committee.[7] The Code provides that a majority of members should be independent, rather than all, therefore membership can include executive directors such as the chief executive.[8]

---

2   Code Provision 17
3   Code Principle A
4   Code Principles H and K
5   FRC Guidance on Board Effectiveness 2018, paragraph 63
6   Code Provision 17. Guidance on circumstances likely to affect independence is provided in Code Provision 10
7   Code Provision 17. However the chair of the board should not chair the nomination committee when it is dealing with the appointment of their successor as chair
8   Code Provision 17

The company secretary is responsible for helping the board and its committees to function effectively.[9] The company secretary (or their nominee) should act as secretary to the nomination committee. The committee should also have access to the services of the company secretariat on all committee matters, including assisting the chair in planning the committee's work, drawing up meeting agendas, maintenance of minutes, drafting of material about its activities for the annual report, collection and distribution of information and provision of any necessary practical support. The company secretary should ensure that the nomination committee receives information and papers in a timely manner to enable full and proper consideration to be given to the issues.

The frequency with which the committee needs to meet will vary considerably from company to company and may change from time to time. It is, however, good practice to plan a minimum number of meetings each year to cover the review of items that form part of the regular cycle, such as directors subject to annual re-election or retiring by rotation, and senior management succession, and to review the statement of the committee's activities in the annual report. In addition there will need to be ad hoc meetings for the committee to consider new appointments.

Model terms of reference

Note: square brackets contain recommendations which are in line with best practice but which may need to be changed to suit the circumstances of the particular organisation.

1. Membership

1.1   The committee shall comprise at least [three] directors. A majority of the members of the committee shall be independent non-executive directors.[10]

1.2   Appointments to the committee are made by the board on the recommendation of the nomination committee and shall be for a period of up to three years, which may be extended for up to two additional three-year periods, provided the director still meets the criteria for membership of the committee.

1.3   Only members of the committee have the right to attend committee meetings. However, other individuals such as the chief executive, the head of human resources and external advisers may be invited to attend for all or part of any meeting, as and when appropriate.[11]

1.4   The board shall appoint the committee chair who should be either the chair of the board or an independent non-executive director. In the absence of the

---

9   FRC Guidance on Board Effectiveness 2018, paragraph 79
10   Code Provision 17
11   FRC Guidance on Board Effectiveness 2018, paragraph 64

committee chair and/or an appointed deputy, the remaining members present shall elect one of themselves to chair the meeting from those who would qualify under these terms of reference to be appointed to that position by the board. The chair of the board shall not chair the committee when it is dealing with the matter of succession of the chair of the board.[12]

2. Secretary

The company secretary, or their nominee, shall act as the secretary of the committee and will ensure that the committee receives information and papers in a timely manner to enable full and proper consideration to be given to issues.

3. Quorum

The quorum necessary for the transaction of business shall be [two] [both of whom must be independent non-executive directors].

4. Frequency of meetings

The committee shall meet at least [twice] a year[13] and otherwise as required.[14]

5. Notice of meetings

5.1 Meetings of the committee shall be called by the secretary of the committee at the request of the committee chair or any of its members.

5.2 Unless otherwise agreed, notice of each meeting confirming the venue, time and date, together with an agenda of items to be discussed, shall be forwarded to each member of the committee and any other person required to attend no later than [five] working days before the date of the meeting. Supporting papers shall be sent to committee members and to other attendees, as appropriate, at the same time.

6. Minutes of meetings

6.1 The secretary shall minute the proceedings and decisions of all committee meetings, including recording the names of those present and in attendance.

6.2 Draft minutes of committee meetings shall be circulated to all members of the committee. Once approved, minutes should be circulated to all other members of the board and the company secretary unless, exceptionally, it would be inappropriate to do so.[15]

---

12 Code Provision 17
13 Some small companies may not need more than one scheduled meeting of the nomination committee each year.
14 The frequency and timing of meetings will differ according to the needs of the company. Meetings should be organised so that attendance is maximised.
15 Guidance on Board Effectiveness 2018, paragraph 65

7. Engagement with shareholders

7.1 The committee chair should attend the annual general meeting to answer any shareholder questions on the committee's activities.[16] In addition the committee chair should seek engagement with shareholders on significant matters related to the committee's areas of responsibility.[17]

8. Duties

The committee should carry out the duties below for the parent company, major subsidiary undertakings and the group as a whole, as appropriate.

The committee shall

8.1 Regularly review the structure, size and composition (including the skills, knowledge, experience and diversity) of the board and make recommendations to the board with regard to any changes.

8.2 Ensure plans are in place for orderly succession to board and senior management positions, and oversee the development of a diverse pipeline for succession[18], taking into account the challenges and opportunities facing the company, and the skills and expertise needed on the board in the future.

8.3 Keep under review the leadership needs of the organisation, both executive and non-executive, with a view to ensuring the continued ability of the organisation to compete effectively in the marketplace.

8.4 Keep up-to-date and fully informed about strategic issues and commercial changes affecting the company and the market in which it operates.

8.5 Be responsible for identifying and nominating for the approval of the board, candidates to fill board vacancies as and when they arise.

8.6 Before any appointment is made by the board, evaluate the balance of skills, knowledge, experience and diversity on the board and, in the light of this evaluation, prepare a description of the role and capabilities required for a particular appointment and the time commitment expected. In identifying suitable candidates the committee shall

    8.6.1 use open advertising or the services of external advisers to facilitate the search

    8.6.2 consider candidates from a wide range of backgrounds

    8.6.3 consider candidates on merit and against objective criteria, having due regard to the benefits of diversity on the board and taking care

---

16 Guidance on Board Effectiveness 2018, paragraph 38
17 Code Provision 3
18 Code Provision 17

that appointees have enough time available to devote to the position.[19]

8.7 Prior to the appointment of a director, other significant time commitments should be disclosed and any additional future commitments should not be undertaken without prior approval of the board.[20] The proposed appointee should also be required to disclose any other business interests that may result in a conflict of interest. These must be authorised by the board prior to appointment and any future business interests that could result in a conflict of interest must not be undertaken without prior authorisation of the board.[21]

8.8 Ensure that, on appointment to the board, non-executive directors receive a formal letter of appointment setting out clearly what is expected of them in terms of time commitment, committee service and involvement outside board meetings.[22]

8.9 Review the results of the board performance evaluation process that relate to the composition of the board and succession planning.[23]

8.10 Review annually the time required from non-executive directors. Performance evaluation should be used to assess whether the non-executive directors are spending enough time to fulfil their duties.

8.11 Work and liaise as necessary with other board committees, ensuring the interaction between committees and with the board is reviewed regularly.[24]
The committee shall also make recommendations to the board concerning

8.12 Any changes needed to the succession planning process if its periodic assessment indicates the desired outcomes have not been achieved.[25]

8.13 Suitable candidates as new directors and succession for existing directors.

8.14 Membership of the audit and remuneration committees, and any other board committees as appropriate, in consultation with the chair of those committees.

8.15 The re-appointment of non-executive directors at the conclusion of their specified term of office having given due regard to their performance and ability to continue to contribute to the board in the light of knowledge, skills and experience required.

8.16 The re-election by shareholders of directors under the annual re-election

---

19 The Code Principle H and Provision 15. See also FRC Guidance on Board Effectiveness 2018, paragraphs 92-95 and The Chartered Governance Institute guidance on liability of non-executive directors: care, skill and diligence; joining the right board: due diligence for prospective directors; and sample non-executive director's appointment letter.
20 Code Provision 15
21 Companies Act 2006 section 175 and in accordance with the company's articles of association
22 FRC Guidance on Board Effectiveness 2018, paragraph 96
23 FRC Guidance on Board Effectiveness 2018, paragraph 109
24 FRC Guidance on Board Effectiveness 2018, paragraph 65
25 FRC Guidance on Board Effectiveness 2018, paragraph 97

provisions of the Code[26] or the retirement by rotation provisions in the company's articles of association, having due regard to their performance and ability, and why their contribution is important to the company's long-term sustainable success in the light of the skills, experience and knowledge required and the need for progressive refreshing of the board, taking into account the length of service of individual directors, the chair and the board as whole.[27]

8.17 Any matters relating to the continuation in office of any director at any time including the suspension or termination of service of an executive director as an employee of the company subject to the provisions of the law and their service contract.

8.18 The appointment of any director to executive or other office.

9. Reporting responsibilities

9.1 The committee chair shall report to the board after each meeting on the nature and content of its discussion, recommendations and action to be taken.

9.2 The committee shall make whatever recommendations to the board it deems appropriate on any area within its remit where action or improvement is needed, and adequate time should be made available for board discussion when necessary.[28]

9.3 The committee shall produce a report to be included in the company's annual report describing the work of the nomination committee, including

9.3.1 the process used in relation to appointments, its approach to succession planning and how both support the development of a diverse pipeline

9.3.2 how board evaluation has been conducted, the nature and extent of an external evaluator's contact with the board and individual directors, the outcomes and actions taken, and how it has influenced or will influence board composition

9.3.3 the policy on diversity and inclusion, its objectives and linkage to company strategy, how it has been implemented and progress on achieving the objectives, and

9.3.4 the gender balance of those in the senior management team and their direct reports.[29]

---

26 Code Provision 18
27 Code Principle K and Provisions 10, 18 and 19. See also FRC Guidance on Board Effectiveness 2018, paragraphs 102-105
28 FRC Guidance on Board Effectiveness 2018 paragraph 62
29 Code Provision 23. Footnote 4 of The Code defines 'senior management' for these purposes as the executive committee or the first layer of management below board level, including the company secretary.

9.4 If an external search consultancy has been engaged, it should be identified in the annual report alongside a statement about any other connection it has with the company or individual directors.[30]

10. Other matters

The committee shall

10.1 Have access to sufficient resources in order to carry out its duties, including access to the company secretariat for advice and assistance as required.[31]

10.2 Be provided with appropriate and timely training, both in the form of an induction programme for new members and on an ongoing basis for all members.[32]

10.3 Give due consideration to all relevant laws and regulations, the provisions of the Code and associated guidance, the requirements of the FCA's Listing Rules, Prospectus Rules and Disclosure Guidance and Transparency Rules sourcebook and any other applicable rules, as appropriate.

10.4 Ensure that a periodic evaluation of the committee's own performance is carried out.

10.5 At least annually, review the committee's constitution and terms of reference to ensure it is operating at maximum effectiveness and recommend any changes it considers necessary to the board for approval.[33]

11. Authority

The committee is authorised by the board to obtain, at the company's expense, outside legal or other professional advice on any matters within its terms of reference.[34]

Further reading

The Chartered Governance Institute and EY report The nomination committee – coming out of the shadows May 2016 (www.icsa.org.uk/assets/files/policy/research/ey-nomination-committee-digital.pdf).

---

30 Code Provision 20
31 Code Provision 16 and FRC Guidance on Board Effectiveness 2018, paragraphs 79-85
32 FRC Guidance on Board Effectiveness 2018, paragraph 81
33 FRC Guidance on Board Effectiveness 2018, paragraph 63
34 FRC Guidance on Board Effectiveness 2018, paragraph 83

Directory

References

Chris Hodge (2018), *A Guide to Better Board Reporting*, ICSA.

Cranfield (2019), *FTSE CEO pay drops: expert explains the rise and fall of executive pay*, Cranfield School of Management.

Elise Perraud (2019), *Why Companies Should Consider Setting Up Advisory Boards*, NEDonBoard.

Elise Perraud (2019), *The 5 Factors that will enable Effective Advisory Boards*, NEDonBoard.

George Anderson, Kevin M. Connelly, Julie Hembrock and Ann Yerger (2019), *Nominating/Governance Committee: Oversight of Board Composition, Function & Evaluations*, SpencerStuart.

HM Treasury (2013), *Infrastructure Carbon Review*, UK Government.

ICSA and Board Intelligence (2017), *Challenges to Effective Board Reporting*, ICSA and Board Intelligence.

ICSA and EY (2014), *The Nomination Committee – Coming out of the shadows*, ICSA, The Governance Institute and EY.

In Touch (2019), *The 2019 Non-Executive Salary Survey*, In Touch.

Jennifer Jordan and Michael Sorell (2019), *Why You Should Create a "Shadow Board" of Younger Employees*, HBR.org.

KPMG (2016), *Chairing an Audit Committee*, www.kpmg.com/globalaci.

KPMG Audit Committee Institute (2017), *Audit Committee Handbook*, www.kpmg/com/globalaci.

KPMG (2019), *Getting Strategic on Environmental, Social and Governance Issues*, www.KPMG.com/us/boardleadershipcenteresg

NEDonBoard (2018), *Board Risk Committee – Financial Services, Board Best Practice®*, NEDonBoard.

NEDonBoard (2018), *Audit Committee – Oversight of Internal Audit, Board Best Practice®*, NEDonBoard.

PWC (2013), *Subsidiary Governance: An Unappreciated Risk*, www.PWC.co.uk.

Robert Myers (2019), *Board Effectiveness: Finding Your Ideal Structure*, Casagrande Consulting LLC.

Referenced published annual reports

Each year The Chartered Governance Institute presents awards that recognise and celebrate excellence in governance and annual reporting. Further information on these awards, the categories and judging criteria, as well as past nominations and winners can be found at: www.icsa.org.uk/awards

Published annual reports, especially those that reflect good governance, are an excellent source of information on reporting on committees. Extracts from annual reports have been included throughout this text, primarily by reference to The Chartered Governance Institute award nominations and winners. The following lists the publicly available annual reports that have been referenced herein:

AA Plc, Annual Report 2019
Astra Zeneca Plc, Annual Report 2018
BAE Systems Plc, Annual Report 2018
Biffa plc, Annual Report 2019
BP, Annual Report 2018
BT Group Plc, Annual Report 2018
Cairn Energy Plc, Annual Report 2018
Compass Group Plc, Annual Report 2018
Experian Limited, Annual Report 2019
Good Energy Plc, Annual Report 2018
Great Portland Estates Plc, Annual Report 2019
Greencore Plc, Annual Report 2019
Hammerson Plc, Annual Report 2018
Just Eat Plc, Annual Report 2018
Legal and General Group Plc, Annual Report 2018
Marks and Spencer Group plc, Annual Report 2019
Provident Financial plc, Annual Report 2018
Prudential PLC, Annual Report 2018
Rolls-Royce Holdings plc, Annual Report 2018
Segro Plc, Annual Report 2018
Smith & Nephew Plc, Annual Report 2018
SSE Plc, Annual Report 2018
SSE Plc, Annual Report 2019
Taylor Wimpey Plc, Annual Report 2018
United Utilities Group Plc, Annual Report 2019
Vodaphone Group plc, Annual Report 2019

Resources

The Chartered Governance Institute knowledge, guidance and resources on governance can be found at: icsa.org.uk.

The Financial Reporting Council provides a number of corporate governance documents on its website at: www.frc.org.uk, including:

- UK Corporate Governance Code (2018) (the 'Code').
- FRC Guidance for Board and Board Committees.
- The Wates Corporate Governance Principles for Large Private Companies.
- Standards and Guidance for Auditors.
- UK Audit Standards.

REGULATION (EU) No 537/2014 OF THE EUROPEAN PARLIAMENT AND OF THE COUNCIL of 16 April 2014 on specific requirements regarding statutory audit of public-interest entities and repealing Commission Decision 2005/909/EC at: eur-lex.europa.eu/legal-content/EN/TXT/PDF/?uri=CELEX:32014R0537

The FCA Handbook can be found at: www.handbook.fca.org.uk/

The Chartered Governance Institute Subsidiary Governance Framework checklist can be found on the website of The Chartered Governance Institute at: www.icsa.org.uk/blog establishing-a-subsidiary-governance-framework-a-checklist

Further information of Pension Trustee Boards can be found on the website of The Pensions Regulator at: www.thepensionsregulator.gov.uk/

The Public Register of Shareholder dissent can be found on the website of The Investment Association at: www.theia.org/public-register

For small and medium sized listed companies, guides to committees can be purchased (free to members) from the Quoted Companies Alliance www.theqca.com/

The Task Force on Climate-related Financial Disclosures: www.fsb-tcfd.org/about/

Further detail of the Three Lines of Defence can be found on the website of The Chartered Institute of Internal Auditors at: www.iia.org.uk/resources/audit-committees/governance-of-risk-three-lines-of-defence/

Links to the Walker Report review of corporate governance in UK banks and other financial industry entities published in 2019 can be found on the website of the ICAEW at:
www.icaew.com/technical/corporate-governance/codes-and-reports/walker-report

Information on whistleblowing can be found on the website of Protect (formerly Public Concern at Work) at: protect-advice.org.uk/

Index

Accounting records
  subsidiary boards 165
Advisers
  committees, and 3
Advisory boards 171–172
Agenda 26
Audit committee 53–72
  audit 60–66
  audit process 60–63
  duties 56–66
  escalation to board 70
  external assessor of audit function 62–63
  external audit 63–66
  fees of audit firm 65
  financial controls and systems 57–58
  financial reporting 56–57
  forward–looking actions 71
  function 53
  interaction beyond 68–69
  internal financial controls 58
  legal compliance 58–60
  liaison with auditor 66
  membership 68
  non–audit services, and 65–66
  oversight 54
  reporting 69–71
  reporting on reviewing audit independence 64–65
  responsibilities 56–66
  role 53–54
  supporting 71
  tasks 56–66
  terms of reference 54–56
  three lines of defence 66–68
  whistleblowing oversight 59
Audit process 60–63

Board and committee responsibilities 32
British Dental Association 154
Business development
  executive committee, and 45–46
Business structure
  executive committee, and 44–45

Chair 12–13, 21
  responsibilities 22
  role 22
Charities
  committees 2
Charity finding boards 175–176
Committee packs 22–26
  authority 25
  collation 25
  content 25
  development 23–24
  distribution 25
  feedback 26
  format 25
  guidance 23–24
  purpose 25
  storage 25
Committee versus project 134–135
Committees 1–6
  advisers, and 3
  benefits 1–2
  charities 2
  consulting 7–8
  culture 4
  decision making 8–9
  definition 7

development, and 4–5
diversity 3–4
dynamics 3–4
external reporting 10
internal governance audit 5–6
legal requirements 2–3
reporting 9–10
values 4
Committees working collectively 35
Compliance committee 137–138
  oversight of ethics and compliance 138
Corporate social responsibility committee 142–145
  affordability and vulnerability 144–145
  approach to plastics 144
  climate change adaptation 144
  climate change mitigation 143–144
  developing young people 145
  diversity and inclusion 145
  early careers 145
  update on community strategy 145
  valuing natural capital 144
Cost calculator 23

Decision making 8–9
Digital impact and sustainability committee 152
Digital meeting support 31–34
  benefits 31

Employee ownership trust board 176–177
Employment committee 150–151
Environmental, social and governance committee 140–142
  strategic report 141
  sustainability 141–142
Ethics and compliance
  oversight of 138
Executive committee 37–51
  business development 45–46
  business structure 44–45
  chair 37
  duties 40–47
  employee engagement 49
  ensuring effective functioning of company 42
  functions 37
  human resources 44
  interaction beyond 48
  meetings 39
  members 38
  membership 48
  objectives 43
  operation 43–44
  performance 43–44
  policies 46–47
  reporting 48–50
    external 48–49
    internal 49
  reporting on 41–42
  responsibilities 40–47
  risk management 44–45
  role 37, 38–39
  service delivery 46
  strategy 43
  supporting 50
  tasks 40–47
  terms of reference 39–40
  transparency of executive roles and responsibilities 40
Executive risk committee 73
External assessor of audit function 62–63
External audit 63–66
  independence 64
  resignation of auditor 64
External committees 153–155
External reporting 10

Financial controls and systems
  audit committee 57–58
Financial reporting 56–57
Financial services risk committee 73–74
Frequency of meetings 18–19

Globally focused committee 152–153

Human resources
  executive committee, and 44

Implementing a committee 11–20
Individual committee membership
	15–16
Industry specific committee 148
Internal audit review 61–62
Internal financial controls
	audit committee 58
Internal governance audit 5–6
Internal non-operating subsidiaries 165
Investigatory Powers Governance
	Committee 152
Investment committee 149
IT and technology committee 145–147
	remit 146

Legal compliance
	audit committee 58–60
Litigation
	unauthorised corporate decisions, and
	8–9

Management committees 33
Markets committees 147–149
	remit 147
Meetings 21
Member tenure 16–17
Members, number of 14–15
Membership 13–14
Minutes 27
Monitoring 28

Niche examples of committees
	152–153
Nomination committee 113–132
	actions taken by 119–120
	board evaluation facilitated by
		company secretary 170
	board tenure 125
	boardroom dynamics and diversity
		126–128
	building director training around board
		meetings 122
	director induction process 123
	diversity 127
	diversity of appointment 114
	duties 117–123
	evaluate 120–121
	extending director appointment 125
	FCA guidance 115–116
	identity 119–120
	information on talent reviews 123
	interaction beyond 128–129
	membership 124–126
	plan 118–119
	reporting 129–130
	responsibilities 117–123
	review of board skills 121
	role 113, 114–115
	shareholder approval of director
		appointments 129
	succession planning for executive
		positions 118–119
	supporting 130–132
	tasks 117–123
	terms of reference 116–117
	train 122–123

Notice of meetings 18–19

Ongoing monitoring 135–136
Operational aspects 21–36
Operational content 24–25
Operational practicalities 135
Overseas subsidiaries 164–165
Oversight of committees 31

Pension trustee boards 174–175
	trustee responsibilities 174–175
PIMFA 153
Policies
	executive committee, and 46–47
Principal risk identification 76–77
	actions taken by management 77
	business change 76–77
	business continuity 76–77
	examples of risks 77
	link to strategy 77
	risk tolerance 77
Project
	committee distinguished from
		134–135
Purpose of committee

clear explanation and documentation 156

Quorum 17–18

Relocation committee 149–150
Remuneration 93–112
  public scrutiny 94
Remuneration committee 93–112
  aligning executive remuneration to employee remuneration 100
  calculation of bonus arrangements 111
  duties 98–102
  elements 93
  external advisers 104–105
  general approach to determining remuneration policy 101–102
  interaction beyond 105–108
    external to company 106–108
    shareholder engagement 107
    within company 105–106
  linking remuneration policy to strategy and wider business 95
  member characteristics 103–104
  membership 103–105
  oversee remuneration strategy of company 97
  policy specifics 102
  remuneration calculations 100–101
  reporting 108–110
    annual general meeting, to 110
    annual report 108–110
    incorporating diversity metrics 109
  responsibilities 98–102
  role 93, 94–97
  set policy for senior remuneration 94–96
  set remuneration for senior management 96–97
  shareholder approval 99–100
  supporting 110–116
  tasks 98–102
  terms of reference 98
  updated remuneration policy provisions 101

Reporting 9–10, 28
Reporting responsibilities 19
Review checklist 29–30
  action plan 30
  administration 30
  committee output 29
  costs 30
  membership 30
  terms of reference 29
Review of terms of reference 28–29
Reviewing and terminating a committee 136
Risk appetite statement 74–75
  current areas of focus 74–75
  risk appetite 74
  risk culture 74
Risk committee 73–91
  ad hoc meetings 79
  advice 80–81
  duties 79–85
  executive 73
  financial services 73–74
  focus for forthcoming year 90
  forms 73–74
  general duties 85
  interaction beyond 87–89
  liaison with other departments 88
  membership 86–87
  new or emerging risk types, and 84
  outsourcing, and 82
  oversight 81–83
  reporting 89–90
  responsibility 75, 79–85
  restrictions on 82
  review 83–85
  review of strategy and business risk appetite 80
  risk/reward framework 75
  risk in general 76–77
  role 78
  strategic discussions 81
  supporting 90–91
  tasks 79–85
  terms of reference 78–79
  transparency risk 76
  whistleblowing policy, and 84–85

Risk Governance Report 87
Risk management
   executive committee, and 44–45
Risk subcommittees 85–86
   examples 85–86
   membership 86
   operational nature of 86
   purpose 86
   specific remit 86

Safety, health and environment
      committees 138–140
Secretary 12–13
Self-assessment tool 23
Service delivery
   executive committee, and 46
Shadow boards 172–174
   company benefit 173–174
   members 172–173
Size of committee 17
Social committee 151
Subcommittees 155–156
   membership 155
   purposes 155
Subsidiary boards 159–169
   accounting records 165
   consistency of approach 162
   informal non-operating subsidiaries
      165
   legal standing 159–160
   members 162–163

   operations of 161
   overseas 164–165
   role of member 163–164
   setting strategy 161–162
   similarities to committees 160
Subsidiary governance 165–167
   Chartered Governance Institute
      framework 166–167
   structure 161
Subsidiary oversight 167–168
Subsidiary rules 168–169
Supporting board and committee 34
Supporting committees 35–36

Technology focused committee
   146
Terms of reference 11–12
Three lines of defence 66–68
   model 67
   role of 68
Time keeping 26–27

Unauthorised corporate decisions
   litigation, and 8–9

Whistleblowing oversight
   audit committee 59
Whistleblowing policy
   risk committee, and 84–85
Wider interaction beyond committee
   34–35

Lightning Source UK Ltd.
Milton Keynes UK
UKHW021842170521
383868UK00003B/72